T0323952

THE BRITISH ECONOMY IN TRANSITION

In the course of the last twenty years, the British economy has changed beyond recognition. In *The British Economy in Transition* the authors examine the nature of these dramatic changes, most of which have been brought about by deindustrialisation and subsequent attempts to regenerate the economy.

Has British industry been modernised? The authors consider this larger question by examining several others which interlock with it:

- Have old industries been replaced by new ones?
- Which traditional industries have survived? What has been the effect of this?
- Is what is left of British industry internationally competitive?

The book also considers the benefits of inward investment as a means of reindustrialisation and job creation. While the volume focuses on the prospects for particular regions and cities, many of the key issues can be seen as central to the economic prospects for Britain as a whole.

The contributors are all leading authorities in their respective areas and the book will be a valuable guide for all those interested in change in British industry and business.

Royce Turner is Research Fellow at the Policy Research Centre, and Senior Lecturer in Public Sector Management at Sheffield Business School, Sheffield Hallam University.

THE BRITISH ECONOMY IN TRANSITION

From the Old to the New?

Edited by Royce Turner

London and New York

First published 1995
by Routledge
11 New Fetter Lane, London EC4P 4EE

Transferred to Digital Printing 2004

Simultaneously published in the USA and Canada
by Routledge
29 West 35th Street, New York, NY 10001

Typeset in Garamond by LaserScript, Mitcham, Surrey

British Library Cataloguing in Publication Data
A catalogue record for this book is available from the British Library

Library of Congress Cataloging in Publication Data
The British economy in transition: from the old to the new?/
edited by Royce Turner.
p. cm.
Includes bibliographical references and index.
ISBN 0–415–11114–5. – ISBN 0–415–11115–3 (pbk.)
1. Great Britain – Economic policy – 1945–??. 2. Great Britain –
Economic conditions – 1945–?? – Regional disparities.
3. Plant shutdowns – Great Britain. 4. Industries – Great Britain.
I. Turner, Royce Logan.
HC256.6.B762353   1994
338.941 – dc20   94-46808
CIP

ISBN 0–415–11114–5 (hbk)
ISBN 0–415–11115–3 (pbk)

For Carlo

CONTENTS

FIGURES

TABLES

CONTRIBUTORS

Peter Baker is senior lecturer in economics in the Department of International Business at the University of Central Lancashire.

Gordon Dabinett is senior lecturer in Urban Policy at the School of Urban and Regional Studies, Sheffield Hallam University. Previously he worked for Sheffield City Council. He works on different aspects of urban economic development and policy evaluation within the Centre for Regional Economic and Social Research.

Mike Geddes is principal research fellow and research manager of the Local Government Centre, University of Warwick. Recent research has included examining the impact of European industrial restructuring on local and regional economies. He is co-author (with John Bennington) of *Restructuring the Local Economy* (Longman, 1992), and co-editor of the journal *Local Economy*.

Anne Green is senior research fellow at the Institute for Employment Affairs, University of Warwick. She is a geographer with particular interests in spatial aspects of economic, demographical, and social change.

John Lovering is professor of human geography, and director of the Centre for Regional Business Development at the University of Hull. He has worked with trade unions, local authorities, training and enterprise councils, and others on responses to defence spending cuts.

Steve Martin is principal research fellow in strategic management at the Local Government Centre, Warwick Business School, University of Warwick. He is currently directing an ESRC-funded project on the Europeanisation of British local governance.

Jonathan Morris is professor of management at the University of Glamorgan. His research interests are in the impact of multinationals upon regional economies and East Asian business systems. He has published widely in both areas, including (with Rob Imrie) *Transforming Buyer-Supplies Relations*

(1991), (with Steve Hill) *Wales in the 1990s* (1991), (with Max Munday and Barry Wilkinson) *Working for the Japanese* (1993), edited *Japan and the Global Economy* (1991), and co-edited *A Flexible Future* (1991).

Garel Rhys, OBE holds the SMMT Chair in Motor Industry Economics at Cardiff Business School, University of Wales, where he is Head of the Economics Section and is also Director of the Centre for Automotive Industry Research.

Ian Stone is reader in economics and head of the Newcastle Economic Research Unit at the University of Northumbria. His research interests are in the areas of regional and industrial development in the UK and European context. Recent work includes a study of inward investment and its impact on local labour markets (for the Employment Department), and the restructuring of defence industries (jointly funded by the European Parliament and the Rowntree Foundation).

Royce Turner is research fellow at the Policy Research Centre, and senior lecturer in public sector management, at Sheffield Business School. He is the author of *The Politics of Industry* (1989) and *Regenerating the Coalfields* (1993).

ABBREVIATIONS

ACE	Annual Census of Employment
A & P	Austin and Pickersgill (former shipbuilders)
ACOM	Association of local and regional authorities in the coal mining areas of the European Community
AEEU	Amalgamated Engineering and Electrical Union
AEU	Amalgamated Engineering Union. Predecessor to AEEU.
ARPA	Advanced Research Projects Agency (USA)
ASTMS	Association of Scientific, Technical and Managerial Staff (trade union merged into MSF, see below)
ASW	Allied Steel and Wire (steel products manufacturer)
ATP	Advanced Technology Programme (USA)
BAC	British Aircraft Corporation
BCE	British Coal Enterprise
BAe	British Aerospace
BEDP	Birmingham Economic Development Partnership
BL	British Leyland
BS	British Steel
CCC	Coalfield Communities Campaign
CEC	Commission of the European Communities
CFBS	Communications, Financial and Business Services
CHP	Combined Heat and Power (Sheffield)
CNC	Computer Numerically Controlled
CND	Campaign for Nuclear Disarmament
COAB	Company Advisory Board
CSO	Central Statistical Office
DESO	Defence Export Sales Organisation
DML	Devonport Management Limited (Devonport Dockyard)
DOE	Department of the Environment
DRA	Defence Research Agency
DTI	Department of Trade and Industry
EC	European Community

EDU	Economic Development Unit (Birmingham)
EEF	Engineering Employers' Federation
EETPU	Electrical Electronic Telecommunication and Plumbing Trade Union
EFA	European Fighter Aircraft
EPOS	Electronic Point of Sale Systems
ERDF	European Regional Development Fund
ESF	European Social Fund
FDI	Foreign Direct Investment
FLA	Future Large Aircraft
FR	Flight Refuelling (defence company)
FTE	Full Time Equivalent
GDP	Gross Domestic Product
GLC	Greater London Council
GMB	General Municipal and Boilermakers (trade union)
HS	Hawker Siddeley
IBC	Isuzu Bedford Corporation (vehicle manufacturer)
ICC	International Convention Centre (Birmingham)
IDOP	Integrated Development Operations Programme. Scheme which allowed for integration of the implementation of the European Structural funds (ERDF and ESF above) and national schemes aimed at regeneration/restructuring
IRC	Industrial Reorganisation Corporation
ISTC	Iron and Steel Trades Confederation
JCCS	Job and Career Change Scheme
JIT	Just-in-time production
KONVER	European Commission fund under which financial assistance for localities suffering contraction in defence industries can be applied for.
LAD	Local Authority District
LLMA	Local Labour Market Area
MEP	Member of the European Parliament
MFA	Multi-Fibre Agreement
MIC	Military-Industrial-Complex
MITI	(Japanese) Ministry for International Trade and Industry
MOD	Ministry of Defence
MSF	Maufacturing Science Finance (trade union formed by a merger of ASTMS and TASS)
NAO	National Audit Office
NAPNOC	No Acceptable Price, No Contract
NCB	National Coal Board
NDC	Northern Development Company
NEB	National Enterprise Board
NEC	National Exhibition Centre (Birmingham)

xiv

NEDC	National Economic Development Council
NESL	North East Shipbuilders Ltd
NIA	National Indoor Arena (Birmingham)
NSTAP	National Strategic Technology Acquisition Programme
NUMMI	New United Motor Manufacturering Inc (USA)
PFB	Pressurised Fluidised Bed (experimental coal fired power station)
R&D	Research and development
RECHAR	*Restructuration des Charbonnages*. A fund of money available from the EC for areas experiencing coal mining decline.
RENAVAL	*Restructuration Chantiers Navals*. A fund of money available from the EC for the restructuring of shipbuilding areas.
ROF	Royal Ordnance Factories
ROSE	Rest of South East England (outside London)
SBAC	Society of British Aerospace Companies
SDE	Statement on Defence Estimates
SEEF	South East Engineering Forum
SEM	Single European Market
SERC	Sheffield Economic Regeneration Committee
SDC	Sheffield Development Corporation
SIC	Standard Industrial Classification
SME	Small and Medium Sized Enterprises
SMMT	Society of Motor Manufacturers and Traders
TASS	Technical Advisory and Supervisory Staff
TEC	Training and Enterprise Council
TGWU	Transport and General Workers Union
T&N	Turner and Newall
TQC	Total Quality Control
TRP	Technology Reinvestment Programme (USA)
TSR-2	Tactical Strike Reconnaisance Aircraft
TTWA	Travel to Work Area
TUC	Trades Union Congress
TWDC	Tyne and Wear Development Corporation
TWO	The Wearside Opportunity
UDC	Urban Development Corporation
WDA	Welsh Development Agency
WSG	World Student Games

1

INTRODUCTION

Royce Turner

It is a commonplace to state that Britain was once regarded as the 'workshop of the world'. Such a description has long been consigned to history. When it was used this phrase meant that Britain was renowned for being a centre of manufacturing, producing goods that were traded throughout the world. Particular places within Britain were seen as being centres of world-class excellence in different kinds of manufacturing. The West Midlands, for example, traditionally the second richest region in Britain after the South East, was renowned for engineering products, particularly the production of motor cars and car components. Sheffield, the birthplace of stainless steel, was also a city associated in the popular consciousness with great industry – steel, steel products, and cutlery, particularly – but, paramountly, with quality. The belief, and the actuality, was that a product stamped 'Made in Sheffield' would be a quality product. Other places, too, could lay claim to a place in this pantheon of great industrial glory: Clydeside and the North East of England with shipbuilding; South Yorkshire, Nottinghamshire, and South Wales, with coal; Lancashire and the East Midlands with textiles and clothing; some places – Hertfordshire, the North West – with defence and aircraft manufacture.

It is also a commonplace to state that this world of global leadership in manufacturing has long ago passed. There is an array of statistics that could be brought to bear, and that have been brought to bear, which seek to confirm this. The percentage of the world export of manufactures captured by British companies has halved in thirty years, for example, from 16.3 per cent in 1960 to 8.4 per cent in 1990. The manufacturing sector within the British economy employs less than half the number of people in 1994 compared to 1966 – down from 8.5 million to 4 million. It makes, proportionately, a far smaller contribution to the country's GDP (Coates, 1994). The share of world trade in manufactures held by companies from the UK fell to 8.6 per cent by 1990. In 1950 it had been 25.5 per cent (Grant, 1993). And so on. That there has been relative economic decline is well known, and needs little rehearsal here.

1

This book is about these changes in the British economy. If manufacturing has been in relative decline what, if anything, has taken its place? Governments at local and central levels have pursued a plethora of policies aimed at reviving both the national economy and in particular local economies. Essentially, one of the basic objectives of these policies – even if it is sometimes unstated – has been to 'modernise' the local and national economies. If the traditional industries – coal, steel, textiles – were 'sunset' industries, then the only way forward for an economy such as Britain's would be to move forward to an economy based on 'sunrise' industries and service-based industries which have potential for growth. Has this happened, or is the British economy simply left with a smaller traditional industrial sector and little to take its place? This is the central issue this book seeks to explore. Alongside that, it examines the nature of the changes in the British economy and the economic and political framework within which they have taken place.

There is obviously both a sectoral and a spatial aspect involved in examining economic and industrial change. In other words, particular industries have changed and, in some cases, disappeared. In this context, this book addresses the situation as it has affected coal, steel, motor vehicles, engineering, textiles, and the defence industry. Alongside this, of course, industries were associated with particular regions and particular cities. What has happened to the places associated with 'traditional' industries? This book examines two cities – Birmingham and Sheffield – and two regions – Wearside and South Wales – and examines the impact of economic change in each.

The changes in the structure and nature of the British economy in the 1970s, 1980s, and early 1990s have had widespread ramifications of a social, political, and economic kind. For example, one effect of the economic restructuring was that it brought in its wake huge numbers of displaced workers, and removed many employment options from people who might otherwise have expected to work in particular industries. In both coal and steel, to cite two examples, there was inter-generational reproduction of labour. In other words, sons followed fathers down the pit, and sons and daughters (usually) followed their fathers into the steel works. That element of economic security has been disrupted, and in many cases lost. In that sense, the industrial economy exhibits less continuity and less stability. The restructuring has changed – sometimes dramatically, always irreversibly – the economies of many regions and localities within the erstwhile 'workshop of the world'. There is no shipbuilding on the Wear in the 1990s, for example. The only coal produced in South Wales came from opencasting, small privately owned pits, and a drift mine – Betws – closed by British Coal in 1993 and bought by a private sector group and re-opened in 1994 (*The Guardian*, 15 January 1994). Here again, the ownership restructuring serves to emphasise the changing fortunes and nature of employment in industry. Betws, a relatively new mine which did not start production until 1978 and which could therefore lay claim to being one of the most 'modern' of the coal industry, had employed 700 in the years before its closure. On re-opening in the private sector, it employed only 100.

Britain had been the first industrialised country. In many ways, it was the *most* industrialised country. The economic restructuring which, in its modern form, began probably in the late 1960s and gathered pace in the following decades changed all that. Hall (1991) commented on this change in the pattern of employment by noting that:

> In the mid-1950s the UK had been perhaps more industrialised than any other country in history, with more workers in industry than in all services; yet by 1983 there were almost two service workers for every industrial worker.

Grant (1993) also notes that 'a greater proportion of the UK workforce is employed in services than in any other major competitor country apart from the United States'. That the relative importance of manufacturing has declined, while the relative importance of services has increased within the economy, is not *necessarily* undesirable. Despite the fact that fewer services are open to international trade, there may be positive aspects to it. The working conditions of people may have improved, for example.

An entire literature has been devoted to examining the reasons for the decline in the world position of British manufacturing, which is attributed to a variety of causes which range from Treasury ineptitude in economic management, poor managerial performance, militant trade unions, a financial sector within the economy too remote in its own interests from the industrial sector, through to an 'exceptionalism' in British social culture which is alleged to have retarded economic progress (see, for example, Aldcroft, 1982; Barnett, 1986; Coates, 1986; Mann, 1988; Pollard, 1982; Wiener, 1981). It is not the intention here to contribute to that already extensive literature in trying to decipher the reasons for the relative decline in the position of British manufacturing. Relative decline is accepted as given.

Nevertheless, what the change in the position of manufacturing *did* do was to stimulate attempts, as noted earlier – sometimes initiated by governments, sometimes by companies – to *modernise* the British economy, or at least sections of it. This book seeks to address that issue. Has the British economy been successfully modernised? Has it made a transition successfully from being an economy reliant on the old 'staples' of coal, steel, shipbuilding, engineering, to being an economy based on high technology industry or on service-based industries, where the prospects for a sustainable and prosperous economic future are much brighter? A great deal rests upon these questions: the future for individuals, the life chances

3

people have, the economic future for localities and entire regions. Thus as well as examining broad economic regeneration activities, chapter 2 also looks at the post-redundancy experiences of displaced mineworkers.

There are at least two kinds of *modernisation* that can be identified, and this work attempts to address both of them. The first kind of modernisation relates to what has happened to individuals and localities where an industry or economic activity has ceased or almost ceased. The classic examples would be coal or shipbuilding, and in some cases steel. In most cases, as a response to industrial decline, there has been a flurry of activity by some combination of government, government agencies, local government, and private sector led enterprise agencies to stimulate the local economy and reskill displaced workers. Sometimes this has taken the form of a contracting nationalised industry establishing a 'job creation' subsidiary: the key examples would be British Coal Enterprise (BCE), and British Steel Industry. Sometimes it has been local government that has tried, within powers which became more limited as the 1980s and 1990s wore on, to take a leading role at least in co-ordinating economic regeneration efforts. Almost all the large local authorities have economic development departments. Sometimes central government has acted as the 'stimulator', establishing enterprise zones, or promoting other policies designed to regenerate the economies of localities. For example, enterprise zones were announced in the 'coal town' of Pontefract in 1981 (Turner, 1992), and in the Dearne Valley in South Yorkshire, Mansfield in Nottinghamshire, and Easington in the North East – all areas traditionally heavily associated with coal – in 1993. The 'steel towns' of Scunthorpe and Corby had similar assistance granted in the early 1980s. Part of Wearside was granted enterprise zone status after the end of shipbuilding in the early 1990s.

The second kind of modernisation relates to sectors that *have* survived, but have had to change significantly in order to survive. The most obvious examples are motor vehicles, textiles, steel manufacture, and parts of the engineering industry, including the defence industry. In chapter 3, Morris, for example, relates the story of how the steel industry has been modernised in Wales: modern technology is employed; high value added steels are produced; new methods of working are employed; employment levels have been reduced on a major scale.

All the industrial sectors mentioned above have been significant sectors in the British economy. All have been subject to pressures which have initiated changes implemented by both public sector and private sector owners and managers. Often, the most drastic restructuring was in the public sector *prior* to privatisation, as exemplified by steel and coal.

The impacts of these changes have, in some cases, been profound, and the ramifications widespread. In many instances there have been plant closures or, at least, reductions in the labour force. In some cases there has been a change in the ownership of at least part of the industrial sector. The most obvious example of this is motor vehicle production with the Japanese multinationals Nissan, Toyota, and Honda establishing bases in Britain for manufacture. Management techniques and industrial relations have also been affected by the wider change taking place in the British industrial economy. The implementation of these changes – which have included a burgeoning of 'no-strike' agreements and non-recognition of trade unions – has occurred within an economic and political climate which rendered the introduction of such changes far more easy than it would have been in, say, the 1960s or the 1970s. Quite simply, this was because the massive hike in unemployment from the early 1980s onwards, coupled with legislation that restricted the unions' power, meant that little resistance could be offered to the changes by Britain's once strong trade union movement.

Moreover, the political conditions for the owners and managers of industries and other businesses to implement change were also favourable. The Labour Party, which might be expected to defend the gains of the working class movement in relation to job security and workers' bargaining power, had not won a general election since 1974. The Conservatives, who held governmental office from 1979 onwards, shared the view of some of those who owned and ran British industry that drastic changes were necessary if companies were to survive and compete on a world scale. The central questions in all this, then, are: What has the restructuring achieved? Is the British economy, after sacrifice has been borne by many individuals and localities as a whole, now left with an internationally competitive collection of businesses in the *modernised* sectors? What has been the *politics* of the change? Who has won and who has lost in the process? Who has borne the price of change – the workers, the owners of businesses, individual local economies? In short, putting the two aspects of modernisation together, has Britain entered a new era of a modern, vibrant economy, upon which a sustainable economic future can be built? Or, after years of deindustrialisation, is the economy left with a massive reduction in the size of traditional industry, and the numbers employed by it, but with little to replace it on which a sustainable economic future could be built? Quite clearly, there is no single indisputable answer to these questions. In some cases, the authors in this book consider that much is left to be done to ensure a viable industrial future. Geddes and Green, for example, put forward the outline of a strategy as to how the prospects for engineering in the South East might be enhanced (chapter 6). Similarly, Rhys outlines the steps he believes are necessary if the motor components industry is to achieve higher efficiency, and, by that mechanism, survive (chapter 7). Stone considers that the 'absence of a meaningful industrial strategy at a national level' has contributed to the weakness of the British economy (chapter 8). Baker also sees advantages in a more pro-active role for national and local government in the modernisation of textiles (chapter 4).

The implications of restructuring can be mixed in terms of overall welfare, and what appears to be positive can disguise negative elements. Geddes and Green note, for instance, that the restructuring of engineering in the South East has had the effect of increasing the relative proportion of the workforce engaged in research and development (R&D) activities. On the surface, that appears positive, given that R&D is a sector which would be associated with a 'modernised' economy. The negative aspect to it is that the proportionate rise has been brought about by a shift of the straightforward manufacturing *out* of the South East. In other words, the R&D has stayed in the South East, but a lot of the manufacturing that used to accompany it has gone elsewhere. As Geddes and Green have it: 'While a balanced local economy will benefit from the continued presence of R&D, the sudden disappearance of tens of thousands of jobs in manufacturing will be difficult to counteract.'

Similarly, Morris notes that economic regeneration in Wales has had mixed effects (chapter 3). On the positive side, inward investment has been substantial, a considerable number of jobs have been created, and the economy has diversified. On the negative side, wages have fallen further behind those that are being paid in the rest of the UK. A further finding of Morris's that is worthy of note here is the increasing polarisation of wealth to be found in the 'new' Welsh economy: in other words, there is now a bigger gap between rich and poor areas.

It should be recognised that modernisation efforts within the British economy are not at all a new phenomenon. Various governments have embarked on assorted schemes and policies, sometimes associated with new institutional frameworks aimed at enhancing economic performance by companies and within industries. Central to the political debate on this issue is to what extent governments themselves should be involved in directing and implementing the process, and to what extent this should be left to private companies operating within the context of market forces. The answer of the Conservative government first elected in 1979 was clear: government intervention was to be kept to a minimum, and the free market would reign supreme. Within the government, however, there were quite obviously different degrees of emphasis on this by different ministers. Michael Portillo, first as Chief Secretary to the Treasury and subsequently as Secretary of State for Employment, was the standard bearer of non-intervention and free market ideology. In 1992, for instance, he was said to have opposed further financial assistance for mining areas facing pit closures (*The Guardian*, 18 September 1992). Michael Heseltine, President of the Board of Trade, on the other hand, clearly placed himself on the 'interventionist' wing of the Party. At the 1992 Conservative Party conference he promised, famously, to 'intervene before breakfast, before lunch and before dinner'. In 1994, the two fell out, as it were, in public. In a letter leaked to the press, Portillo expressed his disagreement over several areas of policy being pursued by Heseltine's Department of Trade and Industry (DTI). He advocated the virtual end of financial assistance to firms under regional policy, an end to assistance for aerospace, the faster phasing out of assistance to space technology, and the rationalisation of support for exporters (*The Guardian*, 2 August 1994).

In terms of a history of government efforts to enhance economic performance by firms, some of the most useful early examples to draw on relate to attempts to make the 'high tech' connection. The National R&D Corporation, for example, which was merged with the vastly slimmed down National Enterprise Board in the 1980s to form the British Technology Group, began granting financial support for technological innovation and exploitation of inventions as far back as 1949. The 1970s also saw government schemes to support and encourage the high- technology sector. The Product and Process Development Scheme, for example, was launched in 1977 to accelerate product and process innova- tions through subsidising firms' development costs. A similar scheme, also launched under the Labour government, was the Microprocessor Applications Project, established in 1978, aimed at encouraging microelectronic applications in industry.

A number of policy landmarks can be identified, then, which char- acterise the efforts of both the Conservative and Labour Parties when in power. The major innovation of the Conservatives, under Macmillan in the early 1960s, was to institute the tripartite NEDC as a consultative forum which could advise on economic and industrial policy (Barberis and May, 1993). An application to join the Common Market (as the forerunner of the European Union was then called) was lodged, and a new framework for regulating wages policy was established. Moreover, as Lovering notes in chapter 5, the Macmillan government, in contrast to the rhetoric at least of the later Thatcher-led Conservative government, was actively involved in intervention in industry. He cites as an example how they used the promise of orders for aircraft to encourage mergers in the aircraft production industry. Macmillan's government did not restrict itself to this kind of intervention. It was heavily involved in regional policy – in other words, cajoling or persuading companies to locate in parts of the country which they otherwise might not have considered. The obvious objective here was to bolster economically – and, in the broad sense of the term, to 'modernise' – relatively deprived regions, or regions tied to 'traditional', and usually declining, industries such as coal. This kind of policy was given considerable emphasis in the 1960s. In 1960, for example, the then British Motor Corporation (forerunner of British Leyland and, eventually, the Rover group) announced not one, but three new factories to be built in areas of high unemployment (South Wales, Merseyside, Scotland). Rhys notes in chapter 7 the extent to which the motor industry was scattered across the land under regional policy in the 1960s.

Labour, in the 1960s, was explicitly associated with 'modernisation' efforts. This was encapsulated in the hitching of science to socialism in prime minister Harold Wilson's rhetoric of forging a future in the 'white heat of the technological revolution'. Wilson had an explicit plan in 1963:

> First we must produce more scientists. Secondly, having produced them we must be a great deal more successful in keeping them in this country. Thirdly, having trained them and kept them here, we must make more intelligent use of them. . . . Fourthly, we must organise British industry so that it applies the results of scientific research more purposively to our national production effort.
>
> (quoted in Bealey, 1970)

Institutionally, Wilson's government created the Industrial Reorganisation Corporation (IRC) which encouraged mergers in the private sector specifically to spur efficiency and create companies that could compete on a global scale. It was under Labour, for instance, that ICL, the computer company, was born out of a merger between ICT and English Electric Computers. The government's carrot was an offer of money to develop a new range of computers. Neither company was particularly keen to merge, but the government was anxious to try to create a 'national champion' that could thrive internationally (*The Guardian*, 8 July 1993). In chapter 5 Lovering also explicitly acknowledges this strategy of encouraging mergers here in relation to defence and the effect that this had of 'enhanc[ing] the influence of the dominant [defence] companies'. Importantly, however, Lovering also makes the point that the these efforts left something to be desired in relation to the long term:

> There was no systematic attempt to arrive at a coherent conception of national military needs, and to relate these to national industrial capacity as a whole.

The 'successor' to the 1960s IRC was the 1970s National Enterprise Board (NEB). The NEB was a state-holding company. In other words, rather than the public-corporation model of public ownership that had characterised Labour's 1945–51 administration – where entire industries such as coal, railways, gas, and electric were taken into state ownership – the NEB would take equity shares in companies. The objective was to provide financial assistance for companies without saddling them with debt, but also that the state would henceforth be involved in helping the expanding, modernising sectors of the economy. Thus, for example, the NEB supported the creation of Inmos in the 1970s to manufacture microprocessors and semiconductors. However, the early ambitious and innovative plans for the NEB were soon overtaken by the need for administrative expedience: the NEB was given jurisdiction over two of the then biggest loss-makers in the public sector, Rolls Royce aerospace, and the car, truck, and bus manufacturer nationalised in 1975, British Leyland.

8

What, then, would a 'modernised' economy look like? How would it be recognisable? There is no direct, unchallengeable answer to this. Modernisation is a value-laden concept. It means different things to different people. There are, however, some broad aspects which would be associated with most people's definition of a 'modernised' economy. First, it would mean a high proportion of the workforce would be employed in high technology industry or in service-based industry. Secondly, it would mean a highly skilled, highly trained workforce, with a substantial proportion of that workforce being well remunerated. Thirdly, it would mean the economy had a modern, efficient, physical, and social infrastructure in terms of communications, transport, health, and education services. Fourthly, it would mean a more mobile labour force: people would have the option and the opportunity to retrain for new employment, and not be trapped in old, obsolescent industries. Anything other than that would produce economic ossification.

DEINDUSTRIALISATION

As the context within which this study of 'modernisation' is located is one of a deindustrialising economy, it would at this juncture be germane to explore the meanings of the term 'deindustrialisation'. This is important because different commentators have placed different emphases on the term. Baker's interpretation in chapter 4, for example, refers largely to declining numbers of people being employed, in this case, in the clothing and textiles industry. Stone, in chapter 8, also follows Caslin (1987), in taking the view that deindustrialisation refers to 'an absolute and proportional decline in industrial employment'. There are, however, varying interpretations of deindustrialisation. For Campbell (1990), for instance, deindustrialisation referred to the *relative* decline of the share of total economic output attributable to the manufacturing sector. Campbell illustrates this by noting that, during the period 1982 to 1988, following the economic recession of the early 1980s, growth in the service sector was nearly 30 per cent, compared to growth of less than 25 per cent in the manufacturing sector over the same period. Singh's (1977) definition, however, is somewhat different. For him, deindustrialisation represented a progressive incapacity to achieve a sufficient surplus of exports over imports of manufactures. There are other interpretations. Bacon and Eltis (1978), in a famous broadside against 'big government', argued that it was politicians who had allowed what they called the 'non-marketed' sector of the economy – activities paid for out of the public purse, rather than by individual private consumers, and therefore largely public sector services – to grow at the expense of the 'marketed' sector. The latter was any part of the economy wherein a business, industry, or organisation had to sell its services or products to a customer in order to survive in the market economy. Governments had connived in this for reasons of political expedience. Re-election to government required full employment, or at least something closely approximating to it, and expanding public sector services was the easiest and quickest way to achieve that. The result was that resources had been pushed away from industry and into, for example, health care, education, local government. The ultimate, and from the point of view of Bacon and Eltis, deleterious effect, was deindustrialisation. For the purposes of this book, deindustrialisation is interpreted in a broad sense: it really refers here to an absolute and/or relative contraction in the *industrial economy*, as opposed to the service sector economy.

Deindustrialisation brought in its wake changes wider than those associated simply with fewer people working in the industrial sector of the economy, although that in itself was obviously damaging to individuals and to the social fabric. Martin notes the catastrophic consequences of unemployment of deindustrialisation on the economy of Birmingham. Rhys notes employment in the vehicle and parts industry falling by nearly 300,000 between 1971 and 1993 (chapter 7). Lovering notes that when defence began to shed jobs – one of the manufacturing industries, alongside, for instance, motor manufacture, which did survive on a large scale in Britain – it was often the 'last major manufacturing sector in these areas' (chapter 5). Geddes and Green also relate the consequences for unemployment of job shedding in the engineering industry (chapter 6). Deindustrialisation changed the social and economic environment within which workers had to operate. In other words, the processes of control over the labour market, and the labour market itself, changed considerably as a consequence of, and partly as a response to, the transformation brought about by deindustrialisation. For example, there is no doubt that one major aspect of the changing labour market has been the proportionate rise in the importance of female labour. Stone, for instance, notes that the jobs that *are* created as part of the 'regeneration' process are often for women (chapter 8). Morris, also, notes the 'feminisation' of the workforce in Wales (chapter 3). There is at least anecdotal evidence of similarly changing conditions in traditional coal mining areas. The importance of these findings is that both Wearside and the coal mining areas, for example, as well as Wales, had traditionally seen the 'dominance' of males in the labour market. These changing patterns are manifested not simply in the economy, but reflect a social culture forced into change under economic pressure. In relation to the overall prospects for economic regeneration, it should be noted that Stone also makes the point that the expansion in job opportunities for women did not make up for the fall off in demand for male labour, at least in Wearside (chapter 8).

A further major change affecting the labour market has been the move away from employment in manufacturing and related industries towards service-based employment. Morris, for example, refers to the dramatic change in the Welsh economy which, in the 1970s, was 'dominated by metal manufacturing', and where, by 1991, 68 per cent of the workforce was employed in the service sector (chapter 3). Dabinett (chapter 10) mentions the change in this direction in Sheffield – particularly in relation to financial and business services – as does Martin in relation to Birmingham (chapter 9). Martin notes, however, that the prospects for this kind of service-based employment actually replacing the numbers of jobs lost – at least in Birmingham – are not auspicious.

Even within the manufacturing industries that have survived there have been major changes within the workforce and in work practices. Lovering (chapter 5) notes the 'typical' worker is now no longer the male, union member in his forties. At the higher end of the scale, the worker is now likely to be better qualified, younger, and not belong to a union. At the other end, in an increasingly polarised workforce, there are likely to be more workers on low pay, often women.

Deindustrialisation brought other changes too, or at least helped them along. Some of them related to changes in industrial relations and, coupled with those, an increased pressure to implement 'flexibility' within the labour market and labour force. It is obvious that the traditional industries referred to above – coal, shipbuilding, steel, defence, engineering, and others – had been bastions of strong, if not always militant, trade unionism. More often than not, this trade unionism was associated with male workers. A series of events and policies conspired in the early 1980s onwards to break this mould.

First, the onset of much higher levels of unemployment – partly a consequence of deindustrialisation, as traditional industries contracted – shifted the balance of workplace power away from organised labour and towards the owners and managements of industries and businesses.

Secondly, throughout the 1980s and into the 1990s there was a raft of legislation designed to restrict the power of trade unions and alter the balance of power *within* them as periodic secret ballots were made compulsory for the election of leaders of unions, and prior to industrial action being embarked upon.

Thirdly, privatisation has served effectively to dismember the unity of some unions where it has led to the break up of the industries within which they organised, such as water, shipbuilding, or electricity generation.

As argued earlier, the political context within which these changes were taking place was that of a governmental commitment to a non-interventionist, free market approach to business and industry. That approach extended to the labour market itself, and that factor, coupled with the enhanced power of employers, ensured that there would be more emphasis on 'flexibility' within the workforce. Flexibility, however, has a number of possible meanings and interpretations, as does modernisation. Flexibility can refer to flexibility of numbers (in which a 'core' and a 'peripheral'

11

workforce are introduced); to tasks (in which workers are expected to be flexible in relation to the jobs they are willing and able to carry out); and to time (in which the organisation operates over what is usually a longer time period which will allow it to maximise efficiency and, if applicable, profits) (Atkinson, 1984).

In terms of the Conservative governments' agenda, and the agenda of corporate management implementing the change, 'flexibility' was equated with 'modernisation'. In other words, to modernise meant the introduction of flexibility. This is at least part of the reason why much of the introduction of flexibility in Britain was pioneered in public sector organisations such as the civil service. Stone argues in chapter 8 that a belief that Wearside was prepared to accept this kind 'flexibility' was used as a mechanism for the promotion of the area to inward investors. Morris demonstrates how flexibility has been implemented by inward investors in South Wales and examines organisational features associated with it (chapter 3). Geddes and Green detail the view of engineering companies in the South East on the objective of attaining flexibility (chapter 6). Rhys sees the adoption of 'modern, flexible manufacturing and new product development processes' as being essential to the survival of the motor components manufacturing industry in the future (chapter 7). As argued earlier, however, there are different interpretations as to how modernisation could be achieved and, probably more importantly, what it would constitute and look like once it had been achieved. This is where economics cannot be separated out from politics, because the decision on which 'model' of modernisation to aim for and implement carries explicit political values. Modernisation from a political perspective is different from the view of those arguing for 'flexibility' as the the key would carry with it a different set of values. This approach would recognise the need for efficiency and flexibility in relation to companies' responses to consumer wishes, but would also emphasise the desirability of a workforce which felt content, and would seek to emphasise the necessity of other factors. A modern infrastructure would be one, good training another, an economy which had the capacity for innovation yet another.

Flexibility, on the positive side, is meant to refer to a more pro-active and multi-skilled workforce, more able to respond effectively to the demands placed upon it, and therefore better equipped to contribute to the overall prosperity of the company. Geddes and Green note in chapter 6, for example, that in the engineering industry in the South East the 'drive for flexibility is best exemplified by the widespread shift from separate skilled craftsmen to multi-skilled technicians'. Looking at flexibility in this positive way, then, there is at least the possibility that the fruits of flexibility would find their way back to at least some of the workers themselves via wages higher than they would be in different circumstances, or via enhanced job security. To be in this relatively happy position, however, one would have to a part of the 'core' workforce, that is, the sector of the workforce necessary for the organisation to continue to exist. It is this section that would benefit from security of tenure, and training investment. To be in the 'periphery' conveys few rights and few attractions.

There is also a more negative interpretation which emphasises that 'flexibility' can result in far greater job insecurity, more arduous work, longer hours, and less worker 'rights'. The introduction of 'flexibility' has been a priority of managements in big companies in the 1980s and early 1990s, ranging from the industrial through to the retail sectors. As noted above, many analysts have argued that this has involved the division of the workforce into the 'core' and the 'peripheral'. The former would represent those seen as being the key workers: these would be offered some job security, though they would make up a much smaller cohort than the workforce as a whole before the reorganisation. The latter would be a group of workers with a much reduced level of job security: they would be liable to be dispensed with when no longer necessary; they might be part-time; they would have few 'rights'. In this fashion, companies would decrease their costs and increase the power of management over the labour force.

Morris notes in chapter 3 the introduction of flexibility in the steel industry in South Wales, and the varying impacts this has had on workers and work organisation. In particular, he deals with how 'flexibility' has had the effect of marginalising the unions. Again, the coal industry provides an example of where attempts have been made to introduce this kind of 'flexibility' in an effort – adopting the most charitable view of it – to 'modernise' the industry. Flexibility here took the form of trying to intro-duce a six-day working week, twelve-hour shifts and more emphasis on productivity payments. The National Union of Mineworkers were bitterly opposed, arguing that conditions of work would suffer. Confidential Department of Trade and Industry documents, leaked to the union in 1994, showed that the government was intending to force the acceptance of the new working conditions on the labour force of the industry in the run up to its privatisation (*The Guardian*, 4 July 1994). Put at its simplest, the alternative view to that of the management was that 'flexibility' was being introduced in order to get more out of the workforce for the same amount of money. In terms of the coal industry, attempts to implement flexibility took a variety of forms. One was the far greater use of subcontractors to work in the mines, as opposed to the direct workforce. Here, the sub-contractors could be seen as the 'peripheral' workers and those – few – who remained on British Coal books, the 'core'. In this particular case, of course, the core could not be said to have enjoyed any vestige of job security. Flexibility in the coal industry also extended to changing patterns of shift work, which served to extend working time in return for longer periods away from work.

It is axiomatic therefore, in relation to the above, that the restructuring of the British economy has had a direct bearing on how work tasks themselves are organised. However, Baker, in his study of textiles in Leicestershire in chapter 4, saw few changes towards flexibility in that industry. It is obvious, then, that the flexibility which has been introduced has been introduced at different speeds and with different levels of intensity. This is bound to be the case in a private sector, capitalist economy. The wider impact of 'flexibility' is on the trade unions: it is obviously far more difficult to organise effectively a workforce which is divided, part-time, insecure as to its long-term job security prospects. Thus the power of trade unions is further diminished. In a sense, this is part of the motivation behind management thinking.

Associated with this is the idea that the changing conditions within the British economy have brought about a more 'ruthless' capitalism, one which, because of economic pressures, has less ability to offer people some of the factors that made up security in the old, post-war consensus era of politics. Central to this was full employment, or at least something closely approximating to it, and job security. Indeed, to emphasise the point by contrast, it is argued and widely accepted that there were certain companies within the British economy which operated a kind of 'paternalistic capitalism'. This was associated for a long time with some famous British companies – Cadbury, Rowntree, Pilkington, Clark's (the shoe manufacturer) – but it had a much wider bearing in the British economy, in the sense that there were many firms, far less well known, which operated something similar. There were, for example, steel mills in Sheffield, engineering works in West Yorkshire, carpet and lock manufacturers in the West Midlands (Ackers and Black, 1991) and others which operated this kind of policy. Martin and Fryer (1973), for instance, devote an entire study to the paternalistic capitalism of a floor-covering manufacturer in a north of England town. This paternalism was suddenly disrupted by economic pressures on the company which forced it to introduce redundancies in 1967. Paternalistic capitalism took various forms, but the main components of it were, as Martin and Fryer put it, that the companies concerned would demonstrate 'social responsibility and concern for their employees'. Essentially, it usually meant that a job was a 'job for life'; that if a worker was unable to work through some kind of disability, a less onerous task would be found, but the worker would not be sacked; that if your father or brother worked at the factory, you were likely to be offered a job too. Sometimes it meant the provision of leisure and recreation facilities. As Martin and Fryer (1973) note in their study of the floor covering company:

> The firm showed a generous attitude towards the sick, the disabled, and the mentally ill, employing more than its quota of disabled personnel – 7 per cent instead of 3 per cent, according to the firm –

and providing a number of quasi-retirement jobs for elderly workers: 'if you could stagger down there you were kept on' commented one warehouseman.

To the extent that this was pervasive – and it did not, by any means, apply everywhere – within British industry, it constituted what was almost a privately organised, if patchily implemented, alternative welfare state. Such paternalism was common in the coal industry, for example, after it had been nationalised in 1947. Here, the industry would very often provide the worker and his family with housing and, at least for certain periods during the 1940s, 1950s, and 1970s, paid employment of long-term tenure.

Studies on the continued existence of paternalistic capitalism are few, although the consensus of opinion seems to be that *aspects* of it, at least, have continued to survive in particular companies. Here they are seen as a means, as Ackers and Black (1991) put it, of 'securing increased loyalty and employee commitment'. Essentially, however, there were a number of pressures which effectively undermined 'paternalistic capitalism' as it had developed within British industry. First of all, as Ackers and Black (1991) note:

the presence of universal, state-provided welfare provisions in education, housing and health . . . undermined the rationale for company-based welfare capitalism.

More importantly, however, from the perspective of examining societal changes brought about by economic transition, it was *economic* pressures which sounded the death knell for the paternalistic company. It is easier to be paternalistic and carry the costs associated with it in times of relative economic prosperity than it is in times of economic strain. The post-war 'long boom' between the 1940s and the 1970s allowed companies the luxury of this kind of paternalistic management structure. When the 'long boom' was over – from the early 1970s, and perhaps the late 1960s onwards – companies could no longer afford to operate in the same fashion. The process of modernisation then, as it occurred in the 1980s and early 1990s, meant that capitalism became more ruthless, and very often more ruthless to those who could least afford it to be so.

Another factor working against the continuation of paternalistic capitalism on a big scale was the increasing *internationalisation* of British capital. In other words, much of the ownership of British business has been moving to foreign interests and, alongside this, British firms have been becoming internationally orientated. The context in which this must be understood is that, as Ackers and Black (1991) note, the 'paternalistic' company was often family-owned, or had a family that had been linked to the company for generations through retaining management or ownership connections. Many of these companies changed ownership or structure in the 1970s and

1980s. Rowntree and Cadbury, for example, became public limited companies after generations of family control. Rowntree was subsequently taken over by the Swiss mulitnational Nestlé. Lever, another 'paternalistic' company became part of a multinational; Pilkington turned itself into a multinational organisation. If the intention here is briefly to document social changes elicited by economic transition, then this move away from a capitalism which had at least some elements of 'paternalism' to it towards a more 'ruthless' capitalism, is worth noting.

Moreover, 'internationalisation' – in the form of inward investment – became a touchstone of economic policy under the Conservative government in power since 1979. Rhys demonstrates in chapter 7 how this was the case in relation to inwardly investing motor manufacturers, and notes the motives of the government as being to substitute exports for imports, and at the same time compensate for the decline of the then domestically owned British Leyland/Rover Group. Rhys also details the factors which led to so many inward investors choosing the UK as a site for investment: among these, the English language figures prominently, as do stable industrial relations (at least in the mid-1980s and early to mid-1990s), relatively low labour costs, and active and warm encouragement from governments at local and central levels. It is worth noting also the 'clustering effect': the existence of some Japanese firms here can attract others. Morris, for example, notes in chapter 3 the increasing internationalisation of the Welsh economy as the 1980s and 1990s progressed, and notes, moreover, the way inward investors were revered by the Conservative government as icons of the new, thrusting, dynamic capitalism. Rhys notes the extent to which ownership of vehicle and vehicle component manufacturers has moved overseas. Inward investment was openly welcomed. An example of this was the £58 million aid package put forward by the British government in October 1994 in order to lure the Korean multinational Samsung to Teesside in the North East of England (*The Guardian*, 18 October 1994). Stone remarks in chapter 8 that the importance of inward investment to Wearside was such that it performed the role of '"engine of growth" in the second half of the 1980s'. Martin also demon- strates the importance of inward investment to Birmingham in the 1980s and early 1990s (chapter 9).

The other way in which internationalisation impinges on economic modernisation in Britain is that the context within which companies are restructuring is, increasingly, globalised. There are two aspects to this. First, companies are operating within a business, economic, and indeed political environment, which is increasingly internationalised. This is clear from a cursory examination of some of the industries examined within this book. For example, international trade in textiles is regulated by the Multi-Fibre Agreement (MFA). Within the context of that agreement, as of 1993, a large number of imports from the world's poorer countries enter the UK market free of tariff, with the exports from the very poorest countries, such as Bangladesh, enjoying virtually unlimited access. By way of a contrast, goods from the UK are virtually excluded from the markets in Egypt, India, and Pakistan. The small quantity of goods which are allowed in are subjected to tariffs of between 100 and 125 per cent. The international trading framework is constantly changing, with new opportunities and new challenges opening up. In textiles, for example, to refer to one of the industries examined in this book, some companies supplying markets in Korea were adversely affected by the decision in 1993 by the Korean government to increase duties on textiles from the UK entering Korea from 9 per cent to 19 (*Yorkshire Post*, 5 January 1994).

Of course, this international trading framework works both ways. Companies based abroad exporting into Britain similarly have to operate within an agreed trading framework. Between 1975 and 1992 Japanese car manufacturers were subject to an agreement between the Society of Motor Manufacturers and Traders (SMMT) of Britain and Japan's car manufacturers to restrict sales by the latter to 11 per cent of total car sales in Britain. After 1992, this agreement was superseded by a new arrangement made between the European Union and the Japanese Ministry for International Trade and Industry (MITI), based on absolute sales numbers rather than a percentage of the market. The purpose of mention- ing these factors is simply to draw attention to the changing international trading environment and the fact that restructuring and modernisation do not take place within what is simply a national context. The international environment – economic *and* political, for it is the political which sets tariff barriers and the like – can have a direct bearing on the prospects for companies and workers in Britain.

Secondly, some companies are responding to this increasingly inter- national trading and political framework by becoming more globalised themselves. Rhys argues, for example, that internationalisation was essential for the motor industry in Britain to survive: 'the main companies active in the UK vehicle sector clearly need to have European and international interests in siting, sourcing and managing their operations' (chapter 7).

Another example is again provided by the textiles industry. For example, one of the biggest textiles companies in the UK, Coats Viyella, saw more than 67 per cent of its operating profits come from overseas trading operations in the 1993 financial year. It had subsidiaries across the globe, in the developed and the developing world: in Argentina, Australia, Canada, Chile, China, Indonesia, Malaysia, Philippines, and elsewhere (Coats Viyella, 1993).

RESPONSES TO CONTRACTION

The contraction of traditional industry in Britain brought a variety of responses from different government, quasi-government, and local government agencies. The decision actively to encourage inward investment, for example, was one of the policy responses from central government. As noted earlier, this policy often entailed changes in established patterns of industrial relations, as well as bringing changes in the style of management in its wake. The rationale behind this was straightforward: the 'new' incoming companies would bring with them all that was best in terms of management practice. In order for domestic companies to ensure survival, they too would have to emulate the incomers and adopt the best possible practice in relation to management techniques, technical processes, and so on. In this sense, the industrial economy as a whole would be 'modernised' and, in theory, everyone would benefit. Rhys discusses the operation of this in practice in the motor industry (chapter 7). John Butcher, Minister of State for Industry in the late 1980s, summed up the Conservative government's view of inward investment as 'a key ingredient in an efficient economy [which] encourages enterprise, more efficient production methods, better management, higher standards of design and quicker responsiveness to changing consumer demands' (*Financial Times*, 10 December 1987). The attraction of inward investment became a central plank of strategy to regenerate areas suffering from the run down of traditional industry, and therefore a major element of the attempt to 'modernise' the British economy.

Another widely implemented policy response to the decline of traditional industry has been to try to stimulate the small business sector. That this was, at a national level, a major part of the Conservative government's micro-economic policy is well known, and the reasons have been widely documented elsewhere. It is also true to say, however, that many private sector led agencies – usually enterprise agencies – as well as local authorities, have regarded the stimulation of the small business sector as a central priority.

At the level of national government, this idea of the stimulation of small business formed at least a part of the thrust towards the creation of a so-called 'enterprise culture'. The thesis held by government, and particularly by Margaret Thatcher, prime minister between 1979 and 1990, was that one of the major reasons for the relatively poor economic performance for so long in the post-war period was the absence of a sufficiently robust 'enterprise culture'. The term was interpreted in a variety of ways (see, for example, Burrows, 1991; Heelas and Morris, 1992; Keat and Abercrombie, 1991).

One aspect of its meaning – as it relates to job provision, at least – can be adequately summarised as follows. The absence of an 'enterprise culture', according to the proponents of this thesis, meant that individuals in Britain had, for far too long, depended on other, already existing, organisations to provide them with paid employment. The opposite of the enterprise culture was said to be a 'dependency culture' which afflicted some British individuals and some sectors of British society. The symptoms of the dependency culture were: dependence on others for the provision of a job, dependence on the state for welfare benefits in the absence of a job through unemployment, old age or infirmity, even, in some cases, dependence on the state for the provision of a home in the form of a council house. It was clear that the Thatcher government, in particular, felt that the breaking of this so-called 'dependency culture' was essential if economic and social progress was to be made. The route to modernisation, therefore, lay through the building of an enterprise culture. The most obvious policy option for taking it forward on the economic side was to try to stimulate the small business sector – according to the theory, this would go some way at least to breaking the dependence of people on existing organisations for work (Turner, 1990). Those seeking to promote the small business sector believed that this was also a policy which might go some way towards denting unemployment, hence its adoption by a wide range of bodies concerned with regeneration who might not always have seen eye to eye politically with the Thatcher government. Chapter 2 on coal, for instance, documents here some of the attempts at the stimulation of small business in coal areas.

The collection of values and ideas that can be subsumed under the rubric of the 'enterprise culture' is, of course, wider than is suggested above. In the 'modern' Conservatism of the 1980s and early 1990s, as represented by Margaret Thatcher and, perhaps, John Major, its values seeped into and informed a much wider and broader range of policies. For example, it infused policies towards education and health where, within the new paradigm, the market was introduced where the market had not been before. Thus those who were previously students or patients were transformed into customers and consumers, supposedly endowed with new rights commensurate with their new status. Alongside this, and as a way of cementing this new creation, the ownership of property, small businesses, and shares were to be the economic reflection of the new social design. Wealth was to be venerated as *the* measure of social success. As Mrs Thatcher herself put it: 'Economics are the method. The object is to change the soul' (quoted in Heelas and Morris, 1992).

If progress towards economic modernisation is dependent upon the creation of an enterprise culture, as the Conservatives believed in the 1980s and early 1990s, what is the evidence that such a cultural paradigm *is* being created? Stone argues in chapter 8 that some of the growth in self-employment is through people being pushed into it by high unemployment. In other words, self-employment is not expressed as a *preference*, as it would have to be in order to demonstrate the emergence of an enterprise culture, rather, people attempt it as an alternative to the dole. Stone's findings are corroborated by studies referred to in chapter 2 on economic regeneration in coal mining areas. Baker also notes that 'among the factors involved in the promotion of the small firm sector is the push factor of unemployment/uncertainty' (chapter 4).

The aim of this introduction has been to highlight some of the salient features of the changing nature of the British economy, and some of their political and economic impacts. Essentially, these can be broadly summarised as follows. First, *power structures* have changed. In other words, although it varies in extent from case to case, power has swung towards the management and owners of companies and away from trade unions and the workforce. A point connected to this is that the *security* of individual workers has declined considerably in terms of job tenure and job 'rights'. Geddes and Green note in chapter 6, for example, how the more competitive economic environment facing defence contractors in the South East has produced 'considerable instability – affecting both employment levels and locational decisions – in what were previously very stable large firms'. Secondly, the nature of employment in the 'new' industrial economy has changed. There is a far greater emphasis on part-time working, and towards the employment of women. Thirdly, there has been a decrease, generally, in the size of plants within which people work. Stone's work, described in chapter 8, corroborates this in relation to Wearside. Baker notes the increasing relative importance of the small firm in relation to textiles and clothing in Hinckley: 'To some extent this has been due to the demise of larger firms, both locally and nationally' (chapter 4). This itself has a bearing on the loci of decision making within industry. For example, Geddes and Green demonstrate the increase in the relative importance of the medium-sized business or the 'autonomous division of a bigger firm' in relation to the defence industry in the South East. They argue that this:

> has interesting implications for the future of the engineering industry, because it entails a weakening of the hegemonic role previously played by a relatively small number of very large firms. Strategic decision-making in the industry may be becoming more diffused among wider and weaker policy networks.

Finally, there has been a change in the relative position of different sectors in the economy. In other words, manufacturing industry is less important than it was, and the service sector is far more important.

Whether or not these changes constitute 'modernisation' in any meaningful sense is at the centre of the debate, and will be discussed in the conclusion. Much depends, of course, on what definition of 'modernisation' is applied. But, at the very least, a modernised economy must demonstrate an efficiency and a prosperity which earlier generations did not enjoy. No one would argue against the benefits of increased prosperity. What also matters, obviously, is the nature of its distribution. There are those who would argue that the best way towards a dynamic and thrusting, 'modernised' economy is through allowing people the prospect of great personal wealth.

This is the incentive to individual, and, on this perspective, collective progress. Others would argue that great wealth sitting alongside grinding poverty creates a potential for societal conflict so great as to make generalised economic progress impossible. Stones notes in chapter 8, for example, how 'flexibility' and the push for further deregulation of labour markets has the potential to throw significant sections of the labour force into poverty. The spectre conjured up is one of a few people desperately clinging on to, and protecting, their wealth while large numbers remain relatively impoverished. It is difficult to see how a 'modernised' economy could be built upon those foundations in any sense meaningful to the mass of the population.

REFERENCES

Ackers, P. and Black, J. (1991) 'Paternalistic Capitalism: An Organization Culture in Transition', in M. Cross and G. Payne (eds) *Work and the Enterprise Culture*, London: Falmer Press.

Aldcroft, D.H. (1982) 'Britain's Economic Decline 1870–1980', in G.W. Roderick and M.D. Stephens (eds) *The British Malaise: Industrial Performance, Education and Training in Britain Today*, Lewes: Falmer Press.

Atkinson, J. (1984) 'Manpower Strategies for Flexible Organisations', *Personnel Management*, August.

Bacon, R. and Eltis, W. (1978) *Britain's Economic Problem: Too Few Producers*, London: Macmillan.

Barberis, P. and May, T. (1993) *Government, Industry and Political Economy*, Buckingham: Open University Press.

Barnett, C. (1986) *The Audit of War. The Illusion and Reality of Britain as a Great Nation*, London: Macmillan.

Bealey, F. (1970) *The Social and Political Thought of the British Labour Party*, London: Wiedenfeld and Nicolson.

Burrows, R. (ed.) (1991) *Deciphering the Enterprise Culture: Entrepreneurship, Petty Capitalism and the Restructuring of Britain*, London: Routledge.

Campbell, M. (1990) 'Employment and the Economy in the 1980s and Beyond', in M. Campbell (ed.) *Local Economic Policy*, London: Cassell Educational.

Caslin, T. (1987) 'De-industrialisation in the UK', in H. Vane and T. Caslin (eds) *Current Controversies in Economics*, Oxford: Basil Blackwell.

Coates, D. (1986) 'The Character and Origin of Britain's Economic Decline', in D. Coates and J. Hillard (eds) *The Economic Decline of Modern Britain: The Debate between Left and Right*, Brighton: Wheatsheaf.

Coates, D. (1994) 'UK Economic Under-performance: Causes and Cures – One-day Conference Report', *Bulletin* No. 4, Spring, Leeds: Centre for Industrial Policy and Performance, University of Leeds.

Coats Viyella (1993) *Report and Accounts 1993*.

Financial Times (1987) 10 December.

Grant, W. (1993) The Politics of Economic Policy, Hemel Hempstead: Harvester Wheatsheaf.

The Guardian (1992) 18 September.

The Guardian (1993) 8 July.

The Guardian (1993) 25 November.

The Guardian (1994) 15 January.

The Guardian (1994) 15 June.

The Guardian (1994) 4 July.

The Guardian (1994) 2 August.

The Guardian (1994) 18 October.

Hall, P. (1991) 'Structural Transformation in the Regions of the United Kingdom', in Lloyd Rodwin and Hidehiko Sazanami (eds) *Industrial Change and Regional Economic Transformation: The Experience of Western Europe*, London: Harper Collins Academic.

Heelas, P. and Morris, P. (eds) (1992) *The Values of the Enterprise Culture: The Moral Debate*, London: Routledge.

Keat, R. and Abercrombie, N. (eds) (1991) *Enterprise Culture*, London: Routledge.

Mann, M. (1988) *States, War and Capitalism: Studies in Political Sociology*, Oxford: Basil Blackwell.

Martin, R. and Fryer, R.H. (1973) *Redundancy and Paternalistic Capitalism: A Study in the Sociology of Work*, London: George Allen and Unwin.

Pollard, S. (1982) *The Wasting of the British Economy: British Economic Policy 1945 to the Present*, London: Croom Helm.

Singh, A. (1977) 'UK Industry and the World Economy: A Case of Deindustrialisation?' *Cambridge Journal of Economics* 1, 113–36.

Turner, R.L. (1990) 'Mrs Thatcher's "Enterprise Culture": Is It Any Nearer?' *Social Studies Review* 5, 3.

Turner, R.L. (1992) 'Industrial Subsidies and the Manipulation of Industrial Culture: The Case of a West Yorkshire Mining Town', *The Journal of Regional and Local Studies* 12, 1, 53–64.

Wiener, M. (1981) *English Culture and the Decline of the Industrial Spirit 1850–1980*, Cambridge: Cambridge University Press.

Yorkshire Post (1994) 5 January.

2

AFTER COAL

Royce Turner

The most significant resistance to the process of deindustrialisation in Britain was marked by the strike action in 1984–85 by the National Union of Mineworkers (NUM). As so often in the past, whether rightly or wrongly, the mineworkers had been in the forefront of action by the labour movement to precipitate or prevent change.

The 1984/85 strike was aimed at preventing large-scale pit closures. As a mechanism for stopping deindustrialisation it failed. Of the 172 coal mines operated by the then National Coal Board (NCB, later British Coal) in 1984, employing 174,000, by mid-1994 there were just fifteen operating and producing coal and one mine under development. In total, these employed about 6,000 administrative staff and about 8,000 mineworkers (*The Times*, 24 August 1994) (see Table 2.1). The strike *did* succeed in one major way, however: it placed on the political agenda, arguably for the first time in a major way, the issue of pit closures, and the wider issue of deindustrialisation.

The NUM – or, at least, sections within it – had been pressing for action by government to prevent pit closures since the mid-1970s, but had met with little success in trying to mobilise its own ranks, or in promoting action by the government to stop contraction (see Turner, 1985). In the mid-1980s, however, pit closures became the major political issue in Britain, a test of strength between the government, supported in the implementation of its policy by the police, and a union which had a reputation for organisational strength and which could call upon its own army of pickets. Following what was, effectively, the defeat of the NUM in 1985, contraction in the coal industry intensified, and was implemented, largely, without much public debate. However, the issue of pit closures returned to the political agenda with a vengeance in October 1992, when the announcement of the closure of thirty-one of the fifty pits being operated by British Coal caused a widespread public outcry.

From the perspective of this book, deindustrialisation in coal cannot be seen in isolation. It was clear that the ramifications of coal industry decline

Table 2.1 British Coal collieries as of October 1994

Longannet (Scotland)
Point of Ayr (North Wales)
Kellingley (Yorkshire)
Maltby (Yorkshire)
Prince of Wales (Yorkshire)
North Selby (Yorkshire)
Riccall (Yorkshire)
Stillingfleet (Yorkshire)
Wistow (Yorkshire)
Whitemoor (Yorkshire)
Bilsthorpe (Nottinghamshire)
Harworth (Nottinghamshire)
Thoresby (Nottinghamshire)
Welbeck (Nottinghamshire)
Daw Mill (Warwickshire)
Asfordby (under development) (Leicestershire)

Source: British Coal, 24 October 1994; *Financial Times*, 14 April 1994.

would reach much further into the heartlands of the British industrial economy. Martin notes in chapter 9, for example, how contraction in the coal industry had a 'marked impact' on companies in Birmingham, a city not usually associated with the coal industry. In 1992, the Association of British Mining Equipment Companies (ABMEC) launched a 'Campaign for Coal' (letter to *The Guardian*, 9 April 1992). Thus a number of the owners and managers of industry – not just sections of labour – were working actively at this time to save the deep-mined coal industry from virtual extinction.

Both the 1984–85 strike, and the 1992 outcry against pit closures put pressure on the government to modify policy on closures. In the first case, the government decided to fight and eventually saw off the NUM challenge. The public outcry in 1992, however, for a brief time, forced the government into what was at least a partial retreat on the number of pits to be closed. Both events precipitated policies from the government aimed at overcoming the economic devastation wreaked by pit closures. This chapter seeks to assess the response of those authorities charged with the economic regeneration of coalfield areas, and to examine which strategies were chosen, and the impact of those strategies. A central and related issue is: what happened to redundant mineworkers? Did they find their way back into the labour market, or did they remain unemployed?

Essentially, this chapter divides into two: the problems facing those authorities charged with regenerating the coalfields, and the impact of the strategies adopted.

24

THE POLITICAL CONTEXT

The first issue to address is the political context in which pit closures were taking place, and the political ramifications of protest. These were of paramount importance in shaping the outcome of policy in the 1980s and 1990s.

As is well known and now needs little rehearsal, the Thatcher-led Conservative government which came to power in 1979 placed a strong emphasis on achieving the primacy of the free market in many areas of policy. The implication of this, so far as policies towards business and industry were concerned, was that there would be a full-scale retreat from the 'old', 1970s practice of providing subsidies to struggling industries or companies. Coupled with this was a firm belief in the superiority of private sector ownership of industry and business. According to this argument, nationalisation had bred inefficiency. Businesses had been kept alive which should have gone to the wall long ago. As was noted in chapter 1, trade unions were also particularly unpopular with this administration, particularly if the union in question was perceived to be a militant organisation.

Two years after the Conservative's election in 1979, Arthur Scargill was elected president of the NUM, with an overwhelming majority of over 70 per cent (see Crick, 1985). Scargill was the most prominent left-wing trade union leader in Britain. He had been at the forefront of the organisation of two successful strikes by the NUM in 1972 and 1974, both of which, it could be argued, humiliated an earlier Conservative administration trying to implement an incomes policy. The latter strike contributed to the Conservatives losing governmental office in 1974.

The coal industry in the 1980s, then, could be seen as a microcosm of everything the Thatcher-led Conservative government saw as being wrong with British industry. It was in state ownership; it was 100 per cent unionised; it had managed to make an overall financial surplus only in the years 1976, 1977, and 1978 across the whole period 1975 to 1990 (NCB, 1981; British Coal Corporation, 1990). In these circumstances, it was inevitable that, sooner or later, there would be a clash between the government and the union.

That clash came in 1981 even before Scargill took over at the helm of the union, when Derek Ezra, then chairman of the NCB, announced that the Corporation was producing 7 million tonnes excess coal, and that production would have to be cut back. Pits would have to close. The proposal was that twenty-three pits should close over the 1981/82 financial year. At the time, the NUM was still a powerful union, commanding bargaining power which, given their monopoly hold on the production of the major fuel for electricity generation in Britain, could cause governments to change policy. The closure announcement precipitated widespread spontaneous action by the mineworkers, particularly in the areas believed to be under most threat, such as South Wales, South Yorkshire, Kent, and Scotland (Allen, 1981). A national strike was threatened, and the government's turnround was swift: it removed the closure threat, and announced further subsidies for the coal industry. The labour movement rejoiced in victory. The government had suffered a humiliating climb down. It was a climb down, moreover, which the government had pledged would not happen to them: 'giving in' to union strength they had identified as being one of the great weaknesses of previous, not least Conservative, administrations. For his part, Scargill was more cautious than overtly jubilant. He believed that to talk of 'complete victory was premature' and that the government had merely postponed the date of battle (Scargill, 1981).

The political ramifications, however, were at least twofold. First, the National Union of Mineworkers were confirmed, however temporarily, as yet again being a trade union which had the power to alter government policy. Secondly, because of this, there is little doubt that the resolve of the government to beat this union once and for all, was deepened.

The final, cataclysmic, battle began in 1984, with the onset of the strike that was to last for a year following the announcement of the closure of Cortonwood colliery in South Yorkshire. That strike has been documented in a variety of different ways, and it is not the intention of this chapter to rehearse its causes, the way it was conducted, or its political, social, and economic consequences (see, rather, Adeney and Lloyd, 1986; Beynon, 1985; Callinicos and Simons, 1985; Coulter *et al.*, 1984; Goodman, 1985). It *is* important at least to mention the strike, however, because of the effect it had on the NUM and, more importantly, on the other trade unions within the land. The once seemingly invincible NUM had been decisively defeated. By 1994, the union was a shadow of its former self. The symbolism of this was profound. If they could be defeated in the battle against economic restructuring, who could possibly win? The retreat of the trade union movement as a whole – in the face of punitive legislation and high unemployment – was further exacerbated. From the government's viewpoint, the 'defeat' of the NUM removed one further barrier to the full implementation of a free market philosophy towards business and industry.

The October 1992 announcement of mass pit closures, however, heralded a surprising degree of support for the mineworkers. Even newspapers usually unflinchingly sympathetic to the Conservative government were prepared to offer vehement criticism. *The Sun*, for example, devoted six full pages to the issue on the day the news broke, leading on the front page with an open letter to the Prime Minister, John Major, headed 'Do you have a plan to get us out of this bloody mess?' (*The Sun*, 15 October 1992). The theme throughout the coverage in this and other tabloid newspapers was of betrayal of a loyal and hard-working labour force. This was a somewhat ironic portrayal given the treatment the miners had received from the same newspaper during the 1984–85 strike but, then again, newspapers are in

26

business to sell papers and *The Sun* had clearly judged the mood of the nation correctly. The other tabloid newspapers adopted a similar tone. The *Daily Star*, for instance, also led on its front page with an open letter to John Major from a redundant miner holding his newborn baby. The headline caption was 'What has my baby done to deserve this?' (*Daily Star*, 15 October 1992). The *Daily Mirror* adopted the headline 'Rotten to the Core' (*Daily Mirror*, 17 October 1992).

The government itself was initially forced to backtrack, announcing that twelve collieries would be reprieved. For a political party so well versed in the art of government, the political mistake of allowing a mass closure announcement to be made was simply incredible. It was, of course, conditioned by the government's desire to reduce the coal industry to a small, profitable, size, in order to successfully privatise it. The previous policy on closures had been to announce contraction in increments: one a week, or one every two weeks. In November 1991, for example, Askern colliery, near Doncaster, closed (*Doncaster Star*, 23 November 1991). The same month saw the announcement of the closure of Thurcroft colliery, near Rotherham (*The Guardian*, 29 November 1991). In February 1992, the closures of Bickershaw colliery, in Lancashire, Sherwood colliery in Nottinghamshire, and Allerton Bywater colliery in Yorkshire, were announced (*The Independent*, 1 February 1992). By these incremental means, substantial contraction could be achieved with little political fall-out. One pit closure by itself has little effect nationally on the political agenda. Its consequences are localised. The closure of thirty-one pits at the same time was always likely to elicit the support of the public, especially against a government which was particularly unpopular. It was seen as picking on people and communities who had already suffered enough, and who were little able to defend themselves. Moreover, the job of a miner has long been associated in the popular consciousness with hard work and danger, and there was always likely to be sympathy for them.

The government's policy reversal on pit closures proved to be only temporary. Within a year, more than the thirty-one collieries originally earmarked for closure had been abandoned by British Coal, in a reversion to the incremental closure policy. The importance of the 1992 outcry against pit closures, however, was that it brought to the forefront of the political agenda the need for economic regeneration in coalfield areas. The announcement of increased efforts in this direction formed a central part of the government's attempts to defuse a politically difficult situation. Nevertheless, efforts to promote economic regeneration in coal mining areas predate October 1992. It is just that many of these efforts – at least in national terms – had a relatively low profile. Given the longevity of some of them, they provide the best examples of what can, or cannot, be achieved. It is important, first, however, to assess the economic context in which these efforts were being implemented.

THE ECONOMIC CONTEXT

There are factors which distinguish deindustrialisation in coal mining areas from deindustrialisation elsewhere, and which make economic regeneration efforts that much more difficult to bring to a successful outcome in coalfields and former coalfields.

First, there has been a rapid shift in the relative prosperity of localities associated, or formerly associated, with coal mining. Thus, although the coal industry has been in continuous decline in terms of numbers of collieries and labour force levels since nationalisation in 1947, albeit with a period of stabilisation and occasional slight upturn in the 1970s, contraction in the 1980s and early 1990s was particularly rapid. One study noted, for example, that of the most deprived districts in the UK in 1983, no locality associated with mining featured among them. Just five years later, there were five localities associated with coal mining in the top thirteen (Beynon, Hudson, and Sadler, 1991). Clearly, this has implications for economic regeneration. The lower the economic base, the greater the haul to achieve some semblance of relative prosperity. The other important impact of such a rapid decline in economic prosperity is the demoralising effect on the local community and, therefore, on the local workforce. This is reflected in lower levels of consumer demand for locally traded goods and services, adding a further depressing element into the local economy, and in the physically run-down appearance of many of the former coal towns. Grimethorpe is a classic example. Situated close to Barnsley, but well off the beaten track, Grimethorpe exhibited the classic social insularity and isolation associated with mining. Here was a small town almost totally reliant, economically, on coal. It had a large colliery complex, NCB administrative offices, a coking plant, a brickworks located there to take advantage of the coal, and two small power stations, one of which was an experimental pressurised fluidised bed unit (PFB). The power stations closed in 1991. The colliery itself finally closed in 1993 (*Barnsley Chronicle*, 7 May 1993). After that, the physical structure and appearance of the place diminished considerably. Petty crime increased dramatically. The employers that remained talked of pulling out. Demoralisation on this scale is hardly conducive to the 'dynamism' widely perceived to be a prerequisite of economic success in the 1990s.

Secondly, it is evident and obvious that certain localities associated with the coal industry in Britain – often referred to as 'pit villages' or 'pit towns' – were one industry economies. The 'pit village' developed solely because the coal industry developed. Indeed, private sector coal mine owners would organise the building of company-owned housing near the pit head in the nineteenth and early twentieth centuries. 'Company villages' were created, for example, in the 1920s in Blidworth, Bilsthorpe, Clipstone, Welbeck, Edwinstowe, Ollerton, and Harworth in Nottinghamshire (see, for example, Field, 1986).

The coal industry, then, bred communities which were steeped in mining, and which had very little need to develop the versatility necessary for other kinds of economic activity. It was an economic and social culture based on hard, manual labour. It was a culture which had been amply drawn upon when it could provide profitability for coal owners, or be used to meet the nation's energy requirements. In an age when coal could not have the same level of input into either, it became one more factor which worked to the disadvantage of coal mining areas: the insurance companies, and other financial service companies which were to provide the employment growth of the 1980s, had no need for a hard, manual labour culture. 'Modernisation' of a local economy in these circumstances would present immense challenges.

The 'one industry' nature of coal mining localities had other ramifications. It meant that where a pit closed, or shed labour, the local economy would have very little else to offer the local population in the way of jobs and economic activity. By and large, the coal industry had a semi-rural setting, with many pits being remote from the major population, and therefore from work centres, so alternative work could be difficult to find. Semi-rurality, however, was not the case in all coalfield localities. There were exceptions, particularly in the Lancashire and Nottinghamshire coalfields, where the pits were often associated with towns and cities (see, for example, Howell, 1989). Nottingham, for example, had coal mines within its city boundaries, Babbington, which closed in 1986, and Clifton, which closed in 1968. The impact of coal mining decline was never going to be so great on a city of that size with a diversified economy as it would be on a small mining village isolated geographically and sometimes even culturally from the major commercial and social centres. The point holds true in sufficient localities for it to be significant, and was one further factor militating against successful economic regeneration in many coalfield localities.

Essentially, then, it can be argued that many coalfields and former coalfield localities have had poorly developed economic structures. The Coalfield Communities Campaign (CCC) (1986), a local authority-based pressure group campaigning *inter alia* for greater regeneration efforts in places associated with coal, argued that:

> The NCB does not appear to generate economic activity among suppliers to the same extent as most manufacturing industries.

Moreover, they argued that the small business sector indigenous to coal mining communities was often underdeveloped. The Conservatives, and others, had invested a huge amount of optimism in the prospects for economic regeneration being built on the back of an expanding small business sector. The existing economic structure in the coalfields seemed to be disadvantageous in this respect. The CCC argued:

In the West Yorkshire coalfield area, for example, in 1981 small firms accounted for only 1 in 20 persons employed compared with 1 in 11 for the country as a whole.

The one industry nature of many localities associated with coal presented problems for any form of economic regeneration strategy. It meant that skills appropriate to other industries and businesses might not have developed or been encouraged. If appropriate skills in the labour market do not exist, inward investment from industries or businesses alternative to coal may be discouraged, as companies are not sure that their labour requirements would be met. There are those who argue – although it seems difficult to substantiate – that governments have deliberately discouraged non-mining companies from investing in coalfields as a method of keeping the workforce 'tied' into mining. The argument is that, if alternative work had been available, the mines would have been starved of labour as the workforce fled the pits (see, for example, Coates, 1992). In these circumstances, what could be called *spontaneous* economic regeneration – where it takes place without government intervention – is less likely, as people were not learning skills in the established dominant industry which could then be transferred into, say, a new entrepreneurial small business which might contribute to a rejuvenation of the local economy. The skills associated with coal mining are usually specific to the coal mining industry.

To appreciate the above point fully, it has to be recognised just how *old* an industry coal actually is. In some communities it provided the majority of employment for over a hundred years. To pick a by no means untypical example, take the 11,000 population 'free standing' pit town of South Kirkby in West Yorkshire, between Wakefield and Barnsley. The shaft of South Kirkby pit was sunk in 1880. In 1984, over 50 per cent of the jobs in the South Kirkby locality were in coal mining. South Kirkby pit was closed in March 1988 on the grounds that it was 'uneconomic'. Such a dominance of one industry over time brought forth a particular kind of social, political, and community culture. This was compounded by the village and small town nature of many coal mining localities: there was an immense *concentration* of one kind of employment in small places. It reduced any chance of cosmopolitanism; and it reduced interaction, socially and economically, with people outside the coal mining *milieu*. Part of this culture was inter-generational employment and skills transference: the son followed the father down the pit. Hence the message of miners' leader Arthur Scargill during the 1984–85 miners' strike: don't take your redundancy and sell your job, it's not yours to sell. The often hazardous working conditions, the terrible accidents and, even after nationalisation, the uncertainty surrounding job security, also contributed to the political and social culture. It was a culture which inspired some to political activity, and nearly all to hold a strong sense of community, based upon the miners' welfare club, loyalty to the union, and the idea of the miner 'providing' for his family. Not voting Labour, the party of collectivism and the working classes, for example, was seen at best as eccentric; at worst as downright disloyal. For obvious political reasons, this was not a culture which would find much favour with the Conservative governments of the 1980s and early 1990s where, at the risk of oversimplification, the ethos encouraged was much more strongly based on social and economic individualism. Nor was it a culture which would be best placed to produce economic revival in the political context of the 1980s and early 1990s. In that period, as noted earlier, the government believed there was a need to reduce trade union power in order to provide conditions suitable for economic modernisation. Similarly, the government believed economic advancement would be best achieved by emphasising individualist progress over and above community progress. Or, at least, it believed that the latter was achievable only as a consequence of the former.

There were two other, connected, problems faced by those charged with the economic regeneration of coalfield localities. The first was image. If the culture referred to above actually did exist, the *perception* of it in the popular consciousness was an exaggerated caricature. Places with a poor image find it difficult to attract inward investment. Perhaps more importantly, from the viewpoint of trying to build a sustainable economic future, it has been argued that companies which showed a potential for expansion would not locate there. Hall (1988), for example, argued that industries which showed potential for growth in the late twentieth and early twenty-first centuries – robotics, biotechnology, 'alternative' energy systems – would be unlikely to locate themselves in the areas formerly associated with traditional industry. Instead these new industries would seek out their own environmentally attractive locations, possibly within the vicinity of an 'entrepreneurial university such as Silicon Valley and Stanford University or the Research Triangle of North Carolina, located between Duke University and the University of North Carolina'.

Some support was offered for this thesis by Champion and Green (1989) who studied 280 Local Labour Market Areas (LLMAs) across Britain. In the study of LLMAs, Champion and Green noted that Barnsley and Mansfield – two towns heavily associated with coal mining since well before the Second World War and into the post-war era – had a proportion employed in producer services[1] and high technology industries which was 'particularly low' in relation to other LLMAs. Barnsley, for instance, had under 4 per cent of its workforce in these sectors as of 1989: a tenth of Bracknell's level.

Poor image then, as a problem, could manifest itself in a number of ways, and militate against the chances of success of economic regeneration efforts. One effect of poor image, for instance, might be outsiders holding a mining locality in low esteem, thus discouraging inward investment. Alternatively, poor image might be reflected in a lack of community and individual self-confidence within the mining, or former mining, localities themselves (see, for example, Derbyshire County Council, 1991).

The second connected problem was sometimes one of geography and isolation, and poor accessibility. There were exceptions to this, as noted earlier, but many coalfield localities suffered from having a transport infrastructure not suited to the needs of modern business. Some of the mining communities in the South Wales valleys, for example, were relatively isolated from the east–west corridor of development along the M4 motorway bound for England (ACOM Secretariat, 1991). Or take the Dearne Valley, in South Yorkshire. The Dearne Valley comprised the small towns and villages of Thurnscoe, Goldthorpe, Bolton-on-Dearne, Mexborough, Conisborough, Swinton, Wath, and Brampton, which straddled the boundaries of Barnsley, Rotherham, and Doncaster. What they had in common was one time extensive coal mining and the River Dearne. In 1976, over 11,000 workers were employed in coal mining in the Dearne (Coopers and Lybrand Deloitte and Sheffield City Polytechnic, 1990). By 1994, the coal mining industry had completely died. Part of the subsequent regeneration efforts were focused on improving the road network.

REGENERATION EFFORTS

Actual regeneration efforts have taken a variety of forms, and have been implemented through a variety of agencies. There has been, first of all, a strong emphasis on the promotion of small businesses and self-employment. British Coal Enterprise (BCE), for example, had this as one of its central objectives. Other agencies, such as local enterprise agencies, pursued this line as well. 'Recharge North East' provided one example. Recharge North East operated in what were the coal mining areas of County Durham, Tyne and Wear, and Northumberland. It was funded by BCE, the European Community, and the DTI, and provided 'management timeshare, pro-marketing, mentoring and the growth potential study' (Recharge North East, undated). Other efforts have involved the establishment of enterprise zones and new industrial and business estates. Langthwaite Grange Industrial Estate, near Pontefract in West Yorkshire, for example, was designated an enterprise zone in 1991. This was in one of the most heavily mined parts of Western Europe. Similarly, the government announced in March 1993 that it would consider the establishment of enterprise zones in the Dearne Valley, Mansfield and Easington in the North East (*The Guardian*, 30 March 1993). By late 1994, these were in the process of implementation, and expected to come on stream in 1995. Other projects have included infrastructure developments. The building of the Dearne Valley link road is one example. The objective of this was to link the towns mentioned earlier with nearby motorways. It was due for completion in 1996, at a cost, along with some other major road improvements, of £39 million (Coopers and Lybrand

Deloitte and Sheffield Business School, 1990). Another example of extensive infrastructural improvements relates to the virtually defunct South Wales coalfield. Here, a central government inspired initiative – perhaps the biggest in any coalfield region – involved a high number of infrastructural and environmental improvement schemes. The Valley Regeneration Towns project, as it was known, was launched in 1988 as a central-government-initiated and co-ordinated regeneration strategy, which also encompassed activity by local authorities, the Welsh Development Agency, voluntary associations and the private sector (Welsh Office, undated; Welsh Office Information Division, 1988). The Valley Regeneration Towns Project was itself a successor to The Valleys Initiative, launched by central government in 1986 (Romaya and Alden, 1987 and 1988).

Mechanisms for regeneration also included efforts directed at training. British Coal Enterprise was involved in this to some extent. Following redundancy, mineworkers could receive training financed by BCE under the Job and Career Change Scheme. The relevant local TECs were also involved in the retraining of mineworkers. Barnsley and Doncaster Training and Enterprise Council made special efforts in the Dearne valley in South Yorkshire, for example (*Barnsley Independent*, 21 July 1992). The government provided additional assistance for mineworkers made redundant from the Bevercotes, Clipstone, and Silverhill pits in Nottinghamshire through the Nottinghamshire Training and Enterprise Council. The funding amounted to £7 million over two years. The TEC's 'normal' budget was £20 million per year, so the increased figures represented a substantial amount. Further money was being made available for the retraining of mineworkers redundant from the Annesley and Ollerton collieries in Nottinghamshire (*Financial Times*, 14 June 1994). One locality associated with mining had a 'task force' assigned to it by central government. Doncaster Task Force existed between July 1987 and September 1990. This was one of sixteen task forces created by Mrs Thatcher's Conservative government in 1986 and 1987, specifically to address the problems of high unemployment in small urban locations. Doncaster Task Force made its highest priority training and retraining (see Turner, 1992a). A detailed analysis of the impact of training measures in mining areas is yet to be carried out. The general view on training, however, is that it can be hardly other than beneficial. Doncaster Task Force's efforts can claim some modest success (Turner, 1992a).

One particular project aimed at securing economic regeneration in the coalfields was directed specifically at promoting innovation: this was the Barnsley Business and Innovation Centre. The innovation centre idea started off in the USA, where the first innovation centres were associated with universities (Leigh and North, 1986). Barnsley Business and Innovation Centre was the second to be established in Britain, in 1988. At the time of writing, it was the only innovation centre to be operating in the heart of what had become a rapidly declining coalfield. The idea behind innovation centres was straightforward: innovative products, processes or services could be turned into 'market winners', thereby stimulating local economic development and aiding the prospect of bringing about economic 'modernisation'. The objective behind this – to contribute towards 'modernisation' via upgrading the local economic and technological base – is undoubtedly worthwhile. Its effects have, as of 1994, yet to be seen as anything other than marginal, however (Turner, 1993a).

The efforts at regenerating the coalfields, then, can be categorised in a number of ways. First those projects that were directed specifically, and mostly exclusively, at straightforward job creation. The enterprise zone activities could be characterised in this way, as could some of the small business promotion activities. A second categorisation relates to those efforts which were directed at 'modernising' the local economy. In the modernisation category could be placed any efforts at moving a local economy from a phase of being dependent on 'traditional' industry, through to a phase of higher technology or producer service orientation. The Barnsley Business and Innovation Centre would certainly fit that criterion. Modernisation would also include some types of training which would potentially, if successful, provide *individuals* at least with a route from one economic phase to another. Similarly, some infrastructural developments could be placed in this category.

CASE STUDIES

This chapter examines regeneration activities in case study fashion drawing in particular on the enterprise zone at South Kirkby; the post-redundancy experiences of mineworkers from Markham Main and Brodsworth collieries; and some of the activities of BCE. No claim is made that these are totally representative of all regeneration efforts taking place in all coalfield areas. However, they *do* represent different efforts in different places and therefore have some claim to being a representative sample of efforts and outcome.

South Kirkby enterprise zone

Enterprise zones have a particular significance in relation to economic regeneration in coalfield areas. This is because three new enterprise zones were announced by the government in response to the public outcry over the October 1992 pit closures, as if they would bring, within a short space of time, economic revival. Few people realised, at the time, that there had already been an enterprise zone in existence for ten years in what was a rapidly declining coalfield, at South Kirkby, mentioned earlier. This allowed for some prognosis to be made as to how the new enterprise zones might fare in their task of helping to bring about an economic regeneration. There was a twist of irony in the government's revival of the enterprise zone idea in the face of continued deindustrialisation. In December 1987, Nicholas Ridley, at that time Secretary of State for the Environment, told the Commons that the government did not intend to establish any more enterprise zones in England, though proposals for other parts of the UK would still be considered. They had been expensive and had not given value for money (Turner, 1989). Clearly, the exigencies of deindustrialisation meant that a policy seen as having limited success in the late 1980s could be dusted off on the grounds of political expediency in the early 1990s. The government, after all, had to be seen to be responding to public disapproval.

South Kirkby was a free standing pit town which had a population of under 11,000 as of the early 1990s. The basic economic outline was sketched earlier: here was a pit town which had had a long-standing dependence on coal and a heavy concentration of employment in the industry. South Kirkby was within the parliamentary constituency of Hemsworth.The constituency could still boast six pits within its boundaries as late as 1985.

By 1992, only one of the six pits – the Frickley-South Elmsall coal mine – remained. While the life of any pit in the 1980s and 1990s was in jeopardy, the death of Frickley itself had not been expected. It had been one of British Coal's most productive collieries. British Coal had said of this pit in August 1990: 'Frickley is a big-hitting colliery – it will last well into the next century' (British Coal, 1990). Frickley was one of the thirty-one coal mines scheduled for closure in October 1992. It eventually closed forever in November 1993, emphasising the extent to which, no matter how good a colliery's performance, no matter how good the quality of its coal, contraction was such that no colliery was safe.

If the effectiveness of enterprise zones in the economic regeneration of coal mining areas is to be judged, it is to the South Kirkby/Hemsworth area to which an evaluation should be addressed. The policy outcome, however, in terms of the 'creation' of paid employment – in other words, jobs – was modest. When enterprise zone status was granted to Langthwaite Grange industrial estate, in South Kirkby, it already boasted the equivalent of 1,215 full-time jobs. By August 1990, research showed that there were fifty-seven companies providing 2,120 full time jobs. So in nine years, the net 'additional' number of jobs created had been 905 at best. It is well known, moreover, that many of the jobs 'created' in enterprise zones have been simply relocations from the nearby locality. Reviewing an early report from the Roger Tym Partnership, which had monitored the enterprise zone experi- ment on behalf of the government, the *Financial Times* of 18 October 1983, had this to say:

Tym found that nine out of every ten entrants [to zones] had come from the same county. Three-quarters of the companies moving into the zones confessed that they would not have looked outside the county for new premises and an overwhelming 85 per cent said they had no intention of going outside the region.

Companies that were on the industrial estate before its designation as an enterprise zone, or would have been operating in the locality anyway, accounted for more than 77 per cent of the employment in the zone only one year before it ceased to enjoy the status, in October 1990. At least fifteen companies, employing 579 people, could be identified as local relocations. Subtracting those 579 jobs from the 905 'created' left the 'new' employment figure at 326. By way of comparison, so that the context of deindustrialisation is fully exposed, the South Kirkby-Riddings pit complex employed 1,350 in May 1987. This leaves out the substantial numbers of workers employed at the other pits mentioned earlier.

The biggest employer in the enterprise zone in 1990, arriving in October of the same year, was a men's outfitter, providing 370 jobs. On moving into the zone, however, the company closed one factory in South Kirkby itself and one three miles away. This local relocation involved neither an increase nor a decrease in the number of jobs available. There was, therefore, no stimulus to the local economy. Other relocations included a chemical company, a glass recycling company, a security company, and a Christmas hamper packing company, all from close by.

Of the six companies in the zone employing more than 100 people in October 1990, three had been on the estate before its designation as an enterprise zone. A fourth was a local relocation: the men's outfitter. It has to be said that this was hardly the basis on which to build a new, thriving local economy.

One of the companies that was already on the estate before designation was to receive one of the largest subsidies. This was a subsidiary of a Swedish multinational. The subsidy was calculated at something over £2 million in the period 1981 to 1990. This money went to a company whose British operations showed a gross profit of £7.23 million to the year December 1990 (Turner, 1992c). A criticism that is made of industrial subsidies in general – and enterprise zone tax relief can be classed as a industrial subsidy – is that companies obtain money from the government for doing what they would have been doing anyway, without the subsidy (see, for example, Grant, 1985). Here is a classic example. The subvention provided for no increase in economic activity.

In general terms, the most successful enterprise zones have been those that were geographically well situated, and those where there was additional public sector help (see Lawless, 1989). For example, the Corby enterprise zone was relatively successful, but had gained from other benefits available to steel closure areas. The enterprise zone in Swansea was also relatively successful, but this had benefited from the highly interventionist Welsh Development Agency. The Isle of Dogs enterprise zone had benefited from the activities of the public sector funded London Docklands Development Corporation. Thus the success of some of the enterprise zones sounded less like the success of a new flourishing spirit of enterprise and more like good old-fashioned government intervention. On the basis of South Kirkby, it has yet to be proved that enterprise zones can provide much help to small, one industry pit towns. They do represent, however, some effort to address the economic problems facing declining coal mining areas, and it may well be that their impact is augmented by other public sector led activities. The enterprise zone in the Dearne Valley, for instance, will operate under the auspices of the Dearne Valley Partnership, a public sector led body co-ordinating the regeneration efforts there. Moreover, the Dearne Valley was the winner of a £37.5 million aid package in 1991 from central government under the City Challenge scheme, as well as over £100 million from other government sources (Turner, 1993b).

Post-redundancy experiences

One indication of the level of success of secure economic regeneration efforts is the ease or difficulty faced by displaced mineworkers in trying to find their way back into the labour market in alternative jobs. Preferably, from the viewpoint of trying to secure a 'modern' economy, these jobs should be in economic sectors likely to have some capacity for longevity in the economy. How have mineworkers fared?

Obviously, it is impossible to be certain about what has happened to the more than 150,000 mineworkers displaced from their employment throughout the course of the 1980s and early 1990s. Surveys of mineworkers in particular areas at particular times, however, have been carried out. Some of these relate to the 1980s and early 1990s, and these can be compared and contrasted with earlier studies carried out in the 1960s and even before. Witt authored a report on the post-redundancy experiences in the late 1980s of mineworkers in the Barnsley/Wakefield area (Witt, 1990). The Coalfield Communities Campaign (CCC) published a series of studies in 1994 which covered large numbers of mineworkers after pit closures at Grimethorpe; Siverhill, in Nottinghamshire; Vane Tempest, in the North East; and Parkside, in Lancashire (Guy, 1994 a–d). Other reports cover the 1950s and 1960s, and even before. One of the pioneering studies, for instance, was on the impact of the closure of Ryhope, a colliery near Sunderland closed in 1966. This was a study undertaken jointly by the NCB and the government (Department of Employment and Productivity, 1970). An analysis of the economic and social consequences of pit closures in the North East of England between 1956 and 1965 was carried out by a research team at the University of Newcastle upon Tyne (House and Knight, 1967).

As far back as 1949, a study was carried out on what happened to displaced mineworkers in Shotts, an area of former pit villages between Glasgow and Edinburgh (Heughan, 1953). Examination of the post-coal career experiences of displaced mineworkers, therefore, is not new. It was rendered more urgent in the 1980s and 1990s, however, by the extent of contraction in the industry.

One of the biggest, and therefore most important, studies was carried out in 1992 and 1993, by Sheffield Business School (Sheffield Business School, 1993). Seventy-seven mineworkers were interviewed between June and October 1992, when their colliery, Markham Main, was still open but facing the prospect of closure. Seventy of those mineworkers were re-interviewed between June and September 1993 following the mine's closure. Additionally, 176 former mineworkers who had worked at the Brodsworth colliery were interviewed between July 1992 and January 1993. Brodsworth had, for many years, been the biggest pit in Yorkshire, traditionally the biggest coalfield, employing 2,907 in 1978, for example (*Guide to the Coalfields*, 1979). Both collieries were near Doncaster. Markham Main was subsequently reopened as a private sector coal mine run by Coal Investments in April 1994. In terms of employment, however, it began its new life as a shadow of its former self, targeted to employ only 150.

The findings relating to the post-redundancy experiences of former mineworkers are illuminating, and are an important aid in for the evaluation of economic and labour market prospects facing those put out of work. At the time of the second interviews, only 40 per cent of the redundant Markham Main mineworkers had managed to find themselves alternative jobs. Importantly, however, a third of those that had found new work were working back in coal mining, this time employed as subcontractors rather than directly by British Coal. In other words, the economic sector they were working in remained the same, as did, largely, the jobs they were doing. There was no semblance of an economic transition. Perhaps even more importantly, the majority of former coal miners had responded to redundancy by effectively *dropping out of the labour market*, either through long-term sick leave, or through long-term unemployment, or through early retirement. Of the total number 25 per cent remained unemployed, and one had retired. The crucial figure to reflect upon, however, is that 23 per cent had gone long-term sick.

These figures have a number of implications, not the least of which is that this cannot be a sound basis upon which to build a new, 'modernised' economy. Exiting from the labour market is, rather, a reflection of crisis management by individuals responding to being placed in a difficult situation. The figure of the long-term sick becomes even more significant given the fact that the average age of the redundant mineworkers at Markham Main was 39, not the usual age at which people become too ill to resume any kind of work. Indeed, taking the Markham Main interviewees sample, 20 per cent of those interviewed in the original sample said that health problems had restricted the kind of work they were able to engage in. This increased to a dramatic 46 per cent at the follow-up interview. Interestingly, Stone notes in chapter 8 that a large number of workers – particularly those in the older age group – have effectively dropped out of the labour market and are classified as 'permanently sick'. Using census data from 1991, Stone shows that nearly 25 per cent of Wearside men in the 45–65 age group are classified in this way. Morris, too, notes here the quadrupling of those classified as 'permanently sick' in certain local authority wards in Wales which have seen large-scale industrial transform-ation (chapter 3). Perhaps exiting from the labour market has become a common response to the problems presented by rapid structural economic change. Obviously, however, it is not a good portent for the economy as a whole. It means that human resources are not being utilized properly. Nor is it auspicious for individuals who see their earning power, and the sense of identity that employment can confer, totally removed.

THE 'ENTERPRISE CULTURE'

It was noted in chapter 1 that one of the mechanisms to economic recovery much vaunted by the Conservatives was via the creation of an 'enterprise culture'. In concrete terms, as far as economic regeneration is concerned, a major part of the creation of an 'enterprise culture' was the idea that people should set up their own small businesses and/or enter self-employment. It is worthwhile to note, therefore, what the outcome was here in terms of the impact of self-employment. While there was, initially, very strong interest in self-employment among the displaced Markham Main mineworkers – 32 per cent said that they were intending to make moves towards it – only 3 per cent of those interviewed had actually entered into self-employment. A further 5 per cent of those interviewed said that they were intending to make moves which would lead them to self-employment within twelve months. Of the Brodsworth men, only 2.8 per cent had entered into self-employment at the time of the interviews. These figures on actual and potential self-employment remain relatively small. The implication has to be that the construction of an 'enterprise culture' as a mechanism for economic regeneration is a long way off. The inability, or reluctance, of displaced mineworkers to become entrepreneurs is corroborated by Rees and Thomas (1991), studying the South Wales coalfield. The view of the authors of this study was that 'there is no evidence . . . that local people, who would otherwise be members of an industrial working class, are being "converted" into small scale capitalists'.

Witt (1990), in his study of redundant mineworkers in the Barnsley/ Wakefield area, noted, similarly, that:

Among the manual workers, only the craftsmen were well represented in self-employment, particularly electricians. For most non-craftsmen, self-employment does not appear to be a viable response to redundancy.

Studies of Bolsover Enterprise Park, which saw a further attempt to stimulate entrepreneurship, this time in the North Derbyshire coalfield, report a similar low level of self-employment among those who previously worked in the coal industry (Turner, 1993b).

British Coal Enterprise

The survey carried out by Sheffield Business School in 1992 and 1993 also provided important findings on the British Coal Enterprise. BCE had a variety of responsibilities, including helping redundant mineworkers back into the labour market, as well as contributing to retraining, providing business premises, and generally trying to promote economic regeneration in mining and former mining areas. Fewer than 10 per cent of those men interviewed who had been employed at the Brodsworth colliery, however, had found BCE to be the most productive source of aid in obtaining new employment. Of the interviewed sample drawn from Markham Main colliery, the figure finding BCE the most useful mechanism for finding new employment rose to 35 per cent. Obviously, then, these figures indicate that BCE was of *some* help to displaced mineworkers seeking alternative employment. They contrast sharply, however, with the constant upbeat pronouncements by BCE on its own view of its startlingly good performance in objectives such as job creation. BCE claimed in 1994, for example, that 106,029 'employment opportunities arising from BCE's support' had been created since BCE's establishment in 1984 (British Coal Enterprise, 1994). Similarly, the results of the Sheffield Business School survey on the impact of counselling to individual mineworkers indicated only modest success. The relatively low figure of a third of those displaced from Markham Main and who had received counselling by BCE had found it to be of any use now relatively low. Of those displaced from Brodsworth, the figure was slightly higher, at 44 per cent. In a situation, as described earlier, where there are serious economic, social, and sometimes physical barriers to spontaneous economic regeneration, this does not bode well for the chances of many individual displaced mineworkers, who very often obviously need all the help that they can get.

British Coal Enterprise started life in October 1994, half way through the 1984–85 strike against pit closures. It followed the model established by the British Steel Industry, a similar body set up under the previous Labour administration, in its job creation endeavours. BCE has been criticised in the past for allegedly inflating the number of jobs it claims to have had a hand in creating (Hudson and Sadler, 1987). There are a number of studies of British Coal Enterprise which cast a more sceptical eye than BCE itself does on the effectiveness of their operations. It has been criticised, for example, for operating over too wide a region, and giving help to firms where there was little justification in terms of coal mine closures. Owen (1988), for example, noted that assistance had been given to companies in 'a small part of Glasgow, Workington/Whitehaven, the Kent coalfield and two small areas of North Wales' where 'pit closures in recent years have had little effect on regional unemployment rates'.

Elsewhere, the veracity of BCE's claims on job creation figures have been challenged by looking at the local operations of one of BCE's 'Enterprise Parks'. Turner (1992b), for example, examined BCE's activities at Carcroft, near Doncaster. Carcroft is a community of 5,000 people, five miles north of Doncaster. The 1980s and early 1990s saw many pit closures in the nearby locality. Its own pit, Bullcroft, had closed in 1970, taking with it 690 jobs (*Guide to the Coalfields*, 1986). The industry continued to be important to the locality, however. In Carcroft there remained, until after the 1984–85 strike, central stores, workshops, and a repairs depot, employing nearly 400 people, servicing other local collieries and maintaining houses owned by the NCB. Elsewhere in the nearby locality there were a number of pit closures in the 1980s and early 1990s. Brodsworth, referred to earlier, was little more than a mile away. Bentley colliery, which was closed in December 1993, was two miles away. Three miles to the north was Askern colliery, which was closed in 1991.

BCE at Carcroft engaged in retraining displaced mineworkers, as well as providing start-up units for small businesses. There were a number of positive aspects to BCE's activities at Carcroft. First, land vacated by the coal industry was recycled into other uses. Secondly, a modest number of jobs were created in the small business sector. A weaker aspect of its activities there, however, was the absence of a coherent evaluation of its job-creation strategies. Once small businesses had moved away from the Enterprise Park, contact between BCE and the companies was lost completely. Yet the numbers of jobs 'created' by the companies were recorded by BCE as part of the 106,029 'employment opportunities' referred to earlier. Given that some companies that started life in BCE premises will have expanded, while others will have gone to the wall, the upbeat figures for job creation publicised by BCE are bound to be considerably wide of the mark.

CONCLUSION

Achieving success in the creation of thriving, post-coal local economies is extremely difficult. As noted earlier, many factors in the economic, political and social environments militate against success. Despite this, there are some examples of progress. Some places associated with coal, such as

Barnsley and Mansfield, have been successful in attracting inward investment from Japan. Barnsley, for example, attracted a £50 million investment from Koyo Seiko, a Japanese-owned ball bearing manufacturer, in 1991. The early 1990s saw Toray, the Japanese textiles concern, engage in significant investment in Mansfield. South Wales also was the recipient of substantial inward investment, as Morris notes in chapter 3. Following the public outcry after the mass pit closure announcement in October 1992, coal mining areas have been far more successful than before in attracting financial assistance for restructuring from central government and from the European Union. There have been infrastructural improvements and efforts to improve the levels of investment in training, as noted earlier. Aspects of these contribute to what could be seen as a 'modernisation' of some of the local economies that were associated with coal. The economic and social problems associated with coal industry contraction, however, far outweigh the elements of success that have been achieved in promoting economic regeneration. The clearest sign of this is the extreme difficulty faced by many displaced mineworkers in finding alternative employment. There appears to be significant numbers of redundant mineworkers who have dropped out of the labour market altogether. The prospects for mining itself are very bleak. Success in the promotion of innovation and retraining appear to have brought some modest success, but it remains at that level. Derek Fatchett, Labour's industry spokesman, drawing on figures from the House of Commons library, claimed in 1994 that unemployment in many mining areas was more than double that elsewhere. Among other places, he cited Westoe in Tyne and Wear, with 24.2 per cent unemployment; Maltby, in South Yorkshire, with 19.6 per cent; and Bilsthorpe in Nottinghamshire, with 19.9 per cent – these compared with a national average of 9.2 per cent (*The Guardian*, 22 September 1994). A considerable amount needs to be done, therefore, before any of the places associated with coal in the 1980s and 1990s can really claim a successful economic regeneration, let alone an economic 'modernisation'.

NOTE

1 *Producer services* here can be defined as those activities such as banking, advertising, insurance, market research, scientific and professional services, and R&D, which are sold to manufacturing industry or other service-orientated businesses. They can be contrasted as a category with *consumer services*, where the demand for services that is being met is demand from the household (Allen, 1988). The distinction is significant: Daniels (1988), for example, noted that service industry expansion and employment growth took place only selectively in the 1960s, 1970s, and 1980s, and most of it was in the producer services sector.

REFERENCES

ACOM Secretariat (1991) *Europe's Coalfields: Problems, Prospects, Policies*, A report by the ACOM Secretariat, Barnsley. March.

Adeney, M. and Lloyd, J. (1986) *The Miners' Strike 1984–85: Loss Without Limit*, London: Routledge and Kegan Paul.

Allen, J. (1988) 'Towards a Post-industrial Economy?', in J. Allen and D. Massey (eds) *The Economy in Question*, London: Sage Publications in association with the Open University.

Allen, V.L. (1981) *The Militancy of British Miners*, Shipley: The Moor Press.

Barnsley Chronicle (1993) 7 May.

Barnsley Independent (1992) 21 July.

Beynon, H. (ed.) (1985) *Digging Deeper: Issues in the Miners' Strike*, London: Verso.

Beynon, H. Hudson, R., and Sadler, D. (1991) *A Tale of Two Industries: The Contraction of Coal and Steel in the North East of England*, London: Open University Press.

British Coal (1990) Written communication to author, 16 August.

British Coal Corporation (1990) *Report and Accounts 1989/90*.

British Coal Enterprise (1994) *A Review of Activities*. Mansfield.

Callinicos, A. and Simons, M. (1985) *The Great Strike. The Miners' Strike of 1984–85 and Its Lessons*, A Socialist Worker Publication.

Champion, T. and Green, A. (1989) 'Local Economic Differentials and the "North–South" Divide', in J. Lewis and A. Townsend (eds) *The North–South Divide: Regional Change in Britain in the 1980s*, London: Paul Chapman Publishing.

Coalfield Communities Campaign (1986) 'The Written Evidence of the Coalfield Communities Campaign'. Presented to the House of Commons Energy Committee During their investigation into the Coal Industry in February 1986. Prepared by the Secretariat of the Coalfield Communities Campaign, in *Working Papers*, Vol. 4, Barnsley: Coalfield Communities Campaign.

Coates, K. (1992) 'Case for Keeping Pits Open?' Letter to *The Guardian*, 25 September.

Coopers and Lybrand Deloitte and Sheffield City Polytechnic (1990) *The Dearne Valley Initiative, Economic Study and Business Plan*, July.

Coulter, J. Miller, S., and Walker, M. (1984) *State of Siege: Politics and the Policing of the Coalfields: Miners' Strike 1984*, London: Canary Press.

Crick, M. (1985) *Scargill and the Miners*, Harmondsworth: Penguin.

Daily Mirror (1992) 17 October.

Daily Star (1992) 15 October.

Daniels, P. (1988) 'Producer Services and the Post-Industrial Space-Economy', in D. Massey and J. Allen (eds) *Uneven Redevelopment: Cities and Regions in Transition*, London: Hodder and Stoughton in association with the Open University.

Department of Employment and Productivity (with the National Coal Board) (1970) *Ryhope: A Pit Closes: A Study in Redeployment*, Department of Employment and Productivity and the National Coal Board, London.

Derbyshire County Council (1991) *North Derbyshire Coalfield Partnership Project*, Progress on 1990/91 Programme at 31 March.

Doncaster Star (1991) 23 November.

Field, J. (1986) 'New Mining Developments and their Impact on the Community', in J. Field (ed.) *Coal Mining and the Community: Perspective from the Warwickshire Coalfield Debate*, University of Warwick Open Studies Paper number 1.

Financial Times (1983) 18 October.

Financial Times (1994) 14 June.

Goodman, G. (1985) *The Miners' Strike*, London: Pluto Press.

Grant, W. (1985) 'The Politics of Industrial Subsidies', Paper submitted to the ECPR Joint Sessions, Barcelona.

The Guardian (1991) 29 November.

The Guardian (1992) 9 April.

The Guardian (1993) 30 March.

The Guardian (1994) 22 September.

Guide to the Coalfields (1979, 1986) Redhill: Colliery Guardian.

Guy, N. (1994a) *Redundant Miners Survey. Grimethorpe*, February. Barnsley: Coalfield Communities Campaign.

Guy, N. (1994b) *Redundant Miners Survey. Silverhill*, February. Barnsley: Coalfield Communities Campaign.

Guy, N. (1994c) *Redundant Miners Survey. Vane Tempest*, March. Barnsley: Coalfield Communities Campaign.

Guy, N. (1994d) *Redundant Miners Survey. Parkside*, March. Barnsley: Coalfield Communities Campaign.

Hall, P. (1988) 'The Geography of the Fifth Kondratieff', in D. Massey and J. Allen (eds) *Uneven Redevelopment: Cities and Regions in Transition*, London: Hodder and Stoughton in association with the Open University.

Heughan, H.E. (1953) *Pit Closures at Shotts and the Migration of Miners*, Monograph number 1, University of Edinburgh Social Sciences Research Centre, Edinburgh.

House, J.W. and Knight, E.M. (1967) *Pit Closure and the Community: Report to the Ministry of Labour*. Papers on Migration and Mobility in Northern England Number 5. University of Newcastle upon Tyne Department of Geography, Newcastle upon Tyne.

Howell, D. (1989) *The Politics of the NUM: A Lancashire View*, Manchester: Manchester University Press.

Hudson, R. and Sadler, D. (1987) 'National Policies and Local Economic Initiatives: Evaluating the Effectiveness of UK Coal and Steel Closure Area Re-industrialisation Measures', *Local Economy* 2, 2: 107–14.

The Independent (1992) 1 February.

Lawless, P. (1989) *Britain's Inner Cities*, London: Paul Chapman Publishing.

Leigh, R. and North, D. (1986) 'Innovation Centres: The Policy Options for Local Authorities', *Local Economy* 2, 45–56.

National Coal Board (1981) *Report and Accounts 1980/81*, London: NCB.

Owen, G. (1988) *British Coal Enterprise – A First Assessment*, Barnsley: Coalfield Communities Campaign.

Recharge North East (undated, circa 1994) *Practical Help for Small Businesses*, Gateshead: Recharge North East.

Rees, G. and Thomas, M. (1991) 'From Coalminers to Entrepreneurs? A Case Study in the Sociology of Re-industrialisation', in M. Cross and G. Payne (eds) *Work and the Enterprise Culture*, London: Falmer Press.

Romaya, S.M. and Alden, J.D. (1987) *The Valleys Initiative, Impact Evaluation Study*, Preliminary Report. Welsh Office. April.

Romaya, S.M. and Alden, J.D. (1988) *The Valleys Initiative, Impact Evaluation Study*, Final Report. Welsh Office. July.

Scargill, A. (1981) *Marxism Today* 25, 4, April.

Sheffield Business School (1993) *Responding to the Decline of the Coal Industry*, Longitudinal Study. A research study for Barnsley and Doncaster Training and Enterprise Council. Final Report. November.

The Sun (1992) 15 October.

The Times (1994) 24 August.

Turner, R.L. (1985) 'Post-War Pit Closures: The Politics of Deindustrialisation', *The Political Quarterly* 56, 2, 167–74.

Turner, R.L. (1989) *The Politics of Industry*, Bromley: Christopher Helm.

Turner, R.L. (1992a) 'A Task Force in a Locality of Declining Coal Mining: The Case of Doncaster', *The East Midland Geographer* 15, 1, 16–29.

Turner, R.L. (1992b) 'British Coal Enterprise: Bringing the "Enterprise Culture" to a Deindustrialised Local Economy', *Local Economy* 7, 1, 4–8.

Turner, R.L. (1992c) 'Industrial Subsidies and the Manipulation of Industrial Culture: The Case of a West Yorkshire Mining Town', *The Journal of Regional and Local Studies* 12, 1, 53–64.

Turner, R.L. (1993a) 'From Coal Mining to a High Technology Economy? The Case of an Innovation Centre in South Yorkshire', *New Technology, Work and Employment* 8, 1, 56–66.

Turner, R.L. (1993b) *Regenerating the Coalfields, Policy and Politics in the 1980s and Early 1990s*. Aldershot: Avebury.

Welsh Office (undated) *The Valleys: A Partnership with the People.*

Welsh Office Information Division (1988) *A Programme for the People.*

Witt, S. (1990) *When the Pit Closes – the Employment Experiences of Redundant Miners*, A Special Report. Barnsley: Coalfield Communities Campaign.

3

McJOBBING A REGION

Industrial restructuring and the widening socio-economic divide in Wales

Jonathan Morris

McJob: A low-pay, low-prestige, low-dignity, low-benefit, no-future job in the service sector. Frequently considered a satisfying career choice by people who have never held one.

Douglas Coupland, *Generation X*

The Welsh economy in the 1990s is something of an enigma. Central to the apparent paradox is that the economy, with significant state intervention, has been considerably refocused from duo-industry domination to one with a considerable international and tertiary-based focus. As anyone involved in Welsh economic affairs, or indeed anyone in Wales, is constantly reminded, this has led to a significant diversification into high-tech industry, considerable job creation, and an unemployment rate which in the 1990s fell below the national (UK) rate, and occasionally below that of the South East of England. This transformation of the Welsh economic base, however, also implies significant social change, and I will argue that many of these changes are negative. The essence of this chapter is to chart both the economic changes and the accompanying social change, through the major headings in the chapter. The first uses an analysis of various data sets to evaluate the positive and negative implications of change. The second and third parts switch from a macro to micro focus, based on case studies of what represents the 'old' and 'new' in the Welsh economy, that is through research on the steel industry and Japanese inward investment respectively.

A WELSH ECONOMIC MIRACLE?

In the past two decades the Welsh economy has undergone a series of transformations of which three are prominent. First, there has been major structural change in the economy, including shifts in the manufacturing make up and a considerable tertiarisation of the economic structure. Secondly, there has been a considerable internationalisation of the economy in a number of respects. Thirdly, and closely linked to the other two

46

transformations, there has been a feminisation of the workforce. The changes, of course, mirror wider transformations in the UK economy and beyond. However, the changes that have occurred, particularly structural change and internationalisation, have grown at a much faster pace than in the UK generally and Wales is thus an interesting microcosm of change.

The underlying structural change in the Welsh economy is well versed, but worth briefly repeating. By the 1970s, the coal industry in Wales was well on the road to terminal decline, but was still a prominent employer (47,800 or 5 per cent of the workforce in 1972). The economy, however, was dominated by metal manufacturing, predominantly but not exclusively comprised of the steel industry, and the service sector. In 1972, for example, metal manufacture employed 84,900, representing 27 per cent of the manufacturing workforce and 9 per cent of the total workforce. It also employed twice as many of the next biggest manufacturing sector, electronics. By 1991, however, this picture had changed dramatically: the sector now only employed 25,300 and, furthermore, the largest manufacturing sector was now electronics (employing 33,800). The wider story of change is described later in the case studies of the steel industry and Japanese investment.

The service sector, meanwhile, continued to grow. In 1972, it employed 487,200 of a total workforce of 973,000 (50 per cent). By 1991, it had grown to 653,600 of a workforce of 963,700 (68 per cent). However, several caveats should be noted. First, employment growth has not been uniform across the service sector, with much faster employment gains in banking and financial services and that sector of the economy classed as 'other services'. Secondly, these employment figures are job totals, not full-time equivalent jobs; a substantial proportion of these jobs are part-time. Nevertheless, these figures do represent a significant transformation of the Welsh economy over twenty years. In that period, the economy has shifted away from a strong predominance of heavy industry, notably steel and coal, toward services and light manufacturing industry, particularly electronics.

Accompanying this structural/sectoral transformation has been the internationalisation of the Welsh economy. This is most obviously illustrated in the case of inward investment. In the 1970s Wales already had a substantial foreign-owned manufacturing sector, broadly dating back to post-war state efforts to compensate for the loss of coal and metal manufacturing employment with jobs created by inward investment. By 1981, 216 foreign-owned production units were employing 45,400, and throughout the 1980s Wales attracted a disproportionate amount of the UK's inward investment total (Hill and Munday, 1994). By 1993 the number of overseas-owned production units had risen dramatically (to 348) as had employment (68,000), representing over 30 per cent of total Welsh manufacturing employment.

During this growth, the nature of inward investment has changed, both in terms of the source of investment and its sectoral composition. American investment dominated up to the 1980s: in 1974, for example, nearly 70 per cent of foreign-owned plants were US owned. By 1993, however, while there was still a large US presence (36 per cent of foreign-owned plants), there had been a considerable growth in investment from Europe (42 per cent, notably Germany and France) and Japan (19 per cent). The sectoral composition had also changed. In 1981 the key sectors were metal manufacturing and metal goods, engineering and vehicles, chemicals, and electronics. By 1993, however, electronics dominated, with the second largest number of plants but twice the employment found in any other sector. This, of course, was reflective of (and caused) the structural changes outlined earlier.

The final transformation of the Welsh economy has been the feminisation of the workforce. Growing from a relatively low base, female workers have been increasingly incorporated into the Welsh workforce over the past fifty years. There has been a gradual, but marked, increase on a decade by decade basis. In 1972, for example, 342,000 females were employed (35 per cent of the workforce); by 1982 this had increased to 379,000 (42 per cent); and by 1992 to 464,000 (49 per cent). Thus by 1992 the Welsh female workforce was almost as large as its male counterpart. These figures, however, need some important qualifications. Female workers are far more likely to be employed part-time (47 per cent) than are males (11 per cent), and they are also far more likely to be employed in the service sector (84,000 compared to 13,200 in manufacturing) than are males (56,100 compared to 30,700).

This transformation has not occurred, of course, within a political vacuum. The state has played a big role in the Welsh economy since the 1950s, perhaps more so than any other British region. The nationalisation of the coal and steel industries, in addition to the growth of public sector services, ensured that the state dominated employment in Wales sufficiently for Humphrys (1972) to label Wales a 'state managed region'. The state also had a major direct impact on private industry through regional policy efforts to attract foreign (including English) industry to Wales (Morgan, 1979). By the 1990s, the 'quangos' notwithstanding, the state's direct role has diminished considerably as a result of the decline of coal and steel employment, privatisation of major industries and services, the diminution of public services, and a decline in regional aid budgets. Nevertheless, as Morgan (1994) notes, the role of the Welsh Office and the Welsh Development Agency are still considerable.

To what extent has this transformation been a 'success'? To a degree the answer must be affirmative. The economy has undergone considerable diversification and there has been a considerable amount of job creation. This has resulted in an unemployment rate in the 1990s which fell below that of the UK for the first time since the 1930s. In mid-1994, for example, the rate was 9.6 per cent compared to 9.3 per cent for the UK as a whole and 9.1 per cent for the South East of England. However, other data indicate that the miracle is somewhat transparent. Pay is extremely low by UK standards. In 1991, for example, male wages were 86.8 per cent of those in other parts of the country, while female wages were 88.4 per cent. Moreover, the gap in earnings between Wales and the rest of the UK are widening rather than converging, which suggests that the economic transformation that has occurred is exacerbating this wage gap (Simpson, 1992; Simpson and McNabb, 1994). Indeed Wales entered the 1980s near the top of the UK regional pay league but ended it near the bottom.

A DIVIDED WALES?

As we have seen, the Welsh economic 'miracle' has been accompanied by some decidedly negative features, and in particular a job loss/job gain mismatch in terms of occupational and gender profiles and low pay resulting in inevitable social and economic polarisation. One further feature is that this social and economic polarisation has manifested itself spatially: in other words while certain parts of the country have prospered, others have felt little impact from economic growth and indeed have been left behind. This, unsurprisingly, has happened at the intra-urban level in Cardiff, Swansea, and the other urban areas. However, it is also extremely noticeable at the inter-urban level.

Recent survey analysis has highlighted this phenomenon. Morris and Wilkinson (1989, 1993), for example, have used a variety of social and economic data from the 1981 and 1991 national census and the 1986 inter-censal survey to track intra-regional disparities at the local authority district level. Many of their findings were, to someone living in Wales, unsurprising: certain valley districts of industrial south Wales (the former coalfield), for example, fared very poorly. However, other findings were more surprising: undoubtedly, the industrial restructuring of Wales has created a new economic (and social) geography of the country.

To summarise two fairly lengthy reports, perhaps the most striking feature was not the coalfield demise, but the extent of an east–west divide. The new economic geography has favoured two 'corridors' of growth. The first of these is in the south, along the M4 corridor, which has been the focus of much new industry coming into Wales, including the electronics investment talked about later in this chapter, as well as inward investment in the financial services industry. This growth corridor has not extended all the way along the M4, rather it peters out after Bridgend (about twenty miles west of Cardiff). The area west, which has experienced considerable job loss in the coal, metal (ferrous and non-ferrous), engineering, and chemical industries, has experienced little inward investment. Only four of the thirty-two Japanese manufacturers, for example, are located west of Bridgend.

The second corridor of growth is along the A55 road (which runs east to west in North Wales), but again it does not extend far west, being primarily confined to the county of Clwyd. This area has, however, been extremely successful in attracting inward investment. Eight of the country's Japanese plants are found in this area, including Sharp, Brother, and Toyota. Thus the urban areas in the eastern part of Wales such as Cardiff, Newport, Ogwr (Bridgend), and Wrexham scored far higher on the index of socio-economic prosperity than those found in the west and in particular the Swansea Bay area.

The second major feature was the extremely poor performance on this index of the core valley (coalfield) areas, with the four lowest out of the total of thirty-seven local authority districts. However, not all of the coalfield valley areas performed poorly, with certain southern valley areas performing relatively well. These are geographically contiguous to the major urban areas of South East Wales and have developed as commuter belts.

The third feature was a rural–urban divide in economic prosperity. The top five performing districts in 1991 were all rural, while the bottom fourteen were all urban, and the average rural percentage 'score' was 68.9 compared to 43.2 for urban districts. Partly reflecting this there was a general urban–rural population shift between 1981 and 1991.

The final feature was that polarisation seems to be increasing. For example, in 1981 the worst performing district, Rhondda, scored only 2.2 on the index compared to the top score of 88.0 in Monmouth. By 1991 this extreme divide had increased even further, within the context of wider socio-economic divides in Wales generally.

CASE STUDY 1

The steel industry

The steel industry in Wales is frequently characterised, alongside the coal industry, as a 'declining' industry. While this is certainly true of coal (although private mining and opencast operations are burgeoning), the position of the steel industry has been far more complex. There have been steel plant closures and, more importantly, there have been massive employment contractions. However, other indications such as output are not so certain and, after all, virtually every major segment of manufacturing industry has seen employment decline in the past decade and a half (and could therefore be described as declining).

This analysis of the Welsh steel industry will be sub-divided into three parts. The initial section will describe developments in the industry in the 1980s and 1990s. The latter sections look at more qualitative data about, among other things, the nature of employment in the industry. Specifically, this is meant to be used in comparison with the later case study on inward investors and Japanese investors in particular.

The background

The Welsh steel industry, as of 1994, employs approximately 15,500 at Shotton, which compares with 75,000 in the early 1970s. The 1970s were years of restructuring in the Welsh steel industry, with the final remnants of the legacy inherited in the 1940s being reordered alongside the major investment in the major integrated works, Llanwern (Newport) and Port Talbot. As a result there were a number of plant closures in the industry in the 1970s, the prime one being the closure of the East Moors works in Cardiff (3,800 jobs lost) and the ending of steel making (but not the steel industry) at Ebbw Vale (1,000 jobs).

Recession in 1979, and huge cumulative losses, forced the abandonment of the major investment of the 1970s and the introduction of the 'Slimline' programme. The only way that this can be properly characterised is as a savage retrenchment programme, with 22,000 jobs lost in an eighteen month period between 1979 and 1981 in British Steel alone (Fevre, 1989; Morgan, 1983; Morris, 1987), and an overall (UK) capacity reduction of 4½ million tonnes being achieved by 1985. As a result, there was major job loss at Port Talbot (6,800 jobs lost) and Llanwern (4,409). Shotton lost its steel making capacity (7,500) and, in the tinplate division, jobs were lost at Trostre, Ebbw Vale, and Felindre, the last of which closed in the early 1980s (1,500 jobs).

Blyton *et al.* (1993) have described this as the first wave of restructuring in the Welsh steel industry, with the restructuring being implemented at British Steel in particular, and characterised by capacity closure and the reduction of payroll levels. The first wave is the one which is uppermost in the characterisation of the steel industry. However, as Blyton *et al.* have argued, the second wave came to dominate the late part of the 1980s and the 1990s. While there has been continued job loss during this second wave, the primary characteristics are the introduction of major new technology and considerable organisational changes, in particular work organisation which will be discussed later. The principal changes in technology have been the introduction of continuous processes (notably continuous casting or 'concast'), the computerisation of the production process, and moves to produce higher quality and value added steels.

As a result of the second wave of changes, by the 1990s the steel industry in Wales was employing progressively lower numbers, while output remained constant, and thus productivity was dramatically increased. Moreover, as Fevre (1989) noted, a major effort to subcontract work out also exaggerated job loss totals. The characterisation of the industry as 'declining' is therefore considerably misleading; it has declined considerably in its employment impact, but the industry has largely maintained its output and is now modern in terms of its technology, its output (with both high quality and high value added steels), and its forms of working. British Steel (BS) in Wales now comprises two integrated works (of the UK's three) at Llanwern and Port Talbot, the tinplate works at Trostre (Llanelli) and Ebbw Vale, a major coating and finishing plant at Shotton, and five steel finishing plants. As such the activities of British Steel virtually all fall within the Strip Division of the company which in turn is now solely concentrated in Wales (40 per cent of total BS turnover). Moreover, the strip division is seen as the keystone of the domestic growth of BS. This is explained by the fact that nearly half of BS Strip output goes to two industries, automotive and construction, with the former anticipated to grow considerably over the next decade. In addition ASW employs 2,100 in Cardiff in steel production (a mini mill) and various finishing processes for construction steel.

The steel workforce in the 1990s

The workforce in the steel industry is in many ways very different, if not the mirror image, of that in the inward investing companies which are described in the next section. Unsurprisingly, the industry is dominated by male workers, with female workers confined to secretarial and administrative jobs. This male domination is reflected at both managerial and production levels. There is no reason, of course, why managerial positions should be the prerogative of males but this tends to reflect the culture of the industry *and* the region. Indeed, there are some female managers and technical staff. Moreover, the male bias in production jobs no longer reflects the day-to-day reality of work tasks. There has been a considerable shift from 'brawn to brain' as a job requirement in most of the major steel making areas as a result of automation and computerisation as the later description will show. However, males predominate, as said partly due to the culture of the industry and partly due to the fact that there has been little or no recruitment of shopfloor operatives (the production operative workforce is both declining and ageing).

In terms of occupational profile the industry has a fairly balanced and widespread occupational structure. A fairly high percentage of employees are found in management grades: at BS Shotton, for example, 500 of the 2,000 workforce in 1992. Moreover, BS retains a strong commitment to R&D: 250 are employed, for example, at BS R&D Division at Port Talbot, 60 per cent of whom are graduates (Bryan *et al.*, 1994), in what is one of the largest Welsh R&D facilities.

Turning to the production area, there is a high percentage of skilled workers, both in terms of the strict definition as time-served apprentices and in the wider sense. In the strict sense, each BS plant employs a high percentage of time-served skilled workers: at BS Shotton, for example, approximately one third of manual workers are skilled, and similar percentages are found at all BS plants. Further, in contrast to the situation facing the unskilled and semi-skilled production workers, recruitment of skilled workers has been maintained. This, in turn, has a spin-off effect on local vocational education providers: Bryan *et al.* (1994) estimate that the steel industry generates £200,000 plus per annum in fee income for local colleges in South Wales, with 600 students on full- and part-time courses at four colleges and an unspecified number at two further colleges. It should be noted, moreover, that skills training for both skilled and unskilled workers is among the most advanced of any industry in Wales and indeed in the UK, as the next section on work organisation will indicate.

The relatively high skill levels found in the steel industry are in part reflected in wage levels in the industry. Actual wage levels have become increasingly difficult to calculate, given decentralisation of bargaining and the growing importance of bonus payments in wage determination. However, one measure, albeit a slightly crude one, is to compare average gross weekly earnings from the 1993 New Earnings Survey for SIC 22 (dominated by the steel industry) with overall wages, as Bryan *et al.* (1994) do. Thus the average gross weekly earnings for full-time manual males in Wales in SIC 22 was £318.40, compared with overall average weekly gross earnings in Wales for full-time manual males of £258.60.

New ways of working in the Welsh steel industry

As I have already indicated, the steel industry has been characterised by a 'two wave' restructuring process (after Blyton *et al.*, 1993; see also Morris *et al.*, 1992). The description thus far has concentrated upon the 'first wave', which was directly a result of the 'Slimline Agreement' in 1980. This had an initial focus of drastically reducing the numbers employed in the industry. As the 1980s wore on, however, the attention of BS management turned to the ways in which the remaining employees were working, particularly at the shopfloor level. This so-called 'second wave' of changes was intro-duced against a background of major technological change, vertical dis-integration of production via subcontracting, and virtual union impotence. These three contextual factors were combined. The first two, for example, were used as carrot and stick: major new technological investments were dangled in front of workers with the condition for their implementation being the acceptance of new working practices. All this took place against a backcloth of plant closures with, for example, Llanwern being played off against the Ravenscraig plant in Scotland. Similarly, changes were pushed through under threat of possible subcontracting out of activities. Mean-while, in the aftermath of the 1980 strike, management reasserted its prerogative and the unions were continually on the back foot. At the same time, 'divide and rule' tactics were furthered with the decentralisation of collective bargaining and the introduction of major plant-based bonus schemes. In short, the principal changes in work organisation were pushed through by management against the will of the major unions involved (ISTC, AEU, EETPU, and TGWU), with little resistance, or at least effective resistance.

The two principal forms of work organisation change have been, first, flexible working and teamwork and, secondly, multi-skilling. In the first instance, demarcation barriers were gradually eroded throughout the 1980s. This erosion was linked either to pay agreements, or allied to major technological investments in specific major areas of individual steel plants. Effectively, it was erosion by stealth. Not only have production workers been required to be more flexible, but there has been a significant blurring of the demarcation line between craft and production workers. Unskilled production workers are now to be found carrying out routine and the simpler maintenance tasks throughout BS plants and in the other producers.

The ultimate expression of increased flexibility is in teamworking, where small multi-functional groups of workers are led by one team leader. Teamworking, borrowing significantly from Japanese manufacturing systems, has been introduced extensively into the car industry. In the steel industry it has, however, far-reaching consequences in that it transforms traditional forms of work organisation. These date back to the last century and are characterised by a rigid hierarchical gang system with promotion up the gang operating on a strict seniority system. The teamwork concept completely overturns this, with all team members on equal pay and status with the exception of the team leader, who is chosen on merit rather than seniority. The trade unions have fought the introduction of teamworking. In particular, the ISTC, the main production union, has fought the introduction of teamworking perhaps more strongly than any other union. The introduction of teamworking has, therefore, been piecemeal. Indeed its implementation has been more tardy in BS Wales plants than elsewhere, notably Teesside. However, it *has* been introduced in Wales, particularly in parts of plants where there has been major investment in technology. Thus it has been introduced on the 'Zodiac line' at BS Llanwern (a major new galvanising line), for example. At BS Panteg seniority-based promotion has all but disappeared, while at BS Trostre, a hybrid variant of teamworking has been introduced. Nevertheless, in the two big plants of Port Talbot and Llanwern, it has, at the time of writing, largely been resisted, with seniority the rule for production promotion lines at Port Talbot, apart from the 'Zodiac line' at Llanwern.

There are a number of issues for production workers that the imposition of teamwork poses. First, there are questions of equity: a fifty-year old worker who has spent his life working up the promotion ladder is suddenly put on equal footing with a relatively new production worker. In addition, there are questions of worker autonomy: primarily the gangs were autonomous, largely self-regulating and carried out their own experience-based on-the-job training. Teamwork takes away that autonomy and self-regulation. There are also issues of job enlargement versus enrichment. Clearly enlargement is taking place, this is the rationale of teamwork, but teamwork is also increasing the job 'skills' of individual workers. This has been backed up by significant training initiatives. However, while the 'skills' of individual workers are undoubtedly 'upped' by teamwork, they are nevertheless confined to relatively small sections of steelmills and are certainly not transferable out of the industry in the way that new craft skills are.

This takes us on to new forms of work organisation for craft workers. In British Steel, after general moves to reduce demarcation and increase flexibility, 'multi-skilling' has been the prime focus for work reorganisation. 'Multi-skilling' is a much used and abused term in British industry. In most cases it simply refers to job enlargement and work intensification via multi-tasking. In the Welsh (and UK) steel industry it has been gradually introduced in its true sense: here, craft workers are being trained and retrained in a variety of skills under, in BS's case, the term 'craft restructuring'. The plethora of different crafts (there were over seventy at Llanwern in the 1970s) has been reduced to two basic classifications, a 'mechanical' craftsman and an 'electrical' craftsman. This scheme has been introduced at the three BS main plants in Wales (Llanwern, Port Talbot, and Shotton), both for new apprentices and for the majority of existing craftsmen, via major retraining exercises. Again, however, this has not gone uncontested by the main unions involved, the AEU and the EETPU (as they were when the negotiations were taking place). Two major areas of confrontation arose. The first was over the premium pay rates that workers with enhanced skills would receive. The second, probably more important area, was over the number of workers who would be retrained. While one *raison d'être* of multi-skilling is to enhance craftworker skills another, arguably more important, outcome for BS would be intensification of work, following which fewer skilled workers would be required. At one major works 390 of 1,000 skilled workers were retrained with a further 200 in the next and final stage. Those to be retrained were picked on the basis of competence. Given the large sums that were being spent on retraining – £3 million on craft restructuring at Port Talbot, for example – it was clear that workers approaching retirement were not likely to be deemed suitable. Despite these negative factors, however, the craft restructuring programme has considerably enhanced the skills of craft workers and, in a practicable sense, made workers more 'attractive' in the market. As one training manager noted, 'This was a high risk strategy, with Bosch down the road' (referring to the location of a major new inward investor). It is, moreover, a model of training in the Welsh economy – far superior to others – and is in stark contrast to the general levels of training elsewhere.

CASE STUDY 2

Inward investment – a false panacea?

As the previous section outlined, the decline of the Welsh coal industry and the considerable contraction, particularly in employment terms, of the steel industry, has met with a variety of policy responses at a number of representational levels. Overwhelmingly, however, these responses have grouped around two main themes: first, the enhancement of the physical environment through land reclamation, and secondly, the rejuvenation of the Welsh national economy through the attraction of inward investment. These two thematic concerns have been closely interrelated, given that by carrying out the first, it was hoped that the second would be more likely to follow. The principal agents for change have been the Welsh Office, and in particular, the Industry Department within the Welsh Office, and their promotional arm, the Welsh Development Agency.

Two concerns should be noted. First, while the response of government towards deindustrialisation has been fairly uniform temporally, that is, the attraction of inward investment has been the primary tool for change used for at least twenty years, the motivation has been both pragmatic and ideological. The pragmatic concerns have been to provide jobs in large units to mitigate the effects of coal and steel closures. Inward investment provided what can be deemed, in one sense, a series of one-off easy fix solutions. In other words, new jobs were provided, although there was little attention paid to the quality of jobs that were being made available and who – men, women, young, old – they were being taken up by. All this is not to detract from the pragmatic achievement of job creation. The ideological imperative is perhaps more interesting. Arguably, this began to develop in the 1980s as part of the Thatcherite project. This had three broad strands. The market was sacrosanct and the government adopted a *laissez-faire* approach to economics. This led to the second strand, which was a lack of any coherent industrial (and energy) policy which could be applied to the Welsh economy. Finally, inward investors were elevated to a more exalted role than the pragmatic job-creating concerns that they had previously been. They now donned the mantle of role models and competitors embodying all of the positive virtues that British industry, with its pluralistic concerns and its rigidities, lacked. Nowhere was this perhaps better exemplified than at the Nissan plant in Sunderland, which Garrahan and Stewart (1992) have termed an 'enigma'.

The second concern is that this policy strand was extremely centrist. It developed within a context of a (Welsh) democratic vacuum, what has been termed the 'democratic deficit'. Local economic strategies, as developed by local authorities, have been emasculated and extremely marginalised. The two key institutions, the Welsh Office and its conduit the

Welsh Development Agency (WDA), are controlled by Westminster and Whitehall and by the powerful Secretary of State for Wales; in the 1980s and 1990s there have been three successive English Secretaries of State representing English parliamentary constituencies. London-based decision making has been controlled via the Welsh Office through a series of non-elected national bodies, including the WDA. This pervasive centrism is graphically illustrated in Kevin Morgan and Ellis Roberts' work *The Democratic Deficit: A Guide to Quangoland*, in 1993. Thus, despite the degree of discretion which the Secretary of State possesses (Peter Walker's incumbency, for example, saw a far greater level of intervention than was the case for Britain generally), this element of centralisation has served to stifle debate on alternative economic strategies. This has been pervasive; the trade union movement (as represented by the Welsh TUC) in Wales, for example, has been incorporated into this milieu, as part of a 'growth coalition' (Welsh Office, WDA, Welsh TUC) to attract inward investment. As such, this represents a now unfashionable pluralistic tripartism, but one in which the agenda is being firmly set by the Welsh Office. In this instance the trade union movement is caught between the proverbial rock and hard place. Either they accept this agenda or are left out of the process totally. That is, they must accept either incorporation on these terms or complete exclusion.

Despite these concerns, as the introductory section indicated, inward investment flows into Wales have been particularly strong, and have been taking up an increasing percentage of the Welsh manufacturing base. As such, inward investment has been important in the transformation of the Welsh economy. Further, as the following case study will argue, it has also been a vehicle for social transformation, notably within the workplace, but also to a certain degree outside it. The exemplar chosen here is that of Japanese inward investment, partly out of pragmatism in that is has been recently under the scrutiny of considerable research by the author and others, but, more importantly, because it has been growing at a considerable rate. Moreover, it has been the touchstone of change at an economic and social level.

Japanese investment – an introduction

The contention here is that Japanese investment has been a central part of a wider economic and social transformation of the Welsh economy. Furthermore, the claim will be forwarded that this investment has transformed workplace social relations, both in the ways in which work is carried out at the workplace and the nature of workplace employee relations. At first glance this might seem an exaggerated claim, given the scale of Japanese investment in Wales. In 1991, for example, the twenty-nine manufacturing plants employed 12,000, representing only 1 per cent of the Welsh workforce and 6 per cent of the country's manufacturing employment. They represent, therefore, a relatively small presence. However, the sector is rapidly expanding: the 12,000 employed in 1991 is expected to have increased to 17,000 by 1995 (with thirty-one plants) and a further new plant to be opened in 1995 will raise this to nearly 18,000. It is not this rapid growth *per se* which makes the Japanese investment interesting, however, rather it is the exemplar effect of the types of work organisation and employee relations being used, which are being emulated by other organisations in Wales, including other inward investors. For this reason the analysis will focus on three areas: workforce composition, work organisation, and employee relations. Before this analysis, however, a brief thumbnail sketch of the investors will be given.

Of the twenty-nine manufacturing investors studied by Morris *et al.* (1993), the companies fall into two broad industrial categories. The largest group are found in electronics-related activities, comprised of sixteen plants and including household-name companies, such as Sony, Matsushita (Panasonic), Sharp, Hitachi, and Aiwa. The second group are a more heterogeneous group involving plastics, chemicals and related products, and automotive components (the three post-1992 locators are Toyota, an automobile component supplier and supplier of components to the electronics industry). Moreover, the importance of the electronics group is underemphasized by these figures on two counts: first, the plants are the bigger in employee terms (seven of the top ten employers produce electronics) and, secondly, a number of the non-electronics plants are directly related to the electronics plants as suppliers of, for example, plastic mouldings. Indeed, there has been a distinctive 'two wave' development of Japanese investment in Wales with the major finished goods producers locating in the 1970s and first half of the 1980s, and the associated components producers locating, in the main, post-1985. Perhaps the best example of this is Matsushita, which now has five plants in Wales, two producing finished products and three producing components.

Workforce composition

The twenty-nine Japanese manufacturing subsidiaries located in Wales in 1992 employed 13,200 people. In 1994 an estimate would be that this has climbed to 16,700, with two major expansions (Sony and Lucas-SEI) and the new plants, including the Toyota engine plant at Deeside in North East Wales (ironically, on the site of the former Shotton steelmaking unit). While these crude numbers indicate the overall importance of Japanese investment in the Welsh economy, particularly given the recency of much of this investment, they tell us little about possible social changes that are occurring. Perhaps more poignantly the questions should be asked as to what type of jobs have been created, for whom, and under what terms and conditions.

Indeed, this has been a recurring criticism of inward investment into the Welsh economy, that it has provided low wages, low skill work, and jobs which are often held by females.

What evidence does the survey provide? The majority of workers in Japanese plants were female (7,153 to 5,803 males). There is no occupational gender breakdown, but observational impressions (and previous studies) indicate a preponderance of female shopfloor workers, particularly in the larger employing plants. This preponderance of females is a consequence of two factors: first, that the majority of plants are in the electronics and related industry, and, secondly, that many of the plants are primarily high volume assembly production units.

Skill levels are notoriously difficult to ascertain, given widely differing definitions of what 'skills' are. Further, what actually constitutes a 'skill' is socially constructed, and there tends to be a bias against 'female occupations'. However, it is possible to tease out and give a flavour of the type of occupations from other parts of our data set (as well as our observational impressions). In the first instance, for example, employees were overwhelmingly not managerial and/or salaried staff. Managerial and salaried staff constituted only 17 per cent of the workforce. This points to a high proportion of manual type work. In addition, only 4.5 per cent of the workforce were graduates. This, however, tells us little in itself about the manual workers. They could, for example, be 100 per cent apprenticed-served, skilled craftsmen and women. However, apart from the observational analysis, a brief description of the training procedures employed in the companies indicates that almost the reverse is true. Despite production regimes which emphasised strict quality controls, training for production workers, irrespective of experience, was typically on the job, of the 'sitting next to Nellie' variety (thus also typically in-house), learning from an experienced operator or float for a few days. There were exceptions. One company stood out, for example, in having around 100 employees currently on four-year apprenticeships, consisting of one year full-time in college, followed by three years' work experience with one day per week in college. This firm was, however, the exception rather than the rule.

The impression that is conveyed, therefore, is of a generally low skilled, largely female, workforce, working in hum-drum routine assembly jobs. There are partial exceptions to this, with certain of the firms offering a broader occupational spectrum. Sony, for example, has fifty to sixty graduate development engineers based at Bridgend, while Calsonic at Llanelli has around eighty people employed in its R&D function, which does research on materials and processes, as well as product development.

As the introductory section outlined, one of the key debates in the Welsh economy is the low pay question. To what extent has Japanese investment contributed to, or ameliorated, this position? Inevitably, it would seem, Japanese investment has contributed to a degree to this problem of low pay, given the preponderance of lower occupational jobs typically found in the plants. What evidence is there, however, of actual pay levels in these plants? Most of the evidence is fragmentary and the survey by Morris *et al.* is no different in this regard. Systematic pay data by firms were not collected due to the understandable reluctance by many of the firms to disclose this sensitive information. Thirteen companies provided information: seven claimed to pay in the upper quantile, two above average, and four average, in relation to their local labour markets. Perhaps more interestingly, eight companies provided us with wage rates, and in these, basic operators earned between £126 and £202 per week, with an average of £163. This may be compared with the Welsh average wage rates outlined earlier, which were considerably higher.

The general picture of employment creation is, therefore, that Japanese investors have made a substantial contribution to manufacturing employment and, equally importantly, in a Welsh context, this employment has been extremely resilient despite the early 1990s economic recession. However, the stereotypical view put forward in the 1980s still largely holds in the 1990s, that females dominate the workforce, particularly at the operator level, that there is a lack (with a few notable exceptions) of spread across the occupational spectrum, that skill requirements at operator level are low, and that pay levels are somewhat below the Welsh average, which in itself is low.

Reshaping a work organisation

The Japanese form of production organisation is, to a great extent, very different from that found in archetypal British organisations, with an emphasis on team-based work, flexibility, and individual worker acceptance of responsibility for quality. These are, in large part, derived from the use of just-in-time (JIT) production and total quality controls (TQC). This embraces what Peter Wickens, Nissan's personnel director, has termed a Japanese 'tripod' of working practices in quality consciousness, teamwork, and flexibility, over-arched by the concept of 'kaizen' or continuous improvement.

To what extent have Japanese manufacturers in Wales introduced Japanese forms of production organisation into their factories? All were well versed in Japanese production methods, with fifteen of the twenty-two companies using JIT production. Within most factories there were negligible or no stocks within or between processes, thus operating an extremely finely tuned but fragile production environment (see Morris *et al.*, 1993). In the great majority of cases (eighteen of twenty-two) shopfloor workers were organised into teams of between fifteen and thirty workers, each team having a clearly defined responsibility for meeting production/ quality targets, with continuous performance monitoring. While formal 'kaizen' teams were found in only five organisations, continuous improvement was typically built in via industrial engineering and performance measurement and feedback.

An even more popular term in the managers' lexicon was quality. While half of our sample used formal quality circles, even more fundamental to quality control was making operators and teams responsible and accountable for the quality of their work, and the ability of management via supervisors and team leaders to identify and pinpoint faults. Individual and team performance on an hour-by-hour basis in some cases, and on a daily basis in others, were typically prominently displayed.

Although production organisation varies considerably from plant to plant, in most cases the tasks carried out by individual operators were mostly short cycle (typically thirty seconds as the product or component moves down the line). Operators were usually expected to perform more than one task, to allow for flexible and efficient labour deployment in the case of observers. While flexibility was the goal, however, it was not often easy to achieve, due to considerable labour turnover. This, of course, is partly due to the age and gender profile of the production operatives, particularly in electronics, that is young and female.

While there is strict adherence to discipline in terms of quality, this also applies to time keeping and absence. In certain companies peer pressure is used, with absence and lateness publicly displayed. In all companies detailed records are kept and return-to-work interviews carried out. This is typically the first step in a strict disciplinary system and, while procedures vary, it is not unusual for two separate absences within a three-month period to lead to a warning and probation. Illness is not necessarily viewed as a good excuse.

What emerges, therefore, in Wales' Japanese transplants is a high pressure production environment with a high degree of visibility, individual responsibility, and tight discipline supported, of course, by a facilitative industrial relations climate.

Employee relations: new terms of representation

In order to facilitate the forms of work organisation previously outlined, certain forms of employee relations are a prerequisite, including the imposition of a managerial prerogative, and stability of industrial relations. In order to achieve such a framework, Japanese investors have introduced a series of novel features which, it would seem, have achieved their objectives, but at the same time posed a series of fundamental questions for the trade unions and their role and strategy. This, in turn, has caused considerable turmoil among trade unions in Wales and beyond.

Before addressing these questions, however, a brief description of the pattern of employee relations is necessary. Across the UK, Japanese companies have consistently established industrial relations systems with either no union or a single union (Oliver and Wilkinson, 1992). In Wales, the latter has generally prevailed: of the twenty-four companies which responded to this question, only two, both small employers, did not recognise a trade union. Three companies, meanwhile, recognised more than one union; in one case the production union (GMB) had virtually the same agreement with the company as its white-collar section had, and in the other two cases the companies had recently acquired more than one trade union on brown-field sites. The most popular union chosen was the (then) EETPU (on eleven sites). The main other unions included were the GMB, TGWU, and AEU. While the majority of plants were, therefore, unionised, what appeal did the unions have to the workforce? One fairly crude mechanism for determining this is to look at union densities. These varied from between 30 and 100 per cent, while, on average, membership density across the eighteen companies which provided us with data was 63 per cent.

While these background data are interesting, they do not take us to the crux of the matter: that is to what extent does this presage transformation? In the first instance, the fact that so many of the deals are with a single union is innovative, in manufacturing at least, and has been of crucial importance in the changing of the industrial relations scene in Wales, as is argued later. Of equal importance, however, is the nature of the deals, and the features that they included.

Four main features in these collective agreements are of importance: a so-called 'flexibility' clause; a 'communications' clause; the presence of a 'company advisory board', or its equivalent, for collective bargaining; and binding and/or pendulum arbitration. The flexible development of labour is crucial to the operation of the Japanese style manufacturing system outlined earlier. In fifteen of the eighteen collective agreements studied, a flexibility clause unambiguously established management's right to deploy labour as it saw fit. In essence, this means that any employee can be asked to carry out any task within their capability, allowing for safety consider-ations. Given that these plants had few job grades and only one union, this allows for extreme flexibility. Equally importantly, it takes away one of the crucial bargaining rights of the union: for example, in only one company were shop stewards consulted before moving workers between factories on the same site.

Communication clauses were less numerous (eight out of eighteen cases), but had the similar effect of marginalising the union. Broadly, these clauses allow management to communicate directly with shop floor workers on whatever issue it chooses, and pre-empts the possibility of the union taking advantage of a powerful source of influence.

The third key feature is consultation and collective bargaining, arguably the key aspect of industrial relations. In only two cases, both small organisations, were formal consultation mechanisms absent. Eleven firms, meanwhile, of our sample of eighteen conducted consultation through a company advisory board (COAB). In this area agreements signed by the EETPU stood out from the rest. In the case of the EETPU agreements, the consultative forum considers and makes recommendations on issues traditionally the preserve of collective bargaining between company and union. In the other agreements bargaining is a separate event. These boards should not be confused with workers' councils or management/union consultation committees. The union has no automatic right to representation and the board is essentially an institution for the dissemination and discussion of important company information. Source agreements formally commit the board members to consensus recommendations. The trade union is effectively caught between marginalisation (if it disagrees) or incorporation on management terms.

The final key features surround arbitration and can be neatly summed up as 'continuity of production' agreements. This arguably presents the greatest challenge to the union, in that it strips away the ultimate sanction of the union, industrial action. In fourteen out of the eighteen agreements studied, collective procedures ended in binding arbitration. Thus, in effect, industrial action could take place only outside the terms of the agreement. As such, in spirit at least if not legally, these are *de facto* 'no strike' deals.

Clearly, therefore, these deals in themselves amount to a transformation. As has been seen, however, they represent only a small proportion of the Welsh workforce. Nevertheless, it is evident that they have set the pace for other employers: single union, 'no strike' type deals are now the norm for new manufacturers locating in Wales. Bosch, for example, a major investor in recent years, signed a similar deal with the EETPU. A transformation has occurred, therefore, at least in the manufacturing sector.

The last question that arises is whether or not structural change in industrial relations represents a benevolent shift? A superficial impression would suggest that it is, in terms of industrial harmony. The research reported on here documented industrial action in only eight Japanese companies in Wales, and none were for a long duration. This is not to suggest, however, that this transformation has been a totally smooth one. There has indeed been a 'contested terrain', even though the outcome has been a pyrrhic victory for the unions. It is a victory in which the unions have secured recognition but at the cost of marginalisation. Two contextual factors, however, gave the unions little choice over conditions they had to accept. First there were the severe problems of unemployment and associated falling union membership which led to extreme inter-union rivalry in securing recognition. Secondly, this was compounded by the 'beauty parade' mechanism of choosing a union before recruitment. Between the first Japanese manufacturer setting up in 1972 and 1990, there was considerable industrial strife, although this was *between* the unions which, *inter alia*, led to the EETPU's expulsion from the TUC in 1988. In the 1990s, however, this debate has subsided. All of the major unions, including the TGWU, have now signed single union 'no strike' deals. To this extent, the Japanese investors have succeeded in emulating something which, if it is not company unionism, is fairly akin to it.

CONCLUSIONS

The transformation of the Welsh economy from one based on older, declining industries, to one with a broad spectrum of manufacturing and services, has been largely completed in the past decade. Both the physical and economic landscape have changed almost beyond recognition. There are few signs, for example, of the once dominant coal industry, apart from a burgeoning 'heritage' industry of pit museums. The greening of the Valley areas has been repeated in the coastal areas where the ports, constructed for coal export, have been gentrified, and yachts in 'marinas' have replaced colliers on wharfs.

On a superficial inspection, this transformation has been relatively painless. In the rhetoric of politicians and policy makers, this is certainly how it is presented: service sector jobs have replaced mining jobs. The Japanese companies now employ more than the steel industry. There is a neat symmetry in the balance sheet of job statistics, and unemployment rates, at the time of writing, are at a low point, relative to the rest of the country.

However, when one begins to look below the surface of these statistics, and indeed at other data, a very different picture begins to emerge. Most obviously the unemployment statistics definitions have been changed so many times in the past fifteen years as to render them almost useless, other than in plotting trends. During the most recent Morris and Wilkinson (1989) survey, for example, we expressed our surprise, to a local vicar, at how low unemployment rates appeared to be in the 1991 census, in what seemed to be very poor Rhondda wards. His response was to pose the question as to how many people were actually working in these wards. The figures are quite startling. In one such ward, Tylorstown, only one-third of the population is actively employed, compared to 57 per cent in the prosperous Usk ward of leafy Monmouth, which also has a higher percentage of retired people. One answer to this conundrum is the percentage of people who are registered 'permanently sick'; this nearly quadrupled in certain local authority districts between 1981 and 1991.

This is only part of the picture, however. The other is found among those who are working. The working population of Wales is impoverished on average relative to the rest of the UK, with the gap widening. What is more, this is within a context of socio-economic polarisation *and* spatial socio-economic polarisation.

Part of the answer would seem to lie in the nature of this economic transformation; the Welsh economy is, to a certain extent, being 'McJobbed'. The comparison of the steel industry and Japanese investment is illustrative of such a process. Yet, to an extent, this is somewhat unfair on the Japanese firms, for while skill and pay rates in these firms are relatively low, they are much better than in other manufacturing firms, and certainly better than in the service sectors. The high price of economic transformation in Wales is, however, quite clearly apparent.

ACKNOWLEDGEMENTS

I would like to acknowledge two pieces of research from which this chapter borrows. First, the Japanese investment work was carried out with two Cardiff colleagues, Barry Wilkinson and Max Munday. Secondly, the steel case study is, in part, based on work carried out with another Cardiff colleague, Paul Blyton, and with Nick Bacon of Loughborough University.

REFERENCES

Blyton, P., Franz, H.W., Morris, J., Bacon, N. and Lichte, R. (1993) *Changes in Work Organisation in the UK and German Steel Industries: Implications for Trade Unions and Industrial Relations*. Report to the Anglo-German Foundation for the Study of Industrial Society, London.

Bryan, J., Hill, S., Munday, M. and Roberts, A. (1994) *Steel in Wales: The Economic Impact of Steel Production in Industrial South Wales*. Report for the Standing Conference on Regional Policy in South Wales by the Welsh Economy Research Unit, Cardiff Business School.

Coupland, D. (1992) *Generation X*, London: Abacus.

Fevre, R. (1989) *Wales is Closed*, Nottingham: Spokesman Books.

Garrahan, P. and Stewart, P. (1992) *The Nissan Enigma: Flexibility at Work in a Local Economy*, London: Mansell.

Hill, S. and Munday, M. (1994) *The Regional Distribution of Foreign Manufacturing Investment in the UK*, London: Macmillan.

Humphrys, S.G. (1972) *Industrial South Wales*, Newton Abbot: David and Charles.

Morgan, K. (1979) 'State Regional Intervention and Industrial Reconstruction in Post-War Britain', WP16, Urban and Regional Studies Group, University of Sussex, Brighton.

Morgan, K. (1983) 'Restructuring Steel: The Crisis of Labour and Locality in Britain', *International Journal of Urban and Regional Research* 7, 175–201.

Morgan, K. (1994) 'The Fallible Servant: Making Sense of the WDA', Department of City and Regional Planning. Working paper, 151. University of Wales, Cardiff.

Morgan, K. and Roberts, E. (1993) *The Democratic Deficit: A Guide to Quangoland*, Department of City and Regional Planning, UWCC, Cardiff.

Morris, J. (1987) 'The State of Industrial Restructuring: Government Policies in Industrial Wales', *Society and Space* 5, 195–213.

Morris, J., Blyton, P., Bacon, N., and Franc, M.W. (1992) 'Beyond Survival: The Implementation of New Forms of Work Organisation in the UK and German Steel Industries', *International Journal of Human Resource Management* 3, 307–29.

Morris, J., Munday, M., and Wilkinson, B. (1993) *Working for the Japanese: The Economic and Social Consequences of Japanese Investment in Wales*, London: Athlone.

Morris, J. and Wilkinson, B. (1989) *Divided Wales: Local Prosperity in the 1980s*, Report prepared for HTV Wales, Cardiff Business School.

Morris, J. and Wilkinson, B. (1993) *Poverty and Prosperity in Wales*, Report prepared for HTV Wales, Cardiff Business School.

Oliver, N. and Wilkinson, B. (1992) *The Japanisation of British Industry*, Oxford: Blackwell.

Simpson, D. (1992) 'Why are Welsh Wages So Low?' *Welsh Economic Review* 5(1), 54–63.

Simpson, D. and McNabb, R. (1994) 'Pay in Wales: Still Falling Behind England', *Welsh Economic Review* 7(1), 53–8.

4

RESTRUCTURING THE TEXTILES AND CLOTHING INDUSTRIES

Peter Baker

The textiles and clothing industry played a major role in the transformation of Britain to the status of first industrial nation.[1] Indeed it has been argued that the 'industrial revolution was a textiles revolution: the cotton textiles industry was the primary engine of growth' (Dicken, 1992: 233). While the textiles and clothing sectors can no longer claim to be the driving force of the UK economy, they are still major contributors to employment, as can be seen in Table 4.1.

The UK economy has deindustrialised at a faster rate than its major competitors over the period covered in Table 4.1 and the rate of loss of employment in the textiles sector has been more rapid than the general loss of employment in manufacturing in the UK. The loss of employment in clothing over the period, while substantial, has been less marked.

The employment fortunes of different regions have varied within the overall decline of employment in textiles and clothing in the UK. For example, the East Midlands lost over 20,000 jobs in textiles between 1980 and 1989 – the total falling from 82,000 jobs in the sector to below 62,000 – though it increased its percentage of total employment in textiles from 26

Table 4.1 Employment in the UK textiles and clothing industries 1970–90

Year	Textiles (,000)	Clothing (,000)	% of Manufacturing
1970	652.6	356.9	12.6
1975	533.1	280.0	10.9
1980	314.8	317.8	9.7
1985	229.9	267.3	10.0
1989	215.5	251.8	9.4
1990	195.6	234.5	8.9

Source: *Census of Production Report Summary*, volume PA 1002.

per cent to nearly 28.6 per cent. Over the same period, starting from smaller totals in 1980, Yorkshire and Humberside and the North West each lost in excess of 20,000 jobs and both saw a deterioration in their percentage of total employment in textiles. In the footwear and clothing sector,[2] the most marked regional decline was registered in the South East. Over the period 1980 to 1989 the South East lost over 22,000 jobs in the sector declining from 20.8 per cent of total employment to 16.0 per cent. At the start of this period the South East had more employment in footwear and clothing than either the North West or the East Midlands; by the end of the period fewer workers were employed in the South East than in either the North West or the East Midlands. While all other regions lost employment in footwear and clothing the West Midlands showed a marked gain rising from just over 18,000 jobs in 1980 to 21,000 jobs by 1989.

Technology, labour, and the competitive process

The textiles and clothing sectors cover a wide range of industrial activities ranging from the manufacture and treatment of materials to the making-up of garments. While the title clothing clearly indicates that this sector is concerned with the making-up of garments, making-up also takes place within the textiles sector. For example, tights and socks are included in the textiles sector as hosiery and yet the knitting and making-up of these items usually takes place on the same premises. Equally, fabric will often be knitted and made-up on the same premises for a wide range of both outerwear and underwear. The distinction between textiles and clothing for sectoral analysis can therefore obscure the fact that common activities do take place in the two divisions.

The textiles sector in general is more capital intensive than the clothing sector. Areas such as knitting, fabric manufacture, and dying and bleaching have all benefited from technological advances which has facilitated both higher standards and consistency of quality while increasing productivity and improving energy use. Improvements in making-up have been registered but these have been limited by the nature of the activities undertaken. Making-up remains a very labour intensive activity and problems revolve around the nature of garment transfer, the limpness of the material, and the number of intricate processes that have to be performed on an individual garment (Winterton, 1992). Labour costs remain a very substantial element of total costs and in the case of clothing constitute more than half of total costs. The implication of this is that those countries with low labour costs should have a comparative advantage over countries with high labour costs. This is in fact the case and this is a significant element in explaining why the UK industry has suffered a major decline in the post-war period. The UK trade balance in textiles and clothing deteriorated markedly over the 1980s with a substantial growth in imports of clothing coming from low labour cost countries. Import penetration in areas such as men's and boys' and women's and girls' outerwear is well in excess of 50 per cent.

However, labour costs are not the only factors which account for the poor performance of the UK textiles and clothing industry in recent years. Italy, with wage levels reflecting its status as a leading industrial nation, has fared much better than the UK and in the late 1980s was the second most important importer of clothing into the UK after Hong Kong.

Restructuring in the Italian textiles and clothing sectors

Italy's relative success reflects a markedly different approach to industrial organisation, and this in turn depends largely on the nature of the social/cultural/economic milieux. Much of the Italian textiles and clothing is located in industrial districts in Northern Italy. These industrial districts are made up of small- and medium-sized enterprises and are deemed to be both enterprising and dynamic (Piore and Sabel, 1984; Totterdill, 1992). It is argued that these districts were well placed to take advantage of important changes which occurred in the clothing retail markets in the 1980s. The 1980s witnessed a growing segmentation of the clothing retail industry with chains concentrating on particular age groups such as the womenswear segment in the age range twenty-five to forty years. At the same time the fashion year became more fragmented with the increase in the number of 'seasons' in any one calendar year. The result of this was a significant increase in variety of garments and a reduction in batch size. These changes have been facilitated by the development of new technology (Electronic Point of Sales Systems: EPOS) which enables retailers to monitor stock levels and fast selling lines to a high level of precision. Benetton, for example, receives information back from their retail outlets across the world on the sales for that day and organises manufacture in accordance with sales patterns. Indeed Benetton is often cited as an example of the new flexible production in operation (GLC, 1986). The company employs directly only a small fraction of the personnel who earn their livelihood through Benetton's activities. Retail outlets are franchised, and most production takes place on a subcontract basis in independent small and medium-sized firms. As Murray (1985: 30) illustrates 'Benetton provides the designs, controls materials stocks, and orchestrates what is produced according to the computerised daily sales returns which flow back to their Italian headquarters from all parts of Europe'.

The networks of small firms used by Benetton to manufacture their garments have grown up over time in an organic fashion. 'Industrial districts', as first described by the eminent early twentieth-century economist Alfred Marshall, provide a number of benefits, most notably the economies of scale which accrue from the agglomeration of firms in the same industrial sector. In the case of clothing in Italy, small firms in districts exist in a context both of co-operation and competition. Firms undertaking the same functions will often find themselves competing with one another for work, but this does not preclude opportunities for co-operation and the sharing of work, and/or personnel, on occasions. Equally, firms at different points in the production chain will develop networks of a long-term nature which revolve around mutual trust and loyalty. Small firms will tend to specialise in a limited range of functions and through this mechanism are able to achieve economies of scale through specialisation in a given niche. Although performing only a limited number of functions, a firm will achieve a high throughput, thus reaping economies of scale. A garment may then be worked on by several firms, each performing its role before passing it on for further processes. Through specialisation firms can justify expenditure on the latest equipment and can place emphasis on high productivity, high quality, and high value added, rather than relying on sweated labour to gain competitive advantage.

The role of the public sector at the local and regional level is also of importance here. Emilia Romagna in Northern Italy has witnessed a significant growth of small clothing firms over the last twenty years, many of these being started by workers displaced from large firms which have encountered difficulties. Regional Councils have been central to the growth of these firms, providing the pump priming for the formation of specialist services to facilitate the development of small- and medium-sized enterprises. As Totterdill (1992: 42) notes, these firms have 'been supported by the development of a sophisticated infrastructure, capable of delivering a near comprehensive range of services designed to lift the administrative burden on entrepreneurs, encourage innovation, and promote specific sectoral objectives'.

Additional factors here are the legal structure in Italy which promotes the development of artisinal firms, and the tax system, which accords benefits to small firms (Lazerson, 1988). The factors contributing to the success of Italian clothing firms in the 1980s can be seen to be a mixture of history, culture, public sector assistance, legislation, fashion changes, and the problems of large firms. This last factor is perhaps of particular importance. In common with many other European countries, Italy experienced a period of intense labour conflict in the 1970s. Larger companies experienced particular difficulties and one reaction of this was to put out work to small companies (Amin and Robins, 1989). The existing industrial districts were beneficiaries of this strategy and this is a factor in their growth in this period. Furthermore, some commentators have argued that many of the more positive features of such 'flexibly specialised' areas have been exaggerated and that exploitation of workers is more widespread than may be generally recognised (Mattera, 1980; Murray, 1987; Amin and Robins, 1989). More recent work does in fact suggest that the clothing and knitwear sectors in Emilia Romagna are under increasing threat from low wage countries (Cooke and Morgan, 1993). In a dynamic world economy, therefore, the model of the 'Third Italy' requires further evaluation. Nonetheless, regardless of such qualifications, in terms of employment and income generation, the recent performance of the Italian textiles and clothing districts has been impressive, relative to other high wage European nations.

Restructuring in textiles and clothing in the UK

It is apposite to contrast the different fortunes of the Italian and UK industries, especially as the Lancashire cotton industry was identified as being a working example of industrial districts in the early twentieth century and as Alfred Marshall drew much of his inspiration from this area (Sunley, 1992). Quite clearly, however, the subsequent development of the Lancashire cotton industry is markedly different from the trajectory of the textiles and clothing sector in Italy. The reasons for this are partly cultural and partly historical. Magatti (1993) contrasts the performance of the Lancashire cotton industry and that of Ticino Olona, an area in Northern Italy between Milan and Varese. Since the Second World War Lancashire has developed from being a region dominated by cotton with a concentration of hundreds of small firms, into a region where textiles and clothing employment has rapidly diminished. The process of reorganisation has resulted in an industry dominated by a handful of externally controlled large firms. Conversely, Ticino Olona has followed a path which has seen the transformation from an industry dependent upon a few relatively large firms to one which derives its strength from a locally owned, diversified, small firm base.

During the nineteenth and into the current century, the UK textiles and clothing sectors were highly dependent on markets in the British Empire and in particular in India. British companies relied heavily on Indian markets for exports of cotton goods, and secured this position by the destruction, through British colonial policy, of the Indian textiles industry in the early nineteenth century (Hobsbawm, 1969). After the Second World War, competition in textiles and clothing intensified and in the 1950s UK companies found themselves under severe pressure from low cost producers in Asia. The UK industry was left with significant overcapacity, and the reaction of the UK government in the 1960s was to encourage rationalisation. The government encouraged the reduction of capacity by offering financial incentives to firms for scrapping machinery; those firms which remained in the industry were encouraged to re-equip with modern machinery, with the aid of government grants. At this time it was felt that the best way to achieve international competitiveness was to concentrate capacity in a limited number of plants. This was the path followed in the

UK and areas like Lancashire suffered a rash of firm closures and a struggle for dominance between a handful of large firms.

In a context of displacement of labour from textiles and clothing, wages could be kept at low levels and the industry became increasingly unattractive to workers, many of whom sought employment elsewhere. During this period of takeovers and closures and reorganisation of labour processes, greater use of marginalised sectors of the labour force was made. Fevre (1985: 157) notes that the 1971 census showed that wool textiles had the greatest 'absolute concentration of black workers in the UK'. Most of these workers were Asian and the level of concentration increased through the 1970s, notably in areas such as Bradford. Overall, the UK industry lost the opportunity to develop a new dynamic partnership between capital and labour and its decline has continued unabated.

In Northern Italy the form of restructuring encouraged by the state was different. The family as a unit of organisation is strong and this often formed the basis for the development of firms. The Italian government has tended to favour small and artisinal firms and resources were made available in a variety of forms, thus facilitating their growth and development. In addition to providing financial aid to the small firm sector from the second half of the 1950s onwards, the Italian government helped in other ways. As international competition intensified and production costs for firms rose, the Italian government 'preferred to exploit the short-term benefits offered by decentralisation of production, tax evasion, the black economy and informal activities, which were all tolerated or even fostered by the administration as well as by the political system' (Magatti, 1993: 221).

The socio-economic climate for small firms restructuring in Italy, therefore, proved to be favourable and this contrasts markedly with the situation in the UK.

Increasingly in the 1980s, attention was paid to the plight of the UK textiles and clothing sectors, notably by academics and local authorities. Note was made of the more positive features of restructuring in high wage economies such as Italy, with the intention of replicating such features, where possible, in the UK economy. The British sector seemed to be trapped in a low wage, low skill, low value product cycle, and it was evident that ways should be sought to break out of this.

The Greater London Council (GLC), working in collaboration with other local authorities, sponsored research into ways in which the textiles and clothing sectors could move towards a high skill, high wage future (GLC, 1986), and this work has been carried forward since the demise of the GLC in 1986 (Farrands et al., 1990). A survey of Nottinghamshire published in 1990 (Farrands et al., 1990: 2) argued, for example, that 'there are substantial gains to be made from the introduction of multi-skill production methods'. The emphasis here is placed on the need for a co-ordinated strategy and reference is made to the training experience of Germany. The

German textiles and clothing sectors have experienced heavy job losses with the clothing sector shedding 200,000 jobs over the period 1970 to 1992, leaving a total of 150,000 employees (Adler and Breitenachner, 1993). A particular feature here has been the extensive reliance on 'outward processing'[3] to low labour cost countries by German firms; companies in Germany are by far the most reliant of all those in the European Community on outward processing. German firms will often attempt to achieve a 'mix' of processes with the less technical, lower value work, being processed abroad, while the more highly skilled sewing work on higher value garments will be carried out in Germany. In order to compete effectively against low labour cost countries it is emphasised that companies in Germany should concentrate on quality, fashion, flexibility, and rapid delivery, and that innovation must stretch from the production process to encompass areas such as management, organisation, and marketing (Adler and Breitenachner, 1993). The German industry is clearly pinning its future on the production of high value added, quality products.

The German training system provides an output of highly skilled workers who have undertaken lengthy programmes of training extending to three years and beyond. Very few workers in the UK industry, particularly at machinist level, have undergone this length of training. In recent years most clothing trainees in Britain have been employed under the government's youth training scheme and in most cases the extent of full time training is limited to around six weeks. A result of this poor level of training is a lower quality finished British product than the German equivalent, and substantial supervision and rectification requirements. The much greater emphasis on the acquisition and development of skills in Germany adds greatly to the versatility of workers and predisposes German firms to compete effectively in areas where quality, and flexibility of response, are crucial. German productivity, even when allowing for better maintained and more modern machinery, is much higher than that in the UK. Commenting on a number of matched Anglo-German comparison firms, Creigh Tyte and Clay (1993: 30) note 'Across 20 or so clothing manufacturers in Britain and Germany it was apparent that German plants produced smaller quantities of high quality goods in greater varieties, whereas Britain concentrated on longer runs of standard garments'.

In an attempt to strengthen the UK textiles and clothing sectors a number of initiatives have been implemented at the local level in the 1980s. These initiatives include the formation of centres for the provision of advice and information, and access to equipment which small firms cannot afford to equip themselves with. In an attempt to enable firms to compete more effectively, some areas have established Fashion Centres with the financial support of local authorities. These Centres assist in such areas as the marketing and design of garments. The first Fashion Centre was set up in Hackney, in London in 1982, and a similar centre was opened in Nottingham in 1985 (Totterdill, 1992). More recently in 1992, an innovative project entitled the Nottinghamshire Work and Technology Programme was introduced with funding from the County Council and two local Training and Enterprise Councils (TECs). The intention here is to provide both technical and training support to knitwear and clothing companies. This is part of a process with the aim of moving firms away from mass production, towards smaller batch production of higher quality garments. At the core of this project is the introduction of teamworking methods whereby workers are expected to become polyvalent and 'carry out more tasks of a discretionary nature, enjoying greater autonomy and responsibility' (McLellan *et al.*, 1993: 14). The result of such practices, it is hoped, should be higher quality products, greater job satisfaction, and higher financial rewards.

While it is clear that at the local level initiatives are being taken in an attempt to revive the flagging fortunes of the UK industry, it is notable that other forms of restructuring have also been taking place in recent years. It is acknowledged that the long-established textiles and clothing sectors in Leicester have become heavily dependent on ethnic entrepreneurs and workers (initially African Asians displaced from Uganda in the 1960s and 1970s), but another feature is the spread of textiles and clothing manufacture organised by ethnic communities to areas which did not have a tradition of such industrial activities. The West Midlands, long associated with engineering, has recently seen the growth in importance of clothing manufacture, for example. Over the period 1974 to 1987, employment in the clothing sector in Coventry increased from 417 to 1,392 jobs, while the number of firms grew from twenty-two to sixty-six (Healey *et al.*, 1987). If homeworkers are added, then the total of employment comes to 1,524 in 1987. Virtually all of these firms have their ownership in the Asian community and 95 per cent of employees are of Asian origin (Healey *et al.*, 1987). Estimates by the West Midlands Enterprise Board suggest that some 500 small clothing firms are in operation in the metropolitan conurbation of the West Midlands as a whole. The estimated employment in these firms is some 20,000 workers, around twice the officially recorded level: this discrepancy exists due to the scale of unregistered workshops and extensive homeworking. Ram (1992) notes that much of the growth of the clothing sector in the West Midlands is due to the increase in unemployment in the region, and the lack of employment opportunities. However, the products these firms in the main manufacture are fairly simple lower quality garments, including jeans and sports/leisurewear. A problem commented on by both Healey *et al.* (1987) and Ram (1992) is the claimed lack of skilled machinists and yet, as Ram notes, employers 'rarely provided training in any systematic or developmental sense' (Ram, 1992: 506). Mitter (1986) states that wage levels in ethnic businesses are usually low and this may be even more marked among homeworkers. The growth of the clothing sector in non-traditional areas would appear, then, to rely on low skill levels and low wages for its competitive advantage, with the crucial determining market factor being the price of the product.

Restructuring of the textiles and clothing sectors in Hinckley

The current economic and social structure of any locality is a result of factors which have shaped this outcome over time. Massey (1983) refers to the 'local uniqueness' which is manifested at any time through the processes of restructuring. The outcomes for any area at any point in time, with regard to variables such as labour quality and industrial militancy, are dependent on a 'combination of layers' (Massey, 1983: 78) whereby successive waves of investment interact with a locality to shape the division of labour. An example of this can be seen in the siting of electronics assembly plants in the 1970s. As it became increasingly possible to separate higher and lower labour processes so a search for geographical concentrations of suitable labour for lower level processes, such as the assembly of printed circuit boards, arose. It was now common to find a geographical separation of workers, with R&D and high order management categories in one area, and production workers in another. This is typified by the concentration of research related work in the 'M4 Corridor' in the South West of Britain, while assembly work is carried out in peripheral areas of Britain or in other parts of the world. Areas which had lost traditional industrial employment in Scotland and Wales have been particularly attractive for companies seeking low order assembly workers, as they had reserves of female labour with few alternative employment prospects. Sites such as ex-mining areas with limited employment for workers of either sex, held particular attractions.

The locality on which this study of restructuring is based is the small industrial town of Hinckley[4] situated in the East Midlands, and roughly equidistant between Coventry and Leicester (approximately thirteen miles). Hinckley was chosen for this study due to its relatively good economic performance over time and its continuing dependence on the textiles and clothing industry as the major provider of industrial employment.

In 1989 there were 114 firms, with less than 100 employees each, operating in all areas of textiles and clothing in Hinckley, and seventeen firms with more than 100 employees each. This study is based on interviews with thirty-one randomly selected small firms and fifteen large firms.

In an attempt to understand Hinckley's current phase of industrial restructuring, and the role of textiles and clothing within that, it is necessary to place this within a historical context. Hinckley's industrial past stretches back to the seventeenth century. Hinckley's transformation from a conventional market town, into a hosiery town, took place from 1640 when the first stocking frame was introduced into the local economy. The stocking frame revolutionised the production of hosiery, greatly increasing productivity. Such frames were accommodated in the home and hosiery was produced on a cottage basis. By 1778 there were 864 stocking frames in a town of 2,150 people (Henderson, 1981) and by the end of the nineteenth century the transformation from cottage industry to factory system was complete. During the nineteenth century the manufacture of footwear grew in importance in the area and this remained Hinckley's second most important industry until recently. Much of Hinckley's industry grew to serve the needs of the hosiery and footwear industries, and important employers of the 1990s such as Ferry Pickering (printers) and Sketchley (dry cleaners) were founded locally to serve these principal industries.

For more than three centuries the primary source of employment in Hinckley has been the textiles and clothing industry. This has had a marked effect on both the architecture of the town and the disposition of its people. The industry remains concentrated in the older industrial and residential heart of the town with many workers employed in Victorian and Edwardian industrial premises, while still living in the rows of terraced properties which grew up to house the workers who served the mills and footwear factories. The inhabitants of Hinckley have come to accept the textiles and clothing industry as a central part of their lives over generations and the socio-economic culture has been shaped by the dominance of the industry. In a relatively small town of less than 60,000 people, almost all families have traditionally had some association with hosiery manufacture. This has stamped itself on the town's character and even today the unique confluence of events stemming from this industrial association can be evidenced within the town as noted by a local historian: 'The self sufficiency of the past and the sense of a close knit community are still present' (Beavin, 1983: 83).

The rate of decline of employment in textiles and clothing found elsewhere in the UK has not been mirrored in Hinckley. Over the period 1971 to 1981 the number of hosiery and knitwear firms employing over 100 workers declined from twenty-one to sixteen. However, employment in this sector declined by only 800 and when the figures for clothing, hats and gloves, and other textiles are added to this, the reduction in employment is only 600. Textiles and clothing still provided more than 7,000 jobs in 1981, over 60 per cent of total manufacturing employment.

This relatively good performance set in the context of rapid national decline was continued through the 1980s and it is estimated that over 7,000 jobs were still provided by the industry in Hinckley in 1989. The reasons for this relatively good performance stem from a combination of the mix of Hinckley's textiles and clothing activities, resilient locally owned and controlled firms, and a market increase in the importance of the small firm sector, notably in the clothing sector. Hosiery production has not been subject to the levels of global trade that have marked many other lines of production, and as a result hosiery firms have been able to produce for their domestic markets with less hindrance from foreign competition. In 1987 import penetration by volume for tights, pantyhose, and stockings was well below 30 per cent, while for knitwear it was 55 per cent (Knitstats, 1989). This has worked to Hinckley's advantage, as it has a heavy orientation towards hosiery production.

A factor which may have a major bearing on the economic fate of an area is the degree to which the workforce is subject to local direction and control. Areas with a tradition of employment in large externally controlled branch plants demonstrated particularly heavy losses of employment in the 1970s and 1980s (Lloyd and Reeve, 1982). It has been shown that branch plants are more likely to close and experience employment reduction than head office plants (Healey, 1981). Hinckley's current ownership pattern indicates that around 80 per cent of employment in larger firms is subject to ownership/control from within Leicestershire. Furthermore, where ownership extends beyond Leicestershire, the establishments concerned operate as separately constituted firms in Hinckley rather than branch plants. Ownership and control of small firms is almost entirely based in Hinckley. While Hinckley has in the past been subject to the active buying up of companies by firms such as Courtaulds, it has, throughout, maintained a strong base of local ownership and control. The destabilising effects of the buying, selling, and closing down of capacity by large externally owned capital has therefore been moderated within the local economy.

The greatest employment losses by larger firms (100 plus employees) were suffered in the 1970s and early 1980s. By the second half of the 1980s some of the larger knitwear firms in Hinckley were experiencing difficulties, but hosiery firms were generally buoyant. Hosiery firms have been able to take advantage of technology which deskills the labour process and increases productivity. Automatic machines which join legs, seam toes and stitch gussets require an operative to feed them, rather than a trained machinist. While some retailers still insist on a finished product that requires the attention of a machinist, many lines can be produced using automatic machines for all processes. This eases labour problems, as feeding operatives require little training. The main requirement is experience, in order that speed can be built up, and this can be achieved in a relatively short period.

Another factor which has been of particular help in relation to the modernisation of the hosiery sector is the development of computerisation for knitting machines. Setting a pattern manually on a knitting machine can take a skilled individual two to three days, incurring significant 'down time' for that equipment. The expense of pattern changing means that long runs of standard lines are necessary for economic viability. Through computerisation, patterns can be changed in minutes, simply by changing a programme.

This has meant that short runs of varied styles are now economically viable. In turn, this has helped to raise the profile of hosiery as a fashion accessory and has seen an increase in sales. During the 1980s the larger Hinckley hosiery firms invested in the production technology described, along with new equipment which facilitated greater accuracy and productivity at the examining and packing stages.

Developments in the larger knitwear companies have been less encouraging. While the advantages of computerisation in knitting have been widely embraced, there has been relatively little advance in the technology available at the making up stage. The larger knitwear companies in Hinckley still seem to be heavily reliant on longer runs of fairly standard products and, while there is a strong orientation towards the high street stores, there is little evidence of a sustained move to high value added designer lines, targeted at the top income earners. One rather traditional family run firm interviewed bemoaned the demise of the long run in knitwear. It was noted that, whereas long runs of garments were their staple diet in former years, such long runs, where they still exist, are often contracted to overseas firms. Mail order companies which still require fairly long runs will contract these out, usually to firms in low labour cost countries, and will use a UK firm only as a 'top up' resource, once their main stocks are exhausted. Many of the larger firms have found, therefore, that their traditional customers no longer require them for large orders, but they cannot survive on small runs. The adjustment process to changed circumstances is clearly painful and a number of firms are struggling, with limited evidence of new investment being made as an attempt to survive in a hostile climate. The option, where it exists, of 'throwing in your lot' with one or two large retailers and dedicating all production to these limited outlets, removes the need to search constantly around for customers. However, while having certain advantages of seeming security and a guarantee of sales, this business strategy is fraught with dangers. The UK retail market is heavily concentrated, giving a small number of firms immense buying power (Elson, 1990). These firms may dictate production requirements closely with respect to materials used, machinery employed, and processes. The result of this will be closely monitored profit margins and limited freedom of manoeuvre for firms working for their retail masters. This asymmetrical power structure can have dire consequences for firms if they fail to meet standards consistently, or if international forces, in such areas as exchange rate fluctuations and fiscal incentives, conspire to move in favour of foreign producers and against domestic manufacturers. In many cases the end result has been the demise of independent producers.

The role of the small firm in restructuring

Small firms have become increasingly important providers of employment in Britain throughout industry in recent years, both at the national level and in specific localities (Daley *et al.*, 1991; Baker, 1993). However, the mechan- isms at work in promoting the increase in number of small firms are diverse (Keeble, 1990). Among the factors involved in the promotion of the small firm sector is the push factor of unemployment/uncertainty. Indeed, Binks and Jennings (1986) demonstrate that around 50 per cent of all new business starts in the Nottingham area in the early 1980s were due to owner/managers being pushed into self-employment.

While there has been a significant increase in the number of small firms in textiles and clothing in the Hinckley area in the period 1971 to 1989 (Table 4.2) it is notable that a major factor here has been the negative one of recession push. In other words the retrenchment or closure of an existing commercial organisation has been the catalyst for the development of a new small business.

Of the thirty-one small firms in the survey it was possible to speak to the firm founder in twenty-five cases. Nine of these (36 per cent) had started their businesses due to unemployment/redundancy. An equally important factor mentioned was dissatisfaction with previous employment, with a desire for independence following closely behind. It was obvious from discussions with small firms founders that a number had felt insecure in employment in other firms and as pay levels in the industry are generally low, the opportunity cost of setting up in business may not be high for many of the individuals concerned. The majority of those 'pushed' into setting up their own businesses had occupied managerial positions in their previous employment.

The clothing industry is one for which the entry barriers are low. Set up costs can be limited to second-hand sewing machines and basic cutting facilities; premises can be varied and can range from anything from a garage, shed, small lock up or industrial unit, upwards. Operating costs can be further reduced by entering into cut make and trim arrangements (CMT) whereby the firm works for an agent who finds the customers and then supplies and pays for materials. The clothing firm makes up the garments and is then paid on supply.

The significant growth of small clothing firms in Hinckley has been

Table 4.2 Textiles and clothing firms in the Hinckley area

Size of Firm	<100			>100		
	1971	1981	1989	1971	1981	1989
Number of firms	41	89	114	23	18	18
Employment	1,267	2,441	3,340	6,657	4,927	4,380

Source: Hinckley Survey.

facilitated by the sub-division of large factories, often of Victorian or Edwardian vintage. The wealth of large industrial properties owing their origins to the hosiery or footwear industries has provided the opportunity for new firm starts in the clothing industry.

Because there are low barriers to entry there is consequently intense competition between small firms. The clothing industry nationally, demonstrates a high degree of 'turbulence' with high birth and death rates for firms. A survey of small- and medium-sized firms in the London area, covering the time period 1979 to 1989, demonstrated that clothing firms had the worst survival record of all sectors covered, with a survival rate of 24 per cent, set against an average of 58 per cent (North *et al.*, 1991).

Industrial premises

Hinckley, as is the case in other areas such as Leicester and Manchester, has its clothing sector concentrated in the older urban core. The premises from which most of these firms operate were not designed for modern production methods and do not make for full efficiency. Many premises are multi-storey and have a large number of rooms; this, combined with the presence of weight bearing pillars, hinders the efficient distribution of work/materials/stocks.

Further problems are experienced with respect to access to premises for picking up and delivering of items, as vehicles have to thread their way through the urban core. However, while these inefficiencies abound, employers are often constricted in their freedom to locate elsewhere. While clothing production is located in the urban core, so too is the workforce. Many of the workers in the textiles and clothing industry in Hinckley live located in the terraced streets which developed alongside the factories. A large proportion of this predominantly female workforce is spatially limited; their local labour market may well be measured in yards rather than miles. Much of the workforce will have domestic responsibilities which tie them very closely to the locality. Furthermore, textiles and clothing is a low paid industry and workers would be unprepared to spend their limited incomes on travel to and from work. A major advantage to the workforce is that work 'is on the doorstep'.

Impacts of production restructuring on labour

A factor which has been of importance in the growth of small clothing firms in Hinckley is the problems experienced by larger firms. As noted earlier, many larger firms which had been accustomed to large runs of garments have found it difficult to accommodate smaller runs. Retailers and catalogue companies requiring a flexible source of supply for smaller runs have therefore turned to smaller firms.

However, while larger UK firms may have experienced difficulties in the shift from longer runs of garments and the tendency to contract the longer runs of garments overseas, small firms have also faced problems. The shift from a two season fashion year of spring and autumn to seasons which cover several distinct changes within a year has placed a major emphasis on rapid response. Retailers now have precise knowledge of their sales and stock position and if a line is selling well, new stock will be required rapidly. The lead time for manufacturers, consequently, has plummeted. This can mean that, at one moment, a manufacturer has little work, and at another, is then required to fill a major order in a short space of time. The clothing industry continues to operate a reward system for employees largely based upon piece rates. This means that workers are paid according to the number of items they have contributed their services to, and not on hours worked. If there is little work, then the employee's income will suffer; conversely if there is a lot of work to be completed in a short period of time, the worker will be expected to work overtime. Neither situation is satisfactory, with the former upsetting financial planning for the household and the latter causing disruption to domestic routines. The textiles and clothing industry has never been regarded as an attractive industry to work in, but as more employment opportunities open up for females, it has become even less attractive. Females constitute 74 per cent of the work-force in large textiles and clothing firms in Hinckley and 83 per cent in small firms. At the UK level in 1991, women constituted slightly less than 50 per cent of the workforce in textiles and just over 70 per cent in clothing.

A number of the factors that contribute to the deterioration of the attractions of employment in textiles and clothing can be summarised as follows.

1 The nature of the work. Garment manufacture is detailed work, demanding of close attention and concentration. Payment is largely by piece work and this brings pressures which are absent in many other forms of work.
2 The work is irregular and varies in intensity. These are factors brought about by fashion changes.
3 The industry has seen failing relative wage rates. This has been intensified by competition from companies in low labour cost countries. It has also been brought about by shorter runs of garments. Short runs allow machinists less opportunity to build up speeds with experience of the garment. This results in a lower output per period of time; it is argued that earnings potential is correspondingly reduced as piece rates have often not been adjusted to accommodate this.
4 Environmental conditions of work are often poor in the textiles and clothing industry. Premises often date from the nineteenth or early twentieth century and are difficult to heat in winter and to keep cool in summer.

In the late 1980s Hinckley's textiles and clothing firms were experiencing particular problems in recruiting/retaining labour. This was worsened by what would normally be seen as Hinckley's advantageous geographical position, located in the centre of the country with easy access to the motorway system. Distribution plants in particular were being attracted to the area and were making strong demands on the local labour market. In a number of cases they were even prepared to 'bus' labour in at the company's expense. The textiles and clothing sectors were under particular pressure. While many employers complained of a markedly deteriorating labour situation they were not in a position to react effectively. Employers complained of tight profit margins in all outlets, be it high street stores, wholesalers, or agents. This problem is made worse in the UK because of the high concentration of buying power in the retail sector. Overseas producers can easily gain access to the UK clothing market as a handful of firms account for the majority of UK clothing sales. This threat of foreign competition can easily be employed as a rod to beat UK producers with. Under such constraints, producers argued that they had difficulty raising their prices and consequently found it hard to increase wages, or invest in more productive machinery. Small firms also find the expense of training too high a burden and rely in the main on attracting trained staff.

The problems in the labour market experienced in the 1980s in the Hinckley textiles and clothing sectors were common to other areas in the UK. The outcome elsewhere, as noted earlier, has been an increase in the use of marginalised elements of the labour force, such as Asian females. This will often take the form of the increasing use of homeworkers. This has not occurred in Hinckley, probably due to the small ethnic population in the town. Homeworking has always been of importance in the town, particularly for the packing of hosiery. However, there is no evidence of this having become of greater significance in recent years. Equally, while there has been some growth of part-time working, this has not generally been a deliberate strategy of restructuring on the part of employers. Faced with labour shortages, employers have employed workers on a part-time basis when they would have preferred to engage them on full-time contracts. Hinckley's long tradition of the industry has remained of importance in maintaining the high profile of textiles and clothing in the town. An acceptance and understanding of the industry remains. It is evident, however, that in many establishments the workforce is ageing and many of the younger female workers will not return if they leave to bring up children. Hinckley, in common with the East Midlands of Britain generally, has an under representation of service sector activities; female workers in particular have had limited alternative employment opportunities in the past, although this is now changing.

Investment and working practices

The textiles and clothing sectors in Hinckley seem to be fairly conservative in terms of investment and working practices. While larger hosiery companies have made significant investment in new machinery, some larger knitwear companies have been more reticent. Small firms continue to operate with relatively unsophisticated, often second-hand, equipment and place reliance on labour skills. While there has been much debate nationally about increasing flexibility of labour (Atkinson and Gregory, 1986; Pollert, 1988) there was no evidence of significant changes in Hinckley firms. Large firms continue to recruit for particular machining tasks such as overlocking or flatlocking and workers are engaged on these specialisms. Employees will therefore be occupied on their specialist function and will not undertake other operations. There is, however, a *desire* for a greater level of functional flexibility in small firms. The reduction in length of garment runs, and greater complexity in manufacture, means that on occasions a small firm will be faced with heavy demands for a particular function such as overlocking. Large firms are more likely to be able to cope with such periodic imbalances due to their larger number of specialists and greater capacity. In an attempt to prevent the subcontracting out of processes, small firms prefer to retain employees who can switch from one specialism to another, as functional requirements change. An individual who has, for example, achieved piece rate standards in a range of machining skills will be termed a 'floater'. While firms are encouraging workers to achieve such status, it appears that limited progress has been made. This may well be because the reward system for achieving wider competence is not sufficiently attractive. Workers may feel that by working across a range of activities their average piece rate earnings will fall, compared to the rate they can achieve through specialisation.

Large firms in hosiery have been able to deskill through their increased use of automatic machinery in the place of machinists, but some workers such as mechanics, have also experienced a degree of enskilling as they now need to add a knowledge of the computerised functions of machinery to their remit. However, generally, there has been limited enskilling in textiles and clothing in Hinckley, regardless of firm size. Overall, therefore, the proportion of workers in the hosiery industry with traditional machining skills has fallen.

When major new investment takes place it is usually necessary to reconfigure the organisation of work. Massey and Meegan (1982) have shown that new investment may require new ways of working and will often lead to job displacement. However, changes in the organisation of work may also take place in the absence of major new investment. New work flow systems or changes in the labour process and the division of tasks can have results on productivity as can methods of work intensification, such as speeding up the belt on an assembly line, or introducing new inexpensive manual aids to production.

However, in Hinckley, other than with the simultaneous introduction of substantial new investment, there was no evidence of major reviews of working practices. Innovative methods such as teamworking were not in evidence. This is perhaps understandable in small firms, where it might be felt that the disruption caused, even if only shortlived, could mean the difference between life and death for the firm. New methods may mean reduced output and/or reduced quality in the short run and could lead to worker resistance.

Problems and prescriptions

Many of the problems experienced in Hinckley are evident to a greater or lesser degree elsewhere. As noted earlier, each locality is unique owing to its different industrial and social development, and therefore each locality will react to change in a different way. Hinckley seems to have fared well in terms of employment in textiles and clothing in the last twenty years. However, what is noticeable is that much of the restructuring which has taken place has involved an increase in importance for the small firm. To some extent this has been due to the demise of larger firms, both locally and nationally. The demise of large firms has opened gaps for small firms to plug, and the demise of larger local firms in particular has provided a source of both labour and entrepreneurs. Much of this restructuring has therefore been reactive and does not seem to have led to innovation in terms of work organisation, inter-firm arrangements, marketing, or product lines. Small firms seem to be concentrated into relatively low value product areas such as leisurewear (tracksuits, bermuda shorts, etc.) selling predominantly to wholesalers. There is no evidence of new organisational arrangements developing between small firms in the manner described in the Third Italy (Pyke *et al.*, 1990).

While small firms have capitalised on their flexibility and responded rapidly to the needs of customers, this sector is still not addressing the longer-term problems which face the industry. A clear deficiency in Hinckley, as elsewhere in the UK, is the lack of high quality training. In order to make the industry more attractive to workers it is necessary to make the work more interesting and, perhaps crucially, to improve pay levels. This can be achieved only by giving consideration to innovative labour processes and by concentrating on high quality, high value added, garments. While small firms do not usually have the financial resources to purchase facilities such as computer aided design these can be provided collectively, perhaps through the agency of local colleges or the local authorities, as in the Hackney and Nottingham cases mentioned earlier. Equally, design and marketing expertise can be provided collectively, as can aids to facilitate return to work such as creches. The industry in Hinckley, as elsewhere, needs to investigate possibilities for co-operation and pooling, and both local and national government can be of assistance here.

Much of what is happening in Hinckley can be regarded as typical for the industry at large. Small firms generally attempt to compete on cost rather than on style, fabric, and detail. Large firms are much more likely to invest in modern technology while small firms make do with older equipment. There are good examples of high quality training and state of the art equipment, as at the Austin Reed and Chester Barrie factories in Crewe, UK, but much of the industry continues along a low cost/low quality trajectory.

The textiles and clothing industry remains spatially concentrated in particular regions of the UK. For example the UK textiles industry is concentrated in the East Midlands, the North West and Yorkshire, and Humberside. These areas account for some two thirds of total UK textiles employment. These same areas, with the addition of the South East, account for some 60 per cent of total UK clothing employment. Particular regions have particular specialisms; for example the North West has a notable specialism in cotton and silk textile finishing, while the East Midlands has a long tradition of hosiery production.

Hinckley demonstrates the limited 'modernisation' of the UK textiles and clothing industry. As in Hinckley, much production nationally continues to take place in unsatisfactory and inefficient premises. Equally, as in Hinckley, work organisation in much of the industry follows traditional lines, and nationally the incidence of practices such as teamworking is patchy.

Although companies in the UK lead the world in some areas, such as the production of industrial textiles, they lag behind companies in other countries such as Germany and Italy in the production of high quality, high value garments. Companies in Britain cannot hope to compete through the promotion of a marginalised sweat shop sector, and urgent attention needs to be paid to raising skill levels and developing innovative practices. Only then can companies in the UK hope to compete with countries such as Italy and resist the everincreasing threat from Asian producers (*Economist*, 1991).

NOTES

1 Textiles cover a range of activities including spinning, weaving, knitting, and dying and bleaching. Products include cotton, silk, knitted fabrics, hosiery, and carpets. Clothing involves the cutting and assembly of fabric to make garments for wear. This is usually referred to as 'making-up' and in the main involves the stitching together of the constituent parts of a garment to constitute a finished product.
2 Footwear and clothing are not disaggregated at the regional level.

3 Outward processing occurs when a firm temporarily exports items for processing abroad, following which they re-enter the country of export.
4 Hinckley, here, is taken to cover the approximate boundaries of the area covered by the Hinckley Urban District Council prior to local government reorganisation in 1974. This embraces the settlements of Hinckley, Burbage, Earl Shilton, and Barwell.

REFERENCES

Adler, U. and Breitenachner, M. (1993) 'Global Restructuring in Germany: A Pioneer in Subcontracting and Flexible Production Methods'. Paper given at conference Global Restructuring and Local Strategies; The Case of the Clothing Industry, University of Bradford, 22–24 September.

Amin, A. and Robins, K. (1989) 'The Re-emergence Of Regional Economies? The Mythical Geography Of Flexible Specialisation', *Environment and Planning D* 8, 7–34.

Atkinson, J. and Gregory, D. (1986) 'A Flexible Future', *Marxism Today*, April.

Baker, P. (1993) 'The Role of the Small Firm in Locality Restructuring', *Area* 25, 37–44.

Beavin, H. A., (1983) *The Book of Hinckley*, Buckingham: Barracuda Books.

Binks, M. and Jennings, A. (1986) 'Small Firms as a Source of Economic Rejuvenation', in J. Curran, J. Stanworth and D. Watkins (eds) *The Survival of the Small Firm*, Vol. 1, Aldershot: Gower.

Cooke, P. and Morgan, K. (1993) 'Growth Regions Under Duress: Renewal Strategies in Baden Wurttemberg and Emilia Romana', in A. Amin and N. Thrift (eds) *Holding Down the Global: Possibilities for Local Economic Policy*, forthcoming.

Creigh Tyte, S. and Clay, N. (1993) 'SMEs' Training Needs: Is There a Role for Government?' paper given at 16th National Small Firms' Policy and Research Conference, Nottingham Trent University, 17–19 November.

Daly, M., Campbell, M., Gallagher, C. and Robson, G. (1991) 'Job Creation 1987–1989: the Contributions of Small and Large Firms', *Employment Gazette*, November, 589–94.

Dicken, P. (1992) *Global Shift*, London: Paul Chapman Publishing.

Economist, The (1991) 'Textiles – Hard at Home', *The Economist*, 11 May, 32–34.

Elson, D. (1990) 'Marketing Factors Effecting the Globalisation of Textiles', *Textiles Outlook International*, March, 51–61.

Farrands, C., Totterdill, P., Fletcher, D., Gebbert, C., Middleton, D. and Waldman, P. (1990) 'Markets, Production and Machinists in Nottinghamshire's Clothing and Knitwear Industries', report for Nottinghamshire County Council.

Fevre, R. (1985) 'Racism and Cheap Labour in UK Wool Textiles', in H. Newby, J. Bujra, P. Littlewood, G. Rees, and T. Rees (eds) *Recession and Reorganisation in Industrial Society*, London: Macmillan.

GLC (1986) *Textiles and Clothing: Sunset Industries?*, Industry and Employment Branch, Greater London Council.

H.M.S.O., *Census of Production Report Summary*, volume PA 10002, various years, London: H.M.S.O.

Healey, M. (1981) 'Locational Adjustments and the Characteristics of Manufacturing Plants', *Trans. Inst. Br. Geogr.*, NS 6, 394–412.

Healey, M., Clark, D. and Shrivastava, V. (1987) *The Clothing Industry in Coventry*, Industrial Location Working Paper 10, Department of Geography, Coventry Polytechnic.

Henderson, E. (1981) *Milestones of Hinckley 1640–1981*, available from Hinckley public library.

Hobsbawm, E.J. (1969) *Industry and Empire*, Harmondsworth: Penguin.

Keeble, D. (1990) 'Small Firms, New Firms and Uneven Regional Development in the UK', *Area* 22, 234–45.

Knitstats (1989) Information Department, HATRA, Nottingham.

Lazerson, M. (1988) 'Organisational Growth of Small Firms: An Outcome of Markets and Hierarchies?', *American Sociological Review* 53, 330–42.

Lloyd, P.E. and Reeve, D.E. (1982) 'North West England 1971–77: A Study in Industrial Decline and Economic Restructuring', *Regional Studies* 16, 345–59.

McLellan, J., Wigfield, A. and Wilkes, V. (1993) 'Restructuring of the Clothing Industry: The Case of Team Working', Paper given at conference *Global Restructuring and Local Strategies: the Case of the Clothing Industry*, University of Bradford, 22–24 September.

Magatti, M. (1993) 'The Market and Social Forces: A Comparative Analysis of Industrial Change', *International Journal of Urban and Regional Research* 17, 213–31.

Massey, D. (1983) 'Industrial Restructuring as Class Restructuring: Production De-Centralisation and Local Uniqueness', *Regional Studies* 17, 73–89.

Massey, D. and Meegan, R. (1982) *The Anatomy of Job Loss*, London: Methuen.

Mattera, P. (1980) 'Small is Not Beautiful: Decentralised Production and the Underground Economy in Italy', *Radical America*, September/October, 67–76.

Mitter, S. (1986) 'Industrial Restructuring and Manufacturing Homework: Immigrant Women in the UK Clothing Industry', *Capital and Class* 27, 37–80.

Murray, F. (1987) 'Flexible Specialisation in the "Third Italy"', *Capital and Class* 33, 84–95.

Murray, R. (1985) 'Benetton Britain: The New Economic Order', *Marxism Today*, November, 28–32.

North, D., Leigh, R. and Smallbone, D. (1991) 'A Comparison of Surviving and Non-surviving Small Manufacturing Firms in London During the Eighties', Paper given at *14th National Small Firms Policy and Research Conference*, Blackpool, November.

Piore, M.J. and Sabel, C.F. (1984) *The Second Industrial Divide: Possibilities for Prosperity*, New York: Basic Books.

Pollert, A. (1988) 'The "Flexible Firm": Fixation or Fact?', *Work, Employment and Society* 2, 281–316.

Pyke, F., Becattini, G. and Sengenberger, W. (eds) (1990) *Industrial Districts and Inter-Firm Co-operation in Italy*, Geneva: ILO.

Ram, M. (1992) 'The West Midlands Clothing Sector: A Suitable Case for Team Working', *Regional Studies* 26, 503–9.

Sunley, P. (1992) 'Marshallian Districts: The Case of the Lancashire Cotton Industry in the Inter-war Years', *Trans. Inst. Br. Geogr. N. S.* 17, 306–20.

Totterdill, P. (1992) 'The Textiles and Clothing Industry: A Laboratory of Industrial Policy', in M. Geddes and J. Benington (eds) *Restructuring the Local Economy*, Harlow: Longman.

Winterton, J. (1992) 'The Transformation of Work? Work Organisation in the UK Clothing Industry', in A. Kasvio (ed.) *Industry Without Blue-Collar Workers – Perspectives of European Clothing Industry in the 1990s*, Finland: University of Tampere.

5

OPPORTUNITY OR CRISIS?

The remaking of the British arms industry

John Lovering

INTRODUCTION

The British defence industry is worthy of special consideration in this book for two reasons. First, it is unusually large. A high proportion of UK national output has been devoted to military purposes since the late 1940s, and a large defence industry has been a distinctive 'peculiarity' of the British economy (Fine and Harris, 1985). Secondly, the defence industry has changed enormously in the last decade, and the ways in which it has changed reveal much about the political economy of economic development in the UK. Government–industry relations, international connections, the behaviour of leading companies, and the 'culture' of the industry have been transformed. Yet this 'modernisation' (the transformation is by no means complete at the time of writing) is problematical. Within the UK, few workers and fewer communities have benefited. On the international level, the reconstruction of the arms industry is not a cause for rejoicing.

The chapter begins by outlining the difficulties in defining and measuring the defence industry. It then outlines developments during the Cold War before focusing on the restructuring of the 1980s and 1990s. The conclusion draws out some of the theoretical and practical issues which arise.

IDENTIFYING THE DEFENCE INDUSTRY

Those who talk of the defence industry usually have in mind a set of industrial sectors, companies, and workforces, which are committed to the production of weapons and the equipment necessary to deploy them. But while it is possible to identify a core group of major specialist military suppliers, any attempt to define a boundary marking off this 'defence-industrial base' will necessarily be rough and ready (Taylor and Hayward, 1989). The official defence statistics suffer from many deficiencies. For many years major defence programmes went unrecorded for reasons of secrecy (McIntosh, 1990: 199), and it would seem rather optimistic to assume that this practice has come entirely to an end. The published figures concerning exports are particularly unclear. The official publication 'Defence Statistics', including only items which are described as 'purely military', recorded sales worth around £1,500 million in 1992 (DS, 1993: 15). Other sources suggest, however, that the British defence industry secured orders for exports of defence-related equipment worth £5 billion in that year, and £6 billion in 1993 (NAO, 1994: 33; SDE, 1993: 74; SDE, 1994: 66).

Official estimates of the jobs generated by defence spending must also be treated with caution. They are derived from an estimate of the number of jobs created per pound spent in British industry on defence equipment (this ratio being derived from a sample of large contractors). Partly because the true ratio will vary from case to case, and partly because the sample base does not include all the Ministry's purchases, these figures cannot be regarded as more than approximations.

Bearing such reservations in mind, the basic dimensions of the British defence industry in the mid-1990s can be outlined. It employs around half a million workers, three-quarters of whom are engaged in producing weapons or other defence equipment. The others work in industries which do not produce specifically military items. Of the former group, over a third work on export orders (Table 5.1). Defence spending accounts for just over a tenth of all jobs in production industries. However, it is generally considered that its economic significance is much greater than this suggests. First, some economists argue that defence spending 'crowds out' other activities, so that the prosperity of the defence sector is paid for by the impoverishment of other industries (for a review of these arguments, see Dunne, 1990). Others point to the high profile of the leading British defence companies: BAe and GEC are not only the nation's biggest arms suppliers, they are also the leading UK manufacturing exporters. The performance of the defence sector tends to have a major impact on national performance in R&D, high level skills development, high technology manufacturing, and export earnings (Malecki, 1991). To understand how this came to be the case, it is necessary to look briefly at the history of arms production in the UK.

BACKGROUND: THE BRITISH DEFENCE INDUSTRY 1945 TO 1979

The unusual size and strategic significance of the British defence industry is a consequence of the slow decline of the UK's imperial military pretentions.[1] Britain experienced the greatest peacetime rearmament in its history in the early 1950s. The defence industry which this created was not only large, but also unusually self-sufficient in technology. Until the 1970s it was mainly occupied on indigenous products, although some technologies

Table 5.1 Basic dimensions of the British defence industry in the early 1990s (1991–92)

Values	(£,000s)
Production:	
for MOD[1]	8,607
for export[2]	3,000
Research and development[3]	
in industry	1,506
in MOD establishments	933
Total value of output:	14,046
Employment:[4]	
Equipment for MOD	265,000
Exports	145,000
Total equipment	410,000
As proportion of employment in manufacturing industries:[5] 8.7%	
Non-equipment for MOD	150,000
Grand total	560,000
As proportion of employment in production industries:[5] 10.9%	

Sources:
(1) MOD spending on defence production; Defence Statistics, 1993: Table 12.6.
(2) Approximation: near mid-range of estimates given in Defence Statistics, 1993: Table 1.11, and contracts value £5,000 million noted in SDE, 1993: 74.
(3) Defence Statistics, 1993: Table 1.5, combining R&D.
(4) Defence Statistics, 1993: Table 2.24.
(5) Defence Statistics, 1993: Table 2.24, and Annual Abstract of Statistics, 1994: Table 6.2.

(especially rocketry and nuclear weapons) relied heavily on US expertise, and the aircraft industry benefitted from German war-time innovations which were appropriated at the end of the war (Wood, 1986). This self-containedness was echoed in France, but in Germany and other European NATO members the Cold War arms industry was reconstructed around licensed production or adaptation of mainly US equipment (Russian equipment in the case of the former East Germany).

Britain's peculiar version of the 'military industrial complex'[2] was shaped by informal and semi-secret arrangements between politicians, government departments, the armed services, and a small group of fiercely independent companies, some of which were run in an almost baronial style (much the same could perhaps be said of the armed services). The defence industry employed a large workforce which grew accustomed to relatively good pay and considerable influence in bargaining (Croucher, 1982; Pagnamenta and Overy, 1984; Lovering, 1991b). Not for nothing was the famous Ealing film comedy 'I'm All Right Jack', in which Peter Sellers played a truculent trades unionist confronting narrow-minded managers and corrupt politicians, set in an arms factory.

Table 5.2 Employment in the defence industry: national comparisons

		1992 ranking
1.	China	3–5,000,000
2.	Russia	4,500,000
3.	USA	2,750,000
4.	Ukraine	800,000
5.	**UK**	**415,000**
6.	Germany (former East and West)	291,000
7.	France	255,000
8.	Poland	180,000
9.	Belarus	150,000
10.	Spain	100,000
11.	Baltic Reps.	100,000
12.	Italy	80,000
13.	Czechoslovakia	75,000
14.	Sweden	30,000
15.	Hungary	30,000
16.	Turkey	25,000
17.	Belgium	25,000
18.	Switzerland	25,000
19.	Netherlands	20,000
20.	Greece	14,000
21.	Norway	10,000
22.	Finland	10,000

Sources: compiled from CEC, 1992; Renner, 1992: 15, 72.

Unlike France or the USA, however, no British government department or even group of departments ever attempted to orchestrate a long-term strategy for the defence industry (Markusen, 1986). In the decades following the Second World War a succession of civilian and military departments (the Ministry of Aircraft Production, Ministry of Supply, Ministry of Aviation, and eventually the Ministry of Defence and Department of Trade and Industry), had responsibility for one or other policy which impacted on the defence producers (see Edgerton, 1991: 98). Nevertheless, no one ministry and no single government post was ever responsible for overseeing such policies and ensuring that they hung together coherently. This strategic 'gap' was symptomatic of the wider lack of an intellectual and institutional apparatus within the British state which was geared to economic development (Gamble, 1981; Fine and Harris, 1985). The 1964–70 Labour government introduced a Ministry of Technology which had responsibility for both civilian and military technology, but it did not control MOD procurement. The Ministry of Defence was formed only in 1964 (bringing the different services together under one umbrella for the first time in peacetime), and the Procurement Executive within the MOD was created as late as 1972.

The Cold War arms industry in the UK was therefore a curious and characteristically British creature. The connections between the armed forces, state procurement agencies, research labs, investors, and companies tended to be informal, lacking any explicit structure or strategic goals, and as time went by these links were increasingly dominated by the short-term financial priorities of the Treasury.[3] Government–industry relations in defence grew from foundations laid during the 1930s rearmament (Pedern, 1979; Shay, 1977). The 'National' coalition government of 1931–40, conservative in all but name, was as anxious to avoid forms of intervention which might smack of socialism as it was to rearm. The aircraft companies, in particular, energetically exploited this situation, winning the 'McKlintock Agreements' whereby procurement contracts were regulated on terms which were highly advantageous to them (Shay, 1977: 261; Middlemass, 1979: 253). Rearmament was achieved without public ownership, and state direction of the industry was imposed only after the outbreak of war and even then only partially. When Short Brothers was nationalised due to management failures in 1943, it prompted a major political outcry (Edgerton, 1991: 79). Secret US subsidies helped the British government pay for the rearmament, thereby fuelling the generous profits of the companies (Morgan, 1990; Ponting, 1990).

Victory in modern war depends on a combination of technology, industrial capacity, and logistics (Kennedy, 1988; Keegan, 1994: 313). At the end of the Second World War most strategists were convinced that the central instrument of any military apparatus would be air power (Dockrill, 1988; for parallels in the USA see Sherry, 1987; and Markusen, 1991). Despite the election of a Labour government there was never any doubt that the development of this air power would be allocated largely to private enterprise. In 1945 the new government identified eighteen private aircraft companies and three aero-engine producers for exclusive support.[4] The state-owned Power Jets company which had created the jet engine was dismembered and its resources given to selected companies. Private R&D efforts were supported by the creation of a massive public sector R&D infrastructure in the form of the government research establishments, including the Royal Aircraft Establishment and National Physical Laboratory, and the nuclear weapons establishments (Heim, 1988).

The raft linking the military, the government bureaucracy, and private companies was no sooner in place than it was lifted up on a new tide of defence spending. In 1946 the USA discontinued nuclear co-operation with the UK, and the government decided to continue development of the atomic bomb on a national basis, along with three different state-of-the-art jet bomber aircraft to deliver it. By 1949 this programme had been joined by other spending programmes intended to develop a range of associated military technologies including radar and guided missiles.[5] The companies dealing with these long-term developments were then required to meet more immediate demands. The Labour government took it upon itself to turn the UK into a military subordinate of the USA (Barnett, 1972; Chalmers, 1985). From 1947 the British Isles became host to permanent military bases of a foreign power for the first time in a thousand years, acquiring its role as an 'unsinkable aircraft carrier' for the US (Campbell, 1984). In the same year British defence spending began to increase in an attempt to convince the USA that the UK was a serious military actor in the new world of superpowers. The outbreak of the Korean War a year later accelerated the growth in defence spending until by 1952 the UK had experienced the biggest peacetime rearmament in its history. The defence industry needed more additional labour than the total number of people then registered unemployed. The prime minister announced that labour and plant would have to be diverted from civilian work to meet defence objectives. Some companies were diverted away from civil exports, never to recover.

These extraordinary efforts consolidated the leading companies in the defence industry. Hawker, Bristol, Rolls-Royce, English Electric, along with Marconi and Plessey became the corporate core of the UK's Cold War arms industry (Croucher, 1982). Some of the older imperial suppliers, notably shipbuilders such as Cammell Laird, Swan Hunter, and Vickers Barrow yard, joined them as the Navy was re-equipped. Individual companies and localities benefitted not only from the general rearmament but also from their ability to exploit irrational conflicts and rivalries between the armed services.[6]

The bonanza in the defence industry was interrupted in the late-1950s. Many of the military delusions of neo-Elizabethan Great Britain were shattered by the Suez debacle, which contributed to a realisation that the UK was now only a minor player in a global nuclear arms race dominated by the USA and the USSR. The undesired results of the rearmament of the Korean War period were also becoming apparent, including weapons which did not work (such as the Vickers-Supermarine 'Swift' fighter aircraft), duplication of facilities and excess capacity, and the extravagant and sometimes scandalous use of public funds, some of which had been heavily subsidised by the USA (Gregory and Simpson, 1982). The UK's military role, and its defence industry, became the objects of increasingly critical debate. From 1957 the government of Harold Macmillan (who had been one of the 'planning-minded' group of reformist Conservatives MPs in the 1930s) attempted to trim defence spending with the aim of 'deterrence on the cheap' (Dockrill, 1988).

Macmillan and President Eisenhower negotiated the closer subordination of British defence policy to that of the senior partner in the alliance. While the USA readmitted the UK to collaborative work on nuclear weapons and allowed use of US test facilities, US missiles were sited on British soil and British missiles targetting was incorporated into the US Single Integrated Operational Plan. In 1960 the development of the British 'Blue Streak' nuclear missile was abandoned, and the US 'Skybolt' ordered instead. But Eisenhower was replaced by John F. Kennedy, whose cost-conscious Secretary of Defense, Robert McNamara, cancelled the Skybolt project. In the ensuing 1962 Nassau Agreement, Kennedy reluctantly agreed to allow the British to buy Polaris submarine-based missiles instead. This sudden conversion to a nuclear submarine fleet guaranteed a future for the Royal Navy and for the chosen British shipbuilding yards (along with nuclear engineering companies such as Rolls Royce and Babcock). The first section of the first Polaris submarine was laid at Vickers Barrow yard in February 1964, the second at Cammell Lairds on Merseyside the following June (the following year the allocation was repeated for the third and fourth).

The Macmillan government used the promise of a major new military aircraft contract (the TSR-2) to induce a wave of mergers in the aircraft industry (Hastings, 1966). English Electric, Vickers, Bristol, and Hunting-Percival came together within the British Aircraft Corporation (BAC). De Havilland, Folland, and Blackburn, were absorbed into the Hawker Siddeley group which already included Armstrong Whitworth, A.V.Roe, and Hawker aircraft. The Dowty Group absorbed Boulton-Paul and Westlands took over the helicopter businesses of Bristol, Fairey, and Saunders Roe. In the aero-engines sector, Bristol merged with Hawker Siddeley in 1958 to form Bristol-Siddeley. But concentration into large groups did little to change the broader character of the UK's arms industry, which was now regarded by many influential commentators as a major contributor to the increasingly evident weaknesses of the British economy (Brittan, 1966; Pollard, 1983). It symptomised a national failure; Britain had lost an Empire but not found a role more in keeping with modern times (Kaldor, Sharp, and Walker, 1986).

This new scepticism coincided with the re-emergence of a mass peace movement. The apparent absurdity of a military strategy based on a global nuclear suicide pact prompted the formation in 1958 of the Campaign for Nuclear Disarmament (CND). Demands for reduced defence spending became a regular part of the alternative policy package advocated by the left of the Labour Party, despite the fact that Labour had played a key role in the expansion of the industry. But the left had little influence. Denis Healey left the meeting at which CND was formed convinced of a different solution. It was necessary to devise a more technologically sophisticated military apparatus capable of 'flexible response' so that conflicts could be contained without triggering a nuclear holocaust – so wars could still be fought (Healey, 1990). Looking to contemporary developments in the USA, Healey also became convinced of the need for modernisation in the defence industry. As Labour's Minister of Defence from 1964 (holding the post longer than any other post-war politician) he was able to put many of these ideas into effect.

The 1964–70 Labour government cut defence spending sharply by ending most of Britain's East of Suez ambitions and cancelling a tranche of associated weapons projects (including one of the five Polaris submarines, and the TSR-2 bomber). This triggered mass demonstrations of angry defence workers outside Parliament, but by the time Labour left office in 1970 the defence industry was enjoying a new era of stability. Labour's pre-1964 election pledge to scrap the nuclear deterrent was forgotten, partly because the Conservatives had ensured that the contracts were such that to do so would have been enormously costly in terms of money and jobs (McIntosh, 1990: 22). In 1967 the UK played a major role in securing the NATO agreement on the concept of Flexible Response, thereby attaching itself to 'the guiding principle behind a multi-billion dollar military build-up in the US' (Klare, 1989: 154). Meanwhile, the unified Ministry of Defence had been created in 1964, and the procurement system was modified along US lines to modernise the relationship between companies and military customers,[7] shifting the emphasis to longer-term contracts and the favouring of prime contractors (Kaldor, 1982). The aerospace industry was rescued from the post-TSR-2 doldrums with a series of orders, including the adaptation of imported US Phantom aircraft, and the development of the Anglo-French Jaguar, which paved the way to the massive Tornado bomber programme of the 1970s and 1980s.

The 1964–70 Wilson government impacted on the defence industry not only through the demand side, but also through a range of measures which impacted on the supply side. Labour hoped to modernise British industry by encouraging mergers and amalgamations leading to large world class companies. In the defence sector this enhanced the influence of the dominant companies. The precise development of the industry was then shaped by the struggles between these companies. The absorption of Bristol-Siddeley into Rolls-Royce transformed the latter into the monopoly British supplier of military jet engines, as well as in nuclear submarine and rocket technology. The defence electronics industry fell increasingly under the influence of GEC, which began its expansion when Arnold Weinstock became managing director in 1964 (Turner, 1969: 345). In 1967 GEC acquired Amalgamated Electrical Industries, adding English Electric a year later. Since the 1960s GEC has dominated the Cold War defence industry, owning key suppliers in the aerospace and electronics sectors, although it took another decade and a half to absorb Plessey and Ferranti. In the 1990s, perhaps, GEC will finally capture the rest of the aerospace industry.[8]

The creation of giant defence companies did not lead to a rationalisation and a more coherent investment strategy across the British defence industry as a whole. British companies remained competitors rather than collaborators, each increasingly committed to military work rather than to more diverse uses of their technologies and skills (Pollard, 1983). The aircraft industry remained divided into competing camps. In 1966 the government attempted to encourage BAC and Hawker Siddeley to merge, but the companies were able to resist thanks partly to new export orders the government had won for them (see below). Within GEC, the 'Weinstock model' involved a highly decentralised corporate structure in which longer-term potential synergies between constituent companies have generally been given less emphasis than short-term financial returns (Turner, 1969; Leadbetter, 1993). Meanwhile, the apparatus of defence procurement and research remained largely beyond public accountability and Parliamentary control and free from 'contamination' with long-term industrial considerations. Major decisions (such as the 'Chevaline' programme from 1966 to upgrade Polaris missiles) were simply kept secret. There was no systematic attempt to arrive at a coherent conception of national military equipment needs, and to relate these to national industrial capacity as a whole.

Meanwhile, considerable effort was devoted to promoting arms exports (Samson, 1991). The cancellation of the TSR-2 in favour of imports of US Lockheed F-111 bombers increased the urgency of generating export earnings. To this end a new Defence Export Sales Organisation (DESO) was created within the Ministry of Defence, headed by Lord Stokes from the motor industry. Following British pleading, the USA agreed to concede a key export opportunity (Samson, 1991: 185–89; Thayer, 1969: 247). In 1965 the Saudi Arabian government agreed to buy English Electric Lightning aircraft armed with US missiles (Howe, 1980: 687). This opened up four decades of lucrative business.

In the short term the export option diluted the cash problems of the defence industry. But in the longer term it helped entrench the institutional and behavioural characteristics which would eventually lead to a crisis (Kaldor, 1980). The Saudi deal in particular strengthened BAC's resistance to government pressure to merge with the Hawker group. The defence industry became increasingly dependent on sales to a small group of Middle Eastern rulers, conditional upon British and US government approval.

Nationalisation

The trend towards concentration in the defence industry slowed under the Conservative government of 1970–74. Prime Minister Heath brought Derek Rayner from the high-street retailer Marks & Spencer to advise on the reform of procurement, resulting in the creation of the Procurement Executive within the MOD in 1972. The demise of the Ministry of Technology, where procurement questions had previously been considered, weakened the links between defence and other technological and industrial agendas (Edgerton, 1993).

In 1973 Arnold Weinstock proposed merging and rationalising the missile businesses of Hawker Siddeley and BAC, a merger which the Labour government had hoped for but failed to achieve seven years before. The idea was dropped, however, due to resistance by the constituent companies and the fear that Labour would be elected and nationalise the aircraft industry (Baker, 1970: 239). Weinstock was right. The 1974–79 Labour government nationalised BAC and Hawker Siddeley's aircraft and guided weapons interests, along with Scottish Aviation, creating BAe (BAe) with a £42 million capital injection. The major warship yards were nationalised in the form of British Shipbuilders. The Northern Ireland aircraft and shipbuilding companies, Shorts, and Harland and Wolff, had long been state owned, and Ferranti and Rolls-Royce had also been taken under public ownership following financial difficulties earlier in the 1970s.

The Parliamentary debate leading to the 1977 Aerospace and Shipbuilding Industries Act was highly entertaining.[9] The main effect of public ownership, however, was merely to overcome management and shareholder resistance to the merging of the two corporate giants (BAC and HS), and thereby to lay the institutional foundations for rationalisation a decade later (Hayward, 1989). At the same time, it perpetuated the separation of the electronics and aerospace industries. BAe was forbidden to develop avionics and other electronics interests which might compete with GEC-Marconi (this restriction was lifted only when BAe was privatised in the 1980s). The problems of fragmentation and inflexibility with which the British defence industry would have to deal in the late 1980s and 1990s were due partly to the conservative effects of decades of profitable private ownership, and partly to the equally conservative effects of the form of public ownership imposed by the 1974–79 Labour government.

THE RESTRUCTURING OF THE DEFENCE INDUSTRY 1979–94

The restructuring of the defence industry between 1979 and 1994 involved a number of breaks with tradition, in terms both of the role played by government, and of the behaviour of the producers (now private corporations). The changes brought about under a Conservative government have been far more radical than anything achieved under Labour, although this does not mean that the outcomes have been satisfactory to all concerned.

1979–1985: The 'New Cold War': rearmament, and privatisation

The incoming Thatcher government did not appear to have considered it necessary to develop a strategy for the defence industry in any detail. Although it wished to tighten government control of procurement, it never developed a coherent position in relation to the contradictory pressures on the defence industry.

Meanwhile, between 1979 and 1985, real defence spending increased by a fifth, and weapons spending by over a third. Despite the militaristic overtones of the Malvinas/Falklands War, the rearmament over which the Thatcher government presided was not of its own making. In 1977 the Callaghan government had agreed that NATO member countries should increase defence spending by 3 per cent annually, hoping that the costs for the British government would be covered by the forthcoming North Sea Oil revenues. It also secretly extended the enormous 'Chevaline' project to update Polaris with multiple warheads (McIntosh, 1990). In the late 1980s British arms spending had fallen to its lowest share of national output since before the Korean War. Now with the 'new Cold War' of the early 1980s (Halliday, 1983) it began to rise again, leading to a bonanza in the arms industry. The social and geographical impact was exaggerated by the recession which was then devastating civilian manufacturing, thanks largely to the Thatcher government's Medium Term Financial Strategy. The favoured defence industry sites became 'islands of prosperity' in a sea of deindustrialisation and job losses (Lovering, 1988).[10]

In this favourable context the government set out to privatise the defence industry, including not only the companies formed through nationalisation five years earlier (BAe and British Shipbuilders), but also Rolls-Royce and Short Brothers, and the historic Royal Dockyards and Royal Ordnance factories. Peter Levene was brought in from a private defence manufacturer to oversee the privatisation of the Dockyards, winning himself a permanent job at the Procurement Executive as a result. A logjam in the process of industrial concentration and rationalisation having been broken by a period of public ownership, the aerospace industry was returned to private hands. The shipbuilding yards were sold off separately. The government tank factory in Leeds was sold to Vickers (making it the British monopolist). BAe bought the remaining Royal Ordnance plants, becoming the UK's most extensive arms producer and the largest outside the USA (Hayward, 1989: 175). Aircraft work at Short Brothers was sold to the Canadian firm Bombardier, and missiles work became a joint venture with the French company Thomson-CSF.

There was no attempt to frame these privatisations within a broader strategy for the defence industry as a whole (Dunne and Smith, 1992: 106). Meanwhile, changes to the procurement process intended to enhance competition created major disputes, with few benefits emerging by 1986 (McIntosh, 1990: 174). As in other sectors ravaged by the government's ideologically driven conception of the virtues of the market, the most visible result was not to promote cost savings but rather to initiate the creation of larger oligopolies. The newly independent companies began to look beyond Whitehall for their future survival, and from the mid-1980s,

BAe joined GEC and other defence companies in making it a fundamental part of their strategy to court City investors (Lovering and Hayter, 1993). This resulted in a greater emphasis by the defence companies on the short-term need to generate cash, and an emphasis on expanding exports.

1985–early 1990s: modifying the apparatus of government support and passing costs to foreigners

In the early and mid-1980s the major changes in the defence industry were in the form of ownership. From 1985 to the early 1990s declining British defence spending formed the background to a series of corporate efforts to bring about real changes in employment and production.[11] British defence spending on equipment fell by 19 per cent in the second half of the decade. This was twice the decline under Labour twenty years earlier, but it had nothing to do with any rethinking of defence strategy. The second and third Conservative governments focused on cutting back public spending in general, from which defence spending could no longer escape. Defence cuts were imposed without any formal review of defence requirements. Projects were cancelled on an *ad hoc* basis, including the Nimrod anti-submarine warfare aircraft, a stand-off nuclear bomb, and several smaller programmes.

The proportion of MOD contracts (by value) let competitively rose from 22 per cent at the beginning of the 1980s to 38 per cent in mid-decade and 63 per cent in 1991 (DS, 1993: 17). In the new context of declining defence spending, the effects of the new emphasis on competition proved to be much harsher than the companies had anticipated when they had urged these reforms in the early 1980s (Gregory and Simpson, 1982). The RAF in particular appears to have grown more distant from its traditional British suppliers (Hayward, 1989), and more willing to buy foreign equipment (including a Brazilian-designed trainer aircraft). Defence Secretary Michael Heseltine nevertheless insisted that competition, privatisation, and contractorisation were not only useful in saving costs, they were also instruments whereby defence procurement could be used to 'galvanise British industry' (McIntosh, 1990: 149).

In fact, no such transformation occurred. Unlike the USA, the British defence industry has not in general acted as a stimulant to civilian dynamism. And, indeed, the turbulent policy environment of the mid-1980s made it difficult for defence companies to plan for their own modernisation. The aircraft, aero-engine, and electronics companies pressed hard to secure support for their favoured long-term projects[12] towering over which was the European Fighter Aircraft programme (EFA, later rechristened the 'Eurofighter'), a direct follow-on from the Cold War Tornado programme. They found a sympathetic ear in Michael Heseltine who maintained that

Table 5.3 Real UK defence spending 1948–93

(total outlay in constant £, 1991–92)	
1948	14,481
1949	14,622
1950	15,123
1951	18,432
1952	22,425
1953	23,134
1954	22,884
1955	21,517
1956	21,850
1957	20,141
1958	19,407
1959	19,541
1960	19,991
1961	20,658
1962	19,658
1964	21,317
1965	21,908
1966	22,100
1967	23,584
1968	22,784
1969	20,333
1970	20,545
1971	21,158
1972	21,825
1973	22,600
1974	22,934
1975	23,334
1976	24,076
1977	22,959
1978	23,076
1979	21,992
1980	22,742
1981	23,059
1982	24,459
1983	24,801
1984	25,785
1985	25,743
1986	24,851
1987	24,434
1988	23,376
1989	23,384
1990	23,467
1991	24,485
1992	23,286
1993	22,003 (estimate)

Sources: 1948–84 Chalmers, 1985: 193; 1985–92 Defence Statistics, 1993, converted to yearly basis.

some form of long-term state involvement in the defence industry was inescapable, despite the Thatcherite orthodoxy (Heseltine, 1987: 111). EFA was given approval in 1986, promising work for virtually all the leading British contractors to the end of the century, and allegedly creating up to 40,000 British jobs during the production phase in the 1990s. Mrs Thatcher initially called Heseltine to account for this decision, but subsequently endorsed it (White, 1992; Clark, 1993: 257). Like Macmillan with the TSR-2 programme twenty-five years earlier, Heseltine seems to have hoped that this major new military contract could further the 'galvanising' effect of defence procurement, this time triggering a rationalisation and dynamic reorganisation of the defence industry on a European scale thereby challenging the American domination of advanced defence technologies (Heseltine, 1989: 194). His vision was not, however, shared by other members of govern- ment, or by European defence companies.[13]

In the event, the EFA project was disrupted by innumerable political, strategic, and industrial upheavals. In 1990 German doubts about the British partners were deflected by a government-prompted acquisition by GEC of the ailing Ferranti radar division (Clark, 1993: 274). In 1992 Minister of Defence Malcolm Rifkind agreed to reduce the price of the aircraft by almost a fifth in order to meet new German objections. In 1994 the future of the production stage of the programme was still uncertain, but few expected that it would be abandoned entirely.

The Thatcher government hoped both to preserve national military capacity and to reduce the financial burden on the state. This led it on the one hand to encourage the strengthening of favoured companies, and on the other to seek to expand markets through increased arms exports. The government managed to pursue its objectives in ways which satisfied few, however, and from the late 1980s defence companies and unions increasingly complained about the lack of a coherent government strategy for the defence industry. The government was so keen to create strong private defence companies that it indulged in various forms of *ad hocery* at odds with its free market pretentions. The manager of the Astra munitions company told the House of Commons trade and industry committee investigations into the 'supergun' affair[14] of the workings of the 'Savoy Mafia'. This group, so called because it met in the Savoy Hotel in London, included Procurement Minister Peter Levene, defence officials, and directors of the leading defence companies. It apparently sought to influence the consolidation of the British defence industry around a small core of giant internationally oriented firms, pre-eminent among which were BAe and GEC (Warner, 1992; Buckley and Donkin, 1992).

The sale of public assets was manipulated to give financial advantages to BAe which acquired the Royal Ordnance Factories and the Rover car company at give-away prices, and then received further 'sweeteners'.[15] BAe was motivated by financial, rather than industrial or technological, considerations and disposed of Rover as soon as this was legally possible, using the funds from the sale to BMW in 1994 to 'return to basics' and concentrate on military activities (Lovering and Hayter, 1993).

The renewed arms export drive

Underhand industrial intervention was accompanied by dubious attempts to promote arms exports. The Defence Export Services Organisation (DESO) was expanded and the support given by the Export Credit Guarantee Department to the defence companies was extended. The armed services played an increasingly prominent role in acting as marketing agents for British arms companies. Officially, it was hoped that exports would be won by company initiative, but the major deals have been government to government arrangements. In 1985 a new accord, of which the companies heard the details only afterwards, resulted in the 'Al Yamamah' ('Dove') contract with Saudi Arabia. This promised an estimated £5 billion of sales, the largest arms export deal in British history. A follow-up contract thought to be worth twice as much was finalised in 1993 (Betts, 1993). In the late 1980s Malaysia became a major export customer, followed in the 1990s by Indonesia. Since 1993 a series of revelations have revealed the extent of covert interventions in the defence export business, including bribes to Saudi and Malaysian elites, the linking of aid and arms sales over the Pergau dam in Malaysia, and above all the Matrix Churchill affair.

Anticipating a sustained arms race in Pacific Asia, British defence companies and government agencies built up marketing capacities in the region. Arms trade fairs in Kuala Lumpur and aerospace fairs in China and Singapore have become major events. The Eurofighter (now rechristened the EF2000) was talked-up as suitable for overseas markets, despite its very European Cold War origins. From the late 1980s BAe sold more military equipment abroad than to the British government (some 70 per cent of military output is exported). Arabian Gulf and Pacific-Asian customers have also become vital to 'second league' companies such as Short Brothers, FR (formerly Flight Refuelling) and Hunting (Aitken, 1994). The naval shipbuilder Vosper-Thorneycroft exports over 95 per cent of its output. Between 1981 and 1991 the proportion of employment in the British defence industry accounted for by export work rose from a quarter to over a third (Table 5.4).

The cultural politics of defence

The Conservative governments' attempts since 1985 to reform the defence industry have had implications ranging beyond financial or industrial questions. The defence industry, and its large and highly unionised work-force, was quintessentially a product of an earlier era of state intervention. The defence establishment and its close ally the patrician Foreign Office,

Table 5.4(a) Employment dependent on defence spending

| Year | direct only | MOD spending on equipment | | |
		direct plus indirect	non-equipment	exports
1978	220	400	180	130
1979	230	420	180	140
1980	230	420	180	140
1981	240	430	150	140
1982	225	405	160	140
1983	215	375	155	130
1984	225	395	155	120
1985	200	·360	155	110
1986	170	310	155	100
1987	175	325	155	150
1988	160	290	150	130
1989	150	280	155	150
1990	135	225	165	125
1991	135	265	150	145

Table 5.4(b) As % of employment in manufacturing

	MOD equipment (direct + indirect)	Export
1980	61.	2.0
1981	6.9	2.3
1982	6.9	2.4
1983	6.8	2.4
1984	7.3	2.2
1985	6.7	2.1
1986	5.9	1.9
1987	6.3	2.9
1988	5.6	2.5
1989	5.4	2.9
1990	5.0	2.5
1991	5.6	3.1

had long been mainstays of the traditional British civil service elite which was seen by Thatcherites as 'soft' on government spending (Edwards, 1994: 19). The Ministry of Defence was said to be a particularly unattractive posting for an ambitious Conservative (Critchley, 1987).

Liberal economists implicitly assume that the military presence in capitalist societies is attributable to the influence of 'pre-capitalist' social groups.[16] Whether Mrs Thatcher was aware of this or not, her administration eventually began to attack the elites associated with defence. According to one observer, she conspired to limit the information available to the defence establishment in the hope that the latter would be less able to mobilise opposition in the corridors of power and the *Daily Telegraph* (McIntosh, 1990: 139). The appointments of Sir Peter Levene in the Procurement Executive, and Alan Clark as Procurement Minister, symbolised a renewed attempt to carry the Thatcherite cultural revolution into the defence establishments. Clark, whose diaries record the contempt with which he regarded the defence establishment, was authorised to prepare a procurement strategy paper in the light of the impending reduction of European forces. Clark provocatively entitled his brief report 'The 1990 Defence Review', and saw it as the sharp end of a wedge of radical reform (Clark, 1993: 263). In the event the resignation of Mrs Thatcher, the opposition of less radical Defence Ministers (Tom King, and later Malcolm Rifkind), the outbreak of the 1991 Gulf War, and the resilience of the civil service, meant that Clark's efforts petered out. The *de facto* defence review from 1990 known as 'Options for Change' was a more conventional and bureaucratic affair, which had not yielded clear results even as late as 1994 (when the annual Defence White Paper was described by the *Financial Times* (27 April) as no more than another 'holding operation').

1993–94: Front line (and the market) first

While defence strategy remained in limbo, the development of the defence industry was increasingly subordinated to the generic restructuring of British economic management. From 1991 'market testing' became a key element in the reform of the public sector, and this soon affected the armed forces, defence establishments, and the defence industry, no less than local government or the national health service. By the mid-1990s the project of 'marketisation' in defence was well underway.

The defence research laboratories were grouped together under the Defence Research Agency (DRA), which was required to act in a commercial manner. DRA employment was expected to fall by a quarter in the following five years. In 1993 it was announced that defence research spending would fall by a third to the year 2000 (Cabinet Office, 1993), implying further reductions in long-term research and employment. One Conserv- ative minister even proposed privatising the agency, although this was almost universally regarded as ridiculous.

A wide range of other military activities, from catering and transport (including shipping during the Gulf War) to the management of the production of nuclear weapons, were transferred to private companies. This 'marketisation' of defence functions was bitterly opposed by some, notably the RAF engineering wings (*Flight International*, 1994). Nevertheless, a Market Testing Organisation was set up within the MOD, with the aim of drawing private investment into military activities that were formerly exclusively by the government. There were some indications that the drive to 'Market Testing' might be tempered in some sectors where the lack of competitors required that more contracts would be let on the NAPNOC (No Acceptable Price, No Contract) principle. This was especially necessary in shipbuilding, where by 1995 there were effectively only three warship yards, each of which was a specialist in its own sector (VSEL, Yarrow-GEC, and Vosper-Thorneycroft).

Nevertheless, the publication of the 'Front Line First' document in summer 1994 appeared to reaffirm the long-term commitment to the creation of (state administered) markets in defence. In the context of an expected 14 per cent decline of defence spending to the year 2000, the document advocated more leasing of private equipment (for example, in simulators and electronic warfare), and contracting-out to private companies third and fourth line repair in the armed services, and possibly even 'repair and resupply at operational levels'. One trade magazine commented in disgust that the British government seemed to believe 'that the best way of supporting a peacetime air force is to place as much of its care and upkeep in the hands of private contractors' (*Flight International*, 1994).

Restructuring continues

Against this background of changing and unclear policies, and changing markets and competitors, the British defence industry has been engaged since the late 1980s in a violent restructuring. In many ways it is now a very different entity from that of the Cold War era. Employment has been cut, industrial relations and payment patterns have been reconstructed, a new web of international linkages has been established, and companies have slimmed down to concentrate on select niches within the international arms and dual-use markets. Figure 5.1 gives details of over 70,000 job losses in the defence industry in this period.

In terms of job losses and working conditions, the most extreme changes took place in the major contractors. The citadels of the old Cold War arms industry underwent the most radical changes in order to become the spearheads of the new order. The restructuring was generally delayed and less dramatic in the smaller suppliers, partly because many already had footholds in non-defence or overseas markets, and partly because their employment practices were already less institutionalised. But many medium-sized companies, junior partners in the old MIC, were caught in the middle. Lacking the high profile and covert government support enjoyed by the core group, and equally lacking the diversity of markets and flexibility of less defence-specialised companies, many simply went out of business. Among these was the Astra company noted above, which closed its factory in Mrs Thatcher's home town of Grantham, Lincolnshire, with the

Figure 5.1 Major job losses in the British defence industry

1987	
April Westland, Weston-super-Mare	925
May Westland, Yeovil	1,155
Aug. Devonport Dockyard, E. Kilbride	1,400
Aug. Rolls-Royce	250
Sept. Swan Hunter, Tyneside	260
1988	
May Racal, Bracknell	215
May BAe Dynamics	3,500
June Devonport Dockyard	1,900
1987–1990 ROFs	4,300
1989	
Jan BAe Dynamics	2,500
July Westlands	2,000
Nov. Normalair Garrett	300
Various months Dowty	1,200
Dec. Swan Hunter, and Yarrow	550
1990	
March ROF, Blackburn	500
June GEC-Ferranti, Edinburgh	550
July Rolls-Royce, Bristol	800
Oct. VSEL Barrow –	1,500
VSEL/Cammell Laird, Birkenhead	2,100
Nov. BAe military Aircraft division	4,500
Nov. Link-Miles, Lancing	325
1991	
End 1989–Feb. GEC-Ferranti, Scotland	1,450
March VSEL	5,500
1990–March Lucas	2,700 *
March BAe Dynamics	2,420
March Rolls-Royce	3,140
March Babcock-Thorn (Rosyth yard)	1,000
March GEC-Plessey	265
April Dowty, various sites, Fife	1,300
April Rolls-Royce, Bristol	200
May Rolls-Royce, Leavesden	1,400
Bristol	1,250
June ROF, Nottingham	400

Figure 5.1 Continued

1992		
Feb. BAe Dynamics, Stevenage	450	
BAe Military Aircraft Warton	550	
Brough	550	
Kingston	350	
March Denis Ferranti, Bangor	250	
June Marconi	825	
Sept. Vosper, Chelmsford	200	
Nov. Lucas	4,000	*
1991–Oct. VSEL	755	
1993		
Oct. 92–Jan. 93 Lucas Industries	400	
Jan. Rolls-Royce	5,000	*
1992–3 Smiths Aerospace	3,000	
Nov. 1993 ROF	297	
Dec. Ferranti, N. West England	450	

Note: *Not all defence.

loss of 180 jobs. By the mid-1990s the core defence companies had mostly completed their rationalisations. The burden of change now fell most heavily on smaller subcontractors and suppliers where the effects were less visible, as large numbers of small-scale job losses tend to go unreported.

The defence industry is no longer a unified whole, containing a set of companies capable of production 'across the board', protected behind the walls of the military industrial complex. The steps in the 'design-make-sell' chain have been differentiated. The post Cold War British defence industry draws far more extensively on non-defence firms and on workers in other countries. Symptomatic of this is that the famous 'jump-jet' is no longer a British product: future versions of the Harrier are being developed jointly by British and US companies (Rolls-Royce, BAe, and McDonnell Douglas), with the US Marine Corp playing a major role.

Every one of the first league of suppliers (BAe, DML, GEC, Rolls-Royce, and VSEL), is connected to several of the others and to many overseas firms. The BAe–GEC nexus has become even more dominant. Many observers expect this will be formalised in the near future through some form of merger.[8] A number of smaller specialist companies, some long-established, some newcomers, serve the core group of BAe, GEC, ROF, Ferranti, Plessey, VSEL, etc. Many also supply foreign governments and defence companies, and some subcontractors rely entirely on overseas buyers (Lancashire County Council, 1993). The new defence industry includes software and systems integration houses, or other high-technology manufacturers and service companies, whose competitiveness is based on specialist expertise. Some companies have been able to grow by taking sales away from the prime contractors thanks to their lower costs and greater flexibility.

It is likely that East European workers will soon contribute their labour to the international networks feeding into Britain's defence industry. In 1993, representatives of nine Central and East European countries attended a procurement seminar hosted by the MOD (SDE, 1994: 62). The 1994 Farnborough air display included several exhibitions by East European and Asian producers seeking customers. South Africa seems likely to attract offshore production by British defence companies in the next few years.

The 'normalisation' of the defence industry

The defence industry is becoming much less exceptional than it used to be during the Cold War. It now shares many of the key features of civilian industry: internationalisation, concentration, the central position of financiers, the dismantling of established employment norms, and so on (Lovering, 1990). In short, arms production is becoming less 'separate' (Lovering, 1993).

This 'normalisation' poses new problems. The development of coherent corporate strategies is difficult when market conditions, the state of competition, and the degree of long-term government support are unpredictable. While the defence market is still fairly buoyant, few companies expect that world demand will rise again until the end of the current decade.[17] In this context the pressure is on to develop new products: the best way of convincing the armed services governments of the need to buy new equipment is to show that it renders their existing equipment redundant (Keegan, 1994: 312). At company level, this means a greater emphasis on R&D. This is all the more necessary for British firms since it is only through technological ingenuity that they will be able to compete with those who can draw on much cheaper labour. By the mid-1990s the aerospace companies were spending 130 per cent of their profits on R&D (SBAC, 1994). Obviously such a situation can continue only in the short term. The recession of the early 1990s had been so severe that it forced the companies to reduce their R&D spending nonetheless. Defence R&D fell four times as rapidly as did civilian R&D (Table 5.5).

The growing conflict between government and industry

Despite sporadic government attempts to support the leading companies, British defence producers have become increasingly aware that they face problems which some of their competitors do not. High-technology firms, especially in the electronics and aerospace industries, tend to receive close and supportive attention from their host governments in countries ranging

Table 5.5 Change in R&D spending by product groups 1990–92 (in real terms)

	1990	1992	1990–92 (%)
Civil			
Total	6,330	5,916	–6.5
Manufactured products	5,314	5,022	–5.5
Chemicals	1,944	1,871	–3.8
Mechanical engineeering	171	188	+9.9
Electronics	1,703	1,585	–6.9
Other electrical engineering	121	94	–22.3
Motor vehicles	485	473	–2.5
Aerospace	355	360	+1.4
Other manufactured products	536	452	–15.7
Non-manufactures	1,025	894	–12.8
Defence			
Total	1,761	1,265	–28.2
Manufactured products	1,665	1,196	–28.2
Chemicals	14	18	+15.5
Mechanical engineering	139	98	–29.5
Electronics	680	475	–30.1
Other electrical engineering	5	1	–80.0
Motor vehicles	16	15	–6.3
Aerospace	767	565	–26.3
Other manufactured products	44	25	–43.2
Non-manufactures	96	69	–28.1

Source: *British Business*, 7 January 1994.

from the USA to Taiwan, France to Russia, Germany to Brazil (Tyson, 1992). The British government has been more energetic in dismantling the traditional status of defence suppliers than in constructing supportive structures for high-technology industry. From the late 1980s the defence industry increasingly complained that procurement policy was too erratic and vague to allow sensible long-term investment (SBAC, 1992; White, 1992; Weston, 1993; Ernst and Young, 1994, see also NAO, 1994). Different government departments pursued different and sometimes conflicting agendas. The Ministry of Defence blocked some forms of restructuring chosen by the companies, most notably the initial form of the acquisition of Plessey proposed by GEC and Siemens.

Industry complaints reached a diplomatically restrained crescendo in the 1993 House of Commons select committee on Trade and Industry. The report urged the government to examine experience elsewhere in diversifying the defence industry and to fund a National Strategic Technology

Acquisition Programme (NSTAP) in the aerospace industry. Despite a new rhetoric of support for industry associated with Michael Heseltine's move to the Department of Trade and Industry, and a 1993 white paper stressing the importance of high technology, the government rejected these recommendations. Instead it would devote some effort to trying to encourage the USA, Taiwan, Japan, and numerous other governments to reduce their subsidies to aerospace. In 1994 the Ministry of Defence was asked to consider a NSTAP for the defence industry, the prospects for which would seem equally unpromising.

The future of government–industry relations came to a head in late 1994 over the Future Large Aircraft (FLA) with which the RAF was to replace its ageing fleet of Lockheed Hercules transporters. The American company offered 'first refusal' on an updated version, the Lockheed C-130J. Meanwhile BAe, along with French, German, Spanish, and Italian companies, offered a yet-to-be developed aircraft based on the Airbus A300 airliner. At the time of writing the decision was still awaited, although it seems likely that a compromise will be reached, tempered by the MOD's new enthusiasm for off-the-shelf imports. This prospect caused considerable anxiety within the British aerospace industry. According to the industry's collective mouthpiece (the Society of British Aerospace Companies), there was now a serious danger that the critical mass necessary to the survival of the British aerospace and related industries would be lost. The FLA crisis also revealed the degree of fragmentation in the British defence industry. One group of British defence/aerospace companies campaigned for the European proposal, and others allied with Lockheed, which promised a 15 per cent share to British subcontractors. The unified Cold War MIC is being replaced by a thing of parts, in which different companies and workforces are integrated to different international networks of design, production, and sale. In the absence of a policy change, the industry is likely to continue to fragment into unconnected elements.

The longer-term future of the British defence industry is dependent on a number of unknowns. The 'commanding heights' formed by BAe, GEC, and a few others include divisions which have in effect attached themselves to a new global network of producers and buyers. Some of these are likely to be reasonably well placed to survive within the new world arms economy. Others depend on work carried over from the Cold War era (such as the Eurofighter project), the future of which is highly uncertain. Among the wide group of suppliers to the first and second tier companies, few are likely to be able to establish niches in the new global defence market, and many will decline, unless they can successfully diversify out of defence.

The social effects of the end of the military industrial complex

Defence industry employment fell from a million in the late 1960s to half a million in the early 1990s (Table 5.4(a)). In the late 1980s the employment decline accelerated, now due to company restructuring rather than simple cuts in government orders (in the last half of the 1980s, the employment generated fell one and a half times as steeply as the value of equipment spending). Job losses were associated with dramatic increases in productivity (in Rolls-Royce sales per employee increased by 13 per cent in 1992 alone). In the USA, where the restructuring was much more rapid and dramatic, defence company share prices began to rise.[18]

The occupational profile of the defence industry tilted sharply towards high-level occupations (managers, scientists, engineers, technologists, and other business and finance professionals). Employment in these groups grew while employment in all other categories fell (Lovering, 1991a), until the crisis of 1990–92, when companies were forced to dispose even of these staff. Middle-management administration, and shop-floor jobs, have been purged through a sustained assault on overmanning, some introduction of new technology, and above all, the discarding of inherited employment and industrial relations practices.

The leading companies attempted to drive the trades unions out, or at least to drastically reduce their influence (Lovering and Hayter, 1993). As noted above, some smaller companies in which the union influence was always weaker, have grown. These changes have combined to alter the 'typical' defence worker. The stereotypical white male manufacturing worker of the early 1980s was in his forties, a union member, and the son of a defence worker. In the 1990s his place is taken by a much more heterogeneous group. The most sought-after employees tend to be younger, with higher academic qualifications, and less likely to belong to a union. At the other pole, the restructuring has brought into the defence labour market more lower paid workers, including women (formerly notable for their absence). The defence industry is no longer a home for the kind of characters who featured in Peter Sellers' film a generation ago.

The changing geography of military work

All this has had a marked geographical impact. The Cold War defence industry had a distinctive geography due to two unusual factors. First, the defence industry was dominated by the new technologies which had emerged in the inter-war period (aircraft and electrical engineering), based primarily in the South East and the Midlands. Secondly, its location was at times directly influenced by government (Law, 1983; Lovering, 1991a).

Fearing that much of Southern England would be devastated if war broke out with Germany, the Air Council in 1934 designated a 'safe area' lying north and east of a line joining Weston-Super-Mare and Stafford. This zone happily also contained the bulk of the relevant industrial labour in engineering who could work on defence projects. The North West received a third of the floor space in wartime factories built under Ministry of Aircraft Production provision, twice its share of output. The South East, responsible for 32 per cent of GDP, received only 13 per cent of the factory space. The transition from the Second World War to the Cold War involved a shift from mass production to a specialist high-technology defence industry (Markusen, 1991). Accordingly, the geographical centre of gravity shifted back towards the South East, where the headquarter sites of the major companies remained, and where the public and private R&D infrastructure was concentrated. The geographical legacy of wartime public investment remained in the form of a group of defence industry dependent localities elsewhere, notably central Lancashire, the Bristol sub-region, central Scotland, and Barrow. Through the 1980s some 55 per cent of British procurement spending was consumed in the South East and South West, with a further 10 to 12 per cent going to the North West. The construction of the Cold War defence industry in Britain did not generate anything approaching the dynamic regional development spin-offs which characterised US experience, notably in the high-technology development of Southern California (Markusen *et al.*, 1990).

The restructuring of the British defence industry since the 1980s has tended to concentrate remaining activities in two types of locality: high-level R&D establishments are scattered across the semi-rural areas of Southern and Western England, while production work has tended to move Northwards towards cheaper sites and workforces (Lovering, 1991a). The collapse of assembly and manufacturing work has meant that the heaviest burden of job losses fell on the larger defence-dependent towns. In many cases the defence industry was the last major manufacturing sector in these areas. The restructuring from the late 1980s therefore worsened the economic problems affecting some urban areas. Bristol, Preston, and north and south London were prominent examples of this. In the 1990s further job losses tended to hit smaller towns and rural areas, where many suppliers in the North and West were located. Although the absolute number of jobs involved is modest, these often represented a high proportion of local employment. These losses prompted local authorities to apply to Europe for compensatory initiatives (Dabinett, 1993). Due to similar pressure in Germany and France, the European Commission devised the 'KONVER' programme, through which localities suffering from the loss of defence jobs could apply for funding for compensatory initiatives.

THE DEFENCE INDUSTRIES AND THE CHANGING POLITICAL ECONOMY OF BRITAIN IN THE 1980s AND 1990s

The restructuring of the British defence industry can be interpreted in different ways. Some see the Thatcher–Major years in a Schumpeterian light

(Dunne and Smith, 1992). Conservative in name only, governments since 1985 have been the agents of a radical liberalism which has subverted the power of the archaic military strata. This view can draw support from the assault on the 'military culture' which got underway between 1990 and 1994 when the perks, salary scales, and other advantages attached to senior status in the armed services eventually came under review.[19]

But the evidence could also support a different interpretation, which this writer would defend. According to this, British workers and employers are still profoundly influenced by the business of producing the means of violence. However, they are engaged in it in more subtle ways, and the economic benefits are less collectivised. The restructuring of the armed services and the defence industry, and social institutional changes associated with this, amount to a change in the *mode* of militarisation rather than a simple decline in the influence of militaristic groups. The achievement of the Thatcher–Major governments has been to facilitate a transition from one form of economic militarisation to another (and to the new problems it brings). In the process, the defence industry has reconstructed itself on an international level. The old nationally defined military industrial complex may have gone, but a new and less visible international nexus of companies, armed services, and government agencies has emerged in its place.

If this is a reasonable description of recent developments, it follows that the current policy debate concerning the defence industry is radically inadequate. There has been a remarkable consensus among defence economists and public policy analysts that the best policy for the defence industry is to allow the intrusion of market forces (Hooper, 1989; Kennedy, 1989). Even those of a theoretical tradition at odds with the neo-liberal mainstream share this view. Dunne and Smith claim that 'Thatcherism' in the defence industry was beneficial despite itself, since it reduced the economic burden of defence spending, and undermined the strength of the military industrial lobby (Dunne and Smith, 1992). Policy disagreements arise mainly over the finer points of the package of measures which are needed to compensate for job losses in the defence industry. Neo-liberals emphasise micro-economic policies such as retraining and management skills, while Keynesians tend to stress the need for expansionary macroeconomic and regional policies (Dunne and Smith, 1984; Smith, 1990; Willett, 1990). The common ground is the assumption that it is necessary to encourage firms which have grown used to traditional 'uncompetitive' defence markets to become more entrepreneurial. This view is shared by many of those outside the academy who emphasise the need for 'arms conversion'. Advocates of 'conversion' call for a more interventionist approach (CAAT, 1994; Southwood, 1991). They argue that the bias of the British economy towards military production is not only ethically undesirable, it is also economically unhealthy (Kaldor *et al.*, 1986).

However, against the background sketched above, much of the current policy debate, among mainstream free-marketeers, Keynesians, and 'conversionists' alike, is somewhat out of date. Protagonists in each camp still tend to argue as if the problems of the defence industry can be traced to the fact that it is fundamentally 'backward'. It is still asserted that much of the industry is still living in the Cold War years, acclimatised to cost-plus pricing, conservative management cultures, relatively unproductive workforces, and general inefficiency (see, for example, Hartley, 1991; Hooper, 1989; Dunne and Smith, 1992). The implication is that defence company managers are somehow less rational than those in non-defence companies. Although this assumption is widely repeated in the literature, few writers have attempted to give any evidence to back it up. The policy debate on the defence industry tends to be characterised by a curious myopia whereby the lamentable situation within defence companies is described in detail, it is assumed that things are very different in non-defence companies, and the conclusion is drawn that the former are victims of their own evils or foolishness (for recent examples, see Willett, 1990; Southwood, 1991; CAAT, 1994). This demonologising of the defence industry presents a misleading picture of what is happening, and an even more misleading suggestion as to the reasons why.

Many of the features which characterised the British defence industry during the 'Cold War' are no longer present. This is a reflection of a fundamental political-economic change: the Cold War defence industry was constructed in the 1930s and 1940s under the influence of an historic national accord between companies, organised labour, and the state (Gamble, 1981). Arms production is rapidly being reconstructed in the 1990s under the influence of a very different national and international balance of social forces. The result is a different form of economic militarisation, which results in a less identifiable and separate defence sector. The dominant analyses of the defence industry overlook this completely and rework the old agenda of proposals for adjustment at the micro-economic level. In so doing they tend merely to legitimise these tendencies.

The absence of any significant 'arms conversion' in the UK is one result. There is not a single example of a major British defence company turning over a major plant or section of its workforce to non-defence work in the first five years of the post-Cold War era (NEDO, 1991; Schofield et al., 1992). Several small conversion initiatives within the major companies have failed. In the 'second' league, some companies have reduced dependence on defence but none of these efforts represent a significant redeployment of former defence staff and facilities.[20] Very few defence workers have moved into non-defence work other than via the route of unemployment and at the cost of declining incomes and security.

This absence of conversion was entirely predictable. As the defence companies became more like other capitalist corporations, more closely governed by market imperatives, they have been obliged to seek outlets where they have competitive advantages, and these tend to be military markets. For a defence industry structured like that of the UK, privatisation and market forces do not spontaneously lead to conversion. As in the USA, the diversification strategy favoured by companies (and the growing number of policy advisors who reject extreme free-market solutions) focuses on the promotion of 'dual-use' technologies (Tyson, 1992; Walker and Gummett, 1993). A rhetoric of 'dual-use' is also more politically acceptable than an explicit emphasis on arms exports (Markusen, 1991).

As noted above, there is a growing debate among practitioners on the need for a more strategic approach from government towards the defence and aerospace industry as a whole, even if the academics remain some way behind. The government remains unconverted, and the annual Defence white paper regularly reiterates its wish to avoid intervention. The Labour Party has developed a somewhat more interventionist strategy, embodied in the proposal for a Defence Diversification Agency (a proposal which was supported by GEC in its 1993 submission to the select committee investigating aerospace). There is a need for a more detailed and much more public debate which links both micro-economic questions of adjustment and macro-economic questions of demand, and also embraces questions both of national industrial strategy and of national policy towards the global arms market.

A policy for the defence industry might form part of a strategy for a transition to a new growth path, and a new social purpose. In effect, this is what happened in the 1930s and the late 1940s. Conversion, in the sense of a transfer of plant and workers from military to civilian production, is but a special instance of consciously directed industrial restructuring. As such it requires in principle a set of policies designed to alter both the decision makers and their contextual pressures. A coherent conversion policy would include a 'cascade' of measures targetted successively on the plant, the company, the locality, the industrial sector, the macro-economy, and on international economic relations. The 'conversion debate' could represent an engagement with these questions, but it has yet to achieve this in practice.

A conspicuous absence in both the mainstream and the 'conversion' policy debates in the UK, moreover, is the lack of a serious European dimension (Lovering, 1994). The Delors faction within the EC stressed the need for defence conversion in the context of European technology and employment policy (CEC, 1993). The defence industry itself has proposed some radical European initiatives, notably the campaign by Lancashire defence companies for a European aerospace R&D complex, 'Euro-NASA', which they hope to lure to Lancashire. British, and European, experience contrasts sharply with that in the USA. The conversion of part of the defence industry is central to the Clinton administration's competitiveness policy, at least at the level of rhetoric. This includes a $1.7 billion Defense

Reinvestment and Conversion Initiative.[21] A debate over a European equivalent – a debate which has only been hinted at to date – could open up a much more promising agenda than the present bland consensus. The policy debate to date has largely been confined to discussing how best to shut the stable door after the horse has bolted.

CONCLUSION

The British defence industry in the 1990s is restructuring in ways which defy simple generalisations. In terms of technological leadership, exports, and corporate adaptation, parts of it have been remarkably successful, although a major catastrophe is still quite conceivable. But in terms of social needs the restructuring is already profoundly problematic. Employment is continuing to decline, while the production of ever-more effective and cheaper weapons is contributing to a global proliferation of the instruments of violence. Mainstream policy analysts and policy makers simply ignore these developments by emphasising the need to 'follow market forces', and this imperative is reproduced within a different moral discourse by much of the arms conversion literature. This myopic focus on the need for adjustment to market forces rather than on the need to impose some regulation on those market forces, on 'following' rather than 'shaping' the market, has pushed the fundamental questions concerning the purposes of economic life off the agenda of public debate. Meanwhile the restructuring of the defence industries – a triumph or a crisis depending on your point of view – is creating an apparatus which is increasingly beyond public control.

NOTES

1 As late as the mid-1960s, the major weapons project was designed to perform a military role on an imperial scale. The specification for the Tactical Strike Reconnaissance aircraft (TSR-2) was intended to enable the RAF to bomb the Middle East from bases in the English Home Counties (Hastings, 1966).

2 This vague but widely used term indicates the close relationship between agencies of the state, large companies, scientists, and other groups. The term is usually attributed to President Eisenhower, who used it to highlight what he regarded as the threat to open democracy resulting from the concentration of economic and political power arising from high defence spending in the USA. For analysis of the concept of the MIC, see Kennedy, 1983; Kaldor, 1990; and Fine, 1993.

3 In an important contribution David Edgerton (1991) argues that the British state *did* in fact adopt a modernising developmental approach in relation to the defence industry, and Coates in 1994 reproduced this claim. I would argue that this is to over-emphasise the technological obsessions and achievements of a few individuals and organisations concerned with the aircraft and nuclear industries in particular. It focuses on the formal 'top–down' apparatus of defence technology procurement, but largely ignores corporate perceptions

and developments at the 'grass roots' of the industry (for which see Wood, 1986). Throughout the Cold War period as a whole the British state made few attempts to anticipate the long-term effects of its defence industry policy, and procurement policy changed dramatically at intervals. This framework may have engendered some striking technological achievements, such as the silicon chip, but this is not the same as nurturing a dynamic capitalist defence industry. Moreover, some major defence technologies, such as vertical take-off, depended on private initiative, in defiance of government, and on the support of overseas governments rather than the British – in this case the USA (see Hooker, 1984).

4 The first group consisted of Vickers-Weybridge, Vickers-Supermarine, A.V.Roe, Hawker, Bristol, De-Havilland, Handley-Page, and Shorts. The second included Fairey, Armstrong Whitworth, Airspeed, Westland, Miles, Boulton-Paul, Saunders-Roe, English-Electric, Blackburn, and Gloster. By the 1980s all the survivors except Westlands and Shorts had become parts of BAe.

5 The political motive for continuing the programme was notoriously expressed by Foreign Secretary Ernest Bevin as follows: 'I don't want any other Foreign Secretary of this country to be talked at by a Secretary of State in the United States as I have just had in my discussions with Mr Byrnes. We have got to have this thing over here, whatever it costs' (Halliday, 1983: 89).

6 For example, the Army and the RAF were unable to agree to co-ordinate their requirements for ground to air missiles, resulting in orders for both the Bristol Bloodhound and the English Electric Thunderbird. The RAF and the Fleet Air Arm could not agree on a common fighter, resulting in orders for both the Blackburn Buccaneer and the Phantom. These conflicts sustained jobs at Bristol and Stevenage, and in Brough (Hull), Preston, and Kingston.

7 The new procurement apparatus was known as the 'Downey System'. A Staff Target or a weapon concept would be drawn up by the appropriate Service, feasibility studies would be conducted using government research establishments, and if these were favourable matters would eventually proceed to the Project Definition stage, and ultimately to full development.

8 The MoD resisted the merger of GEC and BAe through the late 1980s, apparently to the annoyance of Weinstock, but is thought to have relaxed its opposition in the early 1990s (Betts *et al.*, 1994; House of Commons, 1993). At the time of writing GEC is said to prefer a joint venture combining GEC and BAe defence interests, but BAe is also believed to be interested in purchasing the VSEL submarine yard at Barrow. Defence sales account for the bulk of BAe turnover and profits, and a third of GEC's total sales and a higher share of its profits.

9 It was during this debate that Michael Heseltine earned his nickname of 'Tarzan' by waving the Mace while promising to return the industry to the private sector. Labour MPs sang the Red Flag.

10 In the run-up to the 1983 and 1987 general elections Conservative Central office played on this fact, publishing a list of defence companies by constituency and urging local party workers to convert defence jobs into Conservative votes.

11 The restructuring is described in more detail by Dunne and Smith, 1992; Lovering, 1990, 1991b, 1993, 1994; Quigley *et al.*, 1988; Schofield and Gummett, 1990; Taylor and Hayward, 1989; Walker and Gummett, 1989, 1993).

12 Lobbying in general may have become more important in the 1980s.

13 Heseltine failed to secure a similar 'European solution' for the Westlands helicopter company. Unlike the Eurofighter project, this initiative lacked the support of BAe and other major private actors.

14 The inquiry into the sale of equipment by British engineering companies which

was to be used in the construction of an Iraqi 'Supergun'. Investigations by the Customs Office into this and other sales of equipment for military purposes were confounded by the discovery that these arrangements had been approved by other Departments.

15 BAe acquired Royal Ordnance and Rover at prices which ignored their land values. At the time of the deals, the sale of three of the ROF sites could have yielded two and a half times the sum BAe paid for ROF as a whole, and the sale of two Rover sites could have recovered a third of what it paid for Rover (see Lovering and Hayter, 1993; CAAT, 1994).

16 Schumpeter argued that war-making and preparation for war are 'troublesome distractions, destructive of life's meaning, a diversion from the . . . true task' of the bourgeoisie (Schumpeter, 1955: 69). They are attributable to unproductive social groups 'oriented towards war' which are sustained by the state. At root, a bloated defence industry is therefore a particularly intractable instance of the genus 'state intervention'. For a discussion see Fine, 1993 and Lovering, 1994.

17 In 1992 BAe expected a 10 per cent decline in world defence expenditure in the first half of the decade to £900 billion, of which 25 per cent would be spent on equipment. Spending would begin to grow again in the latter part of the decade. The DESO anticipated a decline in export demand by about 16 per cent over the five years from 1993 (except for a rise of 12 per cent in Pacific Asia) before growth returned. Air equipment will account for about half the market (Thomas, 1994).

18 According to *Business Week* (1994): 'if you were a defense worker in 1993 there's a good chance you lost your job. But if you were an investor odds are you doubled your money as defense stock soared. . . . In 1993 industry cost-cutters raced ahead of the Pentagon, slashing jobs – especially in managerial and engineering ranks – faster than revenues tailed off'.

19 The review of pay and conditions of armed forces 'is expected to transform the culture of service life'. '"There will be a revolution in service culture" said one defence source' (Adams, 1994).

20 Rosyth dockyard diversified into refurbishing London underground trains. Dowty shed its defence units and increased civilian sales. Smiths Industries expanded its medical divisions relative to defence/aerospace. Short Brothers expanded civil aerospace work for the Canadian firm Bombardier, which makes more money from recreational equipment than defence. Some Royal Ordnance plants have attempted to diversify, but none have significantly reduced their dependence on military markets, and thousands of jobs have been lost in the process.

21 The cornerstone of this is the Technology Reinvestment Program (TRP) which provides $472 million through ARPA, the Advanced Research Projects Agency (formerly the *Defense* Advanced Research Projects Agency), to encourage industry-led consortia to develop new technologies with civilian and military applications (Technology Development), for manufacturing programs to deploy existing technology (Technology Deployment), and for colleges and universities to provide manufacturing education and training. In addition the Advanced Technology Programme (ATP) provides $199.5 million for new high-risk technology development.

REFERENCES

Adams, J. (1994) '"Forces" Lavish perks to go in £1bn Budget Cut', *Sunday Times*, 4 September.

Aitken, J. (1994) 'Defence Procurement: Past Present and Future', *RUSI Journal*, February, 39–42.
Annual Abstract of Statistics (1994) London: CSO.
Baker, W.J. (1970) *History of the Marconi Company*, London: Methuen.
Barnett, C. (1972) *The Collapse of British Power*, Gloucester: Alan Sutton.
Betts, B. (1993) 'Hat trick for BAe', *Financial Times*, 30 January.
Betts, P., Gray, B., and Jackson, T. (1994) 'BAe Revives Hope of Forging Defence Link with GEC', *Financial Times*, 5/6 February.
British Business (1994) 7 January.
Brittan, S. (1966) *The Treasury Under the Tories 1951–1964*, Harmondsworth: Penguin.
Buckley, N. and Donkin, R. (1992) 'MOD Knew of Supergun in 1989, MPs Told', *Financial Times*, 6 February.
Business Week (1994) 'Cuts Won't Cut It Anymore', 10 January.
CAAT (1994) *Writing on the Wall*, BAe Shareholder Action Group and Campaign Against Arms Trade, 11 Goodwin Street, London N4 3HQ, April.
Cabinet Office (1993) *Realising Our Potential*, London: HMSO.
Campbell, D. (1984) *The Unsinkable Aircraft Carrier*, London: Michael Joseph.
CEC (1992) *The Economic and Social Impact of Reductions in Defence Spending and Military Forces on the Regions of the Community*, Regional Development Studies, no. 5, CEC, Brussels. Luxembourg.
CEC (1993) *Competition, Growth, Employment*, Commission of the European Communities, Brussels.
Chalmers, M. (1985) *Paying for Defence: Military Spending and British Decline*, London: Pluto.
Clark, A. (1993) *Diaries*, London: Weidenfield and Nicholson.
Coates, D. (1994) *The Question of UK Decline*, Hemel Hempstead: Harvester-Wheatsheaf.
Critchley, J. (1987) *Heseltine: The Unauthorised Biography*, London: Hodder and Stoughton.
Croucher, R. (1982) *Engineers at War 1939–1945*, London: Merlin Press.
Dabinett, G. (1993) 'Markets and the State and the Role of Local Regeneration Strategies: A Case Study of the Defence Sector in the UK in the 1980s', *Local Economy*, 8, 338–51.
Dockrill, M. (1988) *British Defence since 1945*, Oxford: Blackwell.
DS (1993) *Defence Statistics*, London: HMSO.
Dunne, J. P. (1990) 'The Political Economy of Military Expenditure', *Cambridge Journal of Economics* 14, 395–404.
Dunne, J.P. and Smith, R.P. (1984) 'The Economic Consequences of Reduced UK Military Expenditure', *Cambridge Journal of Economics* 8, 297–310.
Dunne, J.P. and Smith, R.P. (1992) 'Thatcherism and the UK Defence Industry', in J. Michie (ed.) *1979–1992: The Economic Legacy*, London: Academic Press.
Edgerton, D. (1991) *England and the Aeroplane*, London: Verso.
Edgerton, D. (1993) 'British R&D after 1945: A Re-interpretation', *Science and Technology Policy*, April, 10–16.
Edwards, J. (1994) *True Brits: The Foreign Office*, London: BBC Books.
Ernst and Young (1994) *The UK Defence Industry – Securing Its Future*, London.
Financial Times (1994) 27 April.
Fine, B. (1993) 'The Military-Industrial-Complex: An Analytical Assessment', *Cyprus Journal of Economics* 6, 26–51.
Fine, B. and Harris, L. (1985) *The Peculiarities of the British Economy*, London: Lawrence and Wishart.
Flight International (1994) 'Market Forces', Editorial, 20–26 July.

Gamble, A. (1981) *Britain in Decline: Economic Policy, Political Strategy, and the British State*, London: Macmillan.

Gray, B. (1994) 'Weinstock to Keep Job at Gec for Another Two Years', *Financial Times*, 13 July.

Gregory, F.E.C. and Simpson, J. (1982) 'Memorandum on Defence Equipment Procurement', House of Commons Defence Committee session 1981–2.

Halliday, F. (1983) *The Making of the Second Cold War*, London: Verso.

Hartley, K. (1991) *The Political Economy of Defence Spending*, London: Brasseys.

Hastings, S. (1966) *The Murder of TSR-2*, London: Macdonald.

Hayward, K. (1989) *The British Aircraft Industry*, Manchester: Manchester University Press.

Healey, D. (1990) *The Time of My Life*, London: Penguin.

Heim, C.E. (1988) 'Government Research Establishments, State Capacity and Distribution of Industry Policy in Britain', *Regional Studies* 22, 375–86.

Heseltine, M. (1987) *Where There's a Will*, London: Hutchinson.

Heseltine, M. (1989) *The Challenge of Europe: Can Britain Win?*, London: Pan Books.

Hooker, S. (1984) *Not Much of an Engineer: An Autobiography*, Shrewsbury: Airlife Publishing Ltd.

Hooper, N. (1989) 'Defending the Defence Industrial Base', *Economic Affairs*, October/November, 12–15.

House of Commons (1993) *BAe Industry*, Trade and Industry Committee, Third Report. Vol. I, 563-I.

Howe, R.W. (1980) *Weapons: The International Game of Arms, Money and Diplomacy*, London: Abacus.

Kaldor, M. (1980) 'Technical Change in the Defence Industry', in K. Pavitt (ed.) *Technical Innovation and British Economic Performance*, Science Policy Research Unit, London: Macmillan.

Kaldor, M. (1982) *The Baroque Arsenal*, London: Andre Deutsche.

Kaldor, M. (1990) *The Imaginary War: Understanding the East–West Conflict*, Oxford: Blackwell.

Kaldor, M., Sharp, M. and Walker, W. (1986) 'Industrial Competitiveness and Britain's Defence', *Lloyds Bank Review*, October, 31–49.

Keegan, J. (1994) *A History of Warfare*, London: Pimlico.

Kennedy, G. (1983) *Defense Economics*, London: Duckworth.

Kennedy, G. (1989) 'Defence; Markets and Bureaucracy', *Economic Affairs*, October/November, 6–8.

Kennedy, P. (1988) *The Rise and Fall of the Great Powers*, London: Unwin Hyman.

Klare, M.T. (1989) 'East–West Versus North–South: Dominant and Subordinate Themes in US Military Strategy Since 1945', in J.R. Gillis (ed.) *The Militarisation of the Western World*, New Brunswick: Rutgers University Press.

Lancashire County Council (1993) *The Defence Industry in Lancashire*.

Law, C.M. (1983) 'The Defence Sector in British Regional Development', *Geoforum* 14, 169–84.

Leadbetter, C. (1993) 'The Old Order Endeth', *Financial Times*, 30 July.

Lovering, J. (1988) 'Islands of Prosperity' in M. Breheny (ed.) *Defence Expenditure and Regional Development*, London: Mansell.

Lovering, J. (1990) 'Defence Spending and the Restructuring of Capitalism: The Military Industry in Britain', *Cambridge Journal of Economics* 14, 453–67.

Lovering, J. (1991a) 'The Changing Geography of the Military Industry in Britain', *Regional Studies* 25, 279–93.

Lovering, J. (1991b) 'The British Defence Industry in the (1990s): A Labour Market Perspective', *Industrial Relations Journal* 22, 103–16.

Lovering, J. (1993) 'Restructuring the British Defence Industrial Base After the Cold War: Institutional and Geographical Perspectives', *Defence Economics* 4, 123–39.

Lovering, J. (1994) 'After the Cold War: The Defence Industry and the New Europe', in P. Brown and R. Crompton (ed.) *A New Europe? Economic Restructuring and Social Exclusion*, London: University of London Press.

Lovering, J. and Hayter. T. (1993) 'BAe: The Ugly Duckling that Never Turned into a Swan', in D. Harvey and T. Hayter (ed.) *The Factory and the City*, London: Mansell.

McIntosh, M. (1990) *Managing Britain's Defence*, London: Macmillan.

Malecki, E.J. (1991) *Technology and Economic Development: The Dynamics of Local, Regional, and National Change*, Harlow: Longmans.

Markusen, A.R. (1986) 'Defence Spending: A Successful Industrial Policy?', *International Journal of Urban and Regional Research* 10, 105–21.

Markusen, A.R. (1991) 'The Military–Industrial Divide', *Environment and Planning D: Society and Space* 9, 391–416.

Markusen, A., Hall P., Campbell S., and Dietrick, S. (1990) *The Rise of the Gunbelt: The Military remapping of Industrial America*, Oxford: Oxford University Press.

Middlemass, K. (1979) *Politics in Industrial Society: The Experience of the British System Since 1911*, London: Andre Deutsch.

Morgan, K. O. (1990) *The People's Peace: British history 1945–1989*, Oxford: Oxford University Press.

NAO (1994) *Ministry of Defence: Defence Procurement in the 1990s*. Report by the Comptroller and Auditor General, National Audit Office, London: HMSO.

NEDO (1991) *Diversifying from Defence: Case Studies and Management Guidelines*. National Economic Development Council, Electronics Industry Sector Group, Millbank, London.

Pagnamenta, P. and Overy, R. (1984) *All Our Working Lives*, London: BBC Books.

Pedern, G.C. (1979) *British Rearmament and the Treasury 1932–1939*, Edinburgh: Scottish Academic Press.

Pollard, S. (1983) *The Wasting of the British Economy*, London: Croom Helm.

Ponting, C. (1990) *1940: Myth and Reality*, Reading: Hamish Hamilton.

Quigley, P., Shofield, S., and Woodhouse, T. (1988) 'The Military in Manufacturing', *Studies in Disarmament and Employment No. 2*, Bradford School of Peace Studies.

Renner, M. (1992) *Economic Adjustments after the Cold War*, United Nations Institute for Disarmament Research, Dartmouth, USA.

Samson, A. (1991) *The Arms Bazaar in the Nineties: From Krupp to Saddam*, London: Hodder and Stoughton.

SBAC (1992) 'The Aerospace Sector of the UK Defence Industrial Base', *SBAC Briefing Papers*, Society of BAe Companies, 29 King St, St James, London SW1Y 6RD.

SBAC (1994) Interview with author. April.

Schofield, S. and Gummett, P. (1990) 'A Challenge to the European Defence Industry', in *European Security: The New Agenda*, SaferWorld Foundation, Bristol 103–12.

Schofield, S., Dando, M. and Ridge, M. (1992) 'Conversion of the British Defence Industries', *Peace Research Report No 30*, Department of Peace Studies, University of Bradford.

Schumpeter, J. (1955) *Imperialism and Social Classes*, New York: Augustus M. Kelley.

Shay, R.P. (1977) *British rearmament in the Thirties, Politics and Profits*, Princeton: Princeton University Press.

Sherry, M.S. (1987) *The Rise of American Air Power: The Creation of Armageddon*, Yale: Yale University Press.

Shonfield, A. (1958) *British Economic Policy since the War*, Harmondsworth: Penguin.

Smith, R. (1990) Defence Spending in the UK', in K. Hartley and T. Sandler (ed.) *The Economics of Defence Spending*, London: Routledge.

Southwood, P. (1991) *Disarming Military Industry: Turning an Outbreak of Peace into an Enduring Legacy*, London: Macmillan.

Statement on Defence Estimates (1993) London: HMSO.

Statement on Defence Estimates (1994) London: HMSO.

Taylor, T. and Hayward, K. (1989) *The UK Defence Industrial Base*, London and New York: Brassey's Defence Publishers.

Thayer, G. (1969) *The War Business: The International Trade in Armaments*, London: Weidenfeld and Nicholson.

Thomas, A. (1994) 'Attacked from all Sides: The UK 20% in the Arms Market', *RUSI Journal*, February, 43–5.

Turner, G. (1969) *Business in Britain*, Harmondsworth: Penguin.

Tyson, L D'A. (1992) *Who's Bashing Whom? Trade Conflict in High-Technology Industries*, London Institute for International Economics, Washington/Longmans.

Walker, M. (1991) 'The Pentagon's Profits of Doom', *The Guardian*, 9 September.

Walker, W. and Gummett, P. (1989) 'Britain and the Armaments Market', *International Affairs* 65, 3, 419–42.

Walker, W. and Gummett, P. (1993) 'Nationalism, Internationalism and the European Defence Market', *Chaillot Papers 9*, WEU, Institute for Security Studies.

Warner, J. (1992) 'Former MOD Chief Rubbishes BAe in City', *Independent on Sunday*, 5 January.

Weston, C. (1993) 'Lord Weinstock Attacks Defence Contracts Policy', *The Guardian*, 22 April.

White, D. (1992) 'The Dog Fight Gets Dirty', *Financial Times* supplement: Aerospace survey, 2 September.

Willett, S. (1990) 'Conversion Policy in the UK', *Cambridge Journal of Economics*, December, 469–82.

Wood, D. (1986) *Project Cancelled*, New York: Janes Publishing Inc.

6

ENGINEERING

Company strategies and public policy in an industry in crisis

Mike Geddes and Anne Green

This chapter is divided into three main sections. The first section provides an overview of past trends, future prospects, and key issues for the engineering industry in the UK, and develops a regional perspective on the engineering industry in South East England. This provides a context for a discussion of company strategies in the second part of this chapter, drawing upon recent primary research with firms and public agencies in parts of the South East[1]. The discussion addresses issues such as the changing business environment and business strategies, rationalisation and reorganisation of plants in multi-locational companies, organisational change, human resource development, technological change, inter-firm linkages, and the changing geography of the engineering industry. The policy implications of these changes are reviewed in the latter part of this chapter, and possible components of a local economic development strategy for securing a healthy engineering industry in the South East and the UK are presented.

THE ENGINEERING INDUSTRY IN THE UK: PAST TRENDS, FUTURE PROSPECTS, AND KEY ISSUES FOR POLICY

The diversity and complexity of the engineering industry

The engineering industry is diverse and complex. It covers a wide range of activities, including mechanical engineering, metal goods, electrical engineering, electronics, instruments, motor vehicles, aerospace, and other transport equipment, covering a multiplicity of products and processes. Some of these activities are more closely linked to industries outside engineering than they are to other activities within engineering itself. Some sectors have been in rapid decline in recent years, while others have grown, such that an aggregate overview may disguise differing trends in the various parts of the engineering industry.

The engineering industry in the UK accounted for a little over 10 per cent of total Gross Domestic Product (GDP) and 42 per cent of manufacturing output at the start of the 1990s. Approximately 2.1 million people worked in engineering in 1991. This represented just over 8 per cent of all employment, but about 43 per cent of jobs in manufacturing. While it is still possible to claim that the engineering industry lies at the heart of the UK economy, it is a long time since the UK could claim to be the 'workshop of the world'. Today engineering is an industry in long-term decline.

Between the mid 1920s and the mid-1950s, as the UK economy changed from one based on the traditional industries such as coal, textiles, and shipbuilding to new mass production industries, engineering output increased by nearly 350 per cent, a growth rate that was considerably faster than that of manufacturing output as a whole. Since at least 1970, however, as the basis of the economy has undergone another structural shift, engineering output has consistently declined as a proportion of GDP, to the present figure of around 10 per cent. Correspondingly, employment has also fallen and in 1993 was only 53 per cent of its 1971 level. This long-term decline of engineering reflects a number of structural changes in the economy including the transition from energy to information-intensity, and from metals to newer materials. These changes have both reduced the relative importance of engineering within the economy as a whole, and have profoundly modified the structure, products, and processes of the industry itself.

Changes in engineering in the 1980s

There was a sharp contrast in the experience of the engineering sector during the 1980s. In the first half of the decade, dramatic reductions of demand in final markets led to widespread plant closures and massive redundancies among engineering companies. By contrast, the second half of the 1980s was a period of relative recovery. Engineering significantly out-performed the economy as a whole as the 'Lawson' consumer boom boosted sales of metal-based products.

However, an underlying trend throughout the 1980s was the above average rate of increase in labour *productivity* in engineering. This not only contributed to the major employment reductions of the early 1980s, but also meant that employment continued to decline even when engineering output growth picked up again in the last half of the decade. Between 1981 and 1991 759 thousand jobs in engineering were shed.

The main features of change in engineering during the 1980s are summarised in Figure 6.1.

Overall job loss disguises important changes in the *occupational structure* of employment during the 1980s. While changes in engineering processes have reduced the importance of many traditional, craft engineering occupational categories, there is clear evidence of an 'upskilling' of

Figure 6.1 The experience of engineering in the 1980s

a below national average increase in the value of sales

the movement from a small surplus in international trade to a substantial balance of payments deficit

very variable performance in different sectors, with electrical and instrument engineering and other transport equipment performing relatively well compared with mechanical engineering, metal goods, and vehicles

an above national average rate of increase in labour productivity

an overall reduction of engineering employment of about one-third (with the majority of the reduction occurring in the early 1980s)

the workforce. This has taken two forms. First, there has been a greater demand for non-manual professional skills in science and engineering, along with managerial skills. Secondly, there has been an upgrading of many previously semi-skilled operative manual occupations to technician status. These trends reflect the increasing professionalisation of engineering and the growth of multi-skilling among the workforce. As a result, the 1980s saw technician employment increase by 97 thousand (20 per cent), while operative jobs and skilled craft employment decreased by approximately 300 thousand (17 per cent) and 200 thousand (14 per cent) respectively.

The experience of engineering during the economic upturn of the latter half of the 1980s revealed worrying portents of problems for the industry in future years. Due to the limited confidence in the durability of the boom, capital re-investment in engineering tended to be focused on the replacement of outdated capacity rather than the creation of new capacity, leaving a problem of capacity shortage which resulted in a growing propensity to import during periods of high levels of demand. Some of the factors contributing to this problem are outlined in Figure 6.2.

As a result, the engineering industry entered the 1990s with capital expenditure per employee well below the average for manufacturing as a whole.

Prospects for the 1990s

The UK engineering industry entered the 1990s at a crossroads. The sharp reversion to recession in the UK economy from 1990 onwards produced an acceleration of job losses: 207 thousand jobs were lost in engineering

Figure 6.2 Key features of the legacy of the 1980s

---

the decimation in the early 1980s of key engineering sectors, such as machine tools, which never subsequently recovered

the technological backwardness of many UK companies – failure to adopt new control technologies as rapidly or as effectively as foreign competitors

a tendency for companies with competitive products to focus on short-term profits, through price increases, rather than maintaining and improving market share

the emphasis placed by the UK capital market on company expansion by merger and acquisition rather than investment

---

between 1991 and 1993. The recession also meant company closures (both large and small) and plummeting business confidence and investment. As a slow recovery begins, there are a number of factors which are likely to have an impact upon the engineering industry in the UK over the remainder of the decade (and beyond). These key factors are summarised in Figure 6.3.

While all of these factors will have some impact upon the engineering sector, their precise impact is uncertain and consequently future employment levels are difficult to estimate with precision. Forecasts of employment in engineering produced by the Institute for Employment Research (IER) (Wilson, 1992, 1994) suggest that employment decline will continue during the 1990s, but not at the pace seen in the earlier decade. After a loss of over 200 thousand jobs in engineering between 1991 and 1993, it is forecast that a further 142 thousand jobs will be shed between 1993 and 2001 (representing a decrease at a rate of 1 per cent per annum). This reduction in the rate of employment loss is partly explained by the increased competitiveness of UK engineering products following the fall in the overseas value of sterling since September 1992.

Mechanical engineering was hardest hit by employment reductions in the early 1990s, and losses are expected to continue, albeit at a reduced rate. Further substantial job losses are forecast in electrical engineering. The historical decline in employment in motor vehicles is projected to come to an end in the mid-1990s, with an average annual rate of employment increase of 0.4 per cent between 1993 and 2001. Nevertheless, the general decline of engineering employment will tend to reduce the demand for all occupations. However, offsetting this trend – at least to some extent – is the 'upskilling' of the workforce, which is forecast to lead to increased demand

Figure 6.3 Key factors impacting on engineering in the 1990s

---

completion of the Single European Market (SEM), and intensified competition in European markets

uncertainty over the future of monetary union in Europe

liberalisation of the former communist countries of Eastern Europe

the impact of major cuts in future defence expenditure

possible changes in government economic strategy

---

for technicians and professional skills in engineering, and reductions in demand for unskilled and semi-skilled operative occupations.

A regional perspective: the engineering industry in South East England

The South East is the largest regional economy in the UK, accounting for approximately one-third of total population, employment, and GDP. As the core of the national economy it has a pivotal role in determining the overall economic performance of the UK. In the 1980s the South East was one of the best economic performers of any region in the UK, largely due to a combination of its favourable industrial and occupational structure (employment being heavily concentrated in services and higher level occupations), and its locational advantages as the closest region to continental Europe and with London at the hub of the national communications network.

Throughout much of the last thirty years the economic performance of Greater London has contrasted with that of the Rest Of the South East (ROSE), as the economic balance of the region has shifted from the former to the latter area. The contrasting economic experiences of Greater London and ROSE reflects the operation of processes of decentralisation of population and employment from the largest urban areas. However, not all areas within ROSE have been affected to the same extent by such decentralisation: the 'western corridor' emerged as a key growth area during the 1980s, while the Eastern Thames corridor shared in the general prosperity of the South East to a lesser extent.

The processes of decentralisation, in combination with the deindustrialisation of the UK, have largely removed engineering activities from Greater London. In 1991, manufacturing as a whole constituted only 11 per cent, and engineering only 4 per cent, of all employment in Greater London. Both manufacturing and engineering are of much greater relative importance in ROSE, where the manufacturing share of total employment amounted to over 18 per cent, of which more than half was in engineering (9 per cent of total employment). Within the engineering sector, the 'core' engineering activities in Greater London and the ROSE are similar, with electrical, electronics, and instrument engineering emerging as dominant. Aerospace is particularly important in ROSE relative to the UK, but is of much less significance in Greater London.

As at the national scale, so within the South East region, the engineering sector has experienced considerable change over the last quarter century. Over the two decades to 1991, engineering output in the region barely changed in real terms, increasing by just over 2 per cent from £9.3 billion to £9.5 billion (measured in 1985 prices). This virtually static level of output, however, masks considerable variation within the sector. Output in the more traditional engineering industries of metal goods, mechanical engineering, and motor vehicles fell by at least a third, while output in electrical, electronics, instrument engineering, and aerospace increased by at least three-quarters. This differential change had the effect of raising the relative share in engineering output of electrical, electronics, and aerospace engineering from just 32 per cent in 1971 to nearly 60 per cent in 1991.

Despite the increases in output in electrical and electronic engineering and in aerospace, employment fell in every sector of the engineering industry between 1971 and 1991. Indeed, while the greatest rates of decline were in those sectors such as mechanical engineering and motor vehicles where regional output was declining, the largest number of net job losses was in electrical and electronic engineering where output was increasing. Overall, engineering employment fell by about half over the two decades. One result of the combination of static output and sharply declining employment was that real GDP per person employed in engineering doubled (from about £8,000 to just over £16,000 per capita). In electrical/ electronic engineering the increase in per capita output more than trebled from £5,500 thousand to £17,000 thousand (all values in 1985 prices). These increases in per capita output reflect both increases in labour productivity and a shift towards higher value-added products such as electronics.

Not only does the engineering industry in the South East have a distinctive sectoral composition, it is also characterised by relative specialisation in non-manual occupational groups compared with the national average. The key feature of the occupational structure of the South East is the high concentration of non-manual occupational groups relative to the national average. Over 40 per cent of all UK employment in associate professional and technical occupations is in the South East, compared with approximately one third of total employment. By contrast, the South East accounts for only about a quarter of UK employment in craft and related occupations, plant and machine operatives, and other (unskilled) occupations. This pattern reflects both regional variations in industrial structure, and inter-regional differences in patterns of occupational specialisation within industries. The sharp reduction in employment in engineering over the past two decades, together with 'upskilling' of the workforce has markedly reduced employment in the region among craft and related skill occupations, which fell by a little under 200 thousand between 1971 and 1991, and among plant and machine operative jobs which declined by around 250 thousand (25 per cent) over the same period.

The South East region was the region most badly affected by the recession of the early 1990s. Greater London bore the greatest share of the misery, with the number of employees falling by over 10 per cent between 1990 and 1992, but even in the more usually prosperous ROSE, employment decline was worse than any other region bar the West Midlands. Forecasts to 2001 suggest that the economic performance of the South East may continue to lag behind that of some other regions in the UK, partly because the service industry bias of the South East provides less scope for any positive impact from the depreciation of sterling. In this regard, the engineering sector could be of critical importance in determining the speed and extent of the region's recovery as the industry represents a major exporting sector.

COMPANY STRATEGIES AND LOCAL DEVELOPMENT: EVIDENCE FROM THE ENGINEERING INDUSTRY IN SOUTH EAST ENGLAND

The importance and value of examining company strategies

The recent trends and future prospects of the engineering industry, outlined above, are the result of the strategic decisions and responses being made by companies, especially the larger companies, in response to their perception of changes in the strategic spheres within which they are operating. In this section research from a survey of engineering companies in South East England undertaken in late 1992 is drawn upon to provide some insights into how engineering companies in the region are reacting to shifts in their competitive environment by altering their company strategies, and the impact of such changing company strategies on the regional economy.

It is now commonplace to argue that the strategies, including the locational strategies, of large firms have undergone structural changes in the transition from the Fordist to a post-Fordist production system (Lipietz, 1986). Moulaert and Demaziere (1994) contend that these structural changes

129

have involved a number of key tendencies, including those outlined in Figure 6.4

In the remainder of this section of the chapter the *ways* in which engineering companies in the South East have responded to change are outlined, and the overall impact of these changes for the engineering industry in the South East are assessed. To make such an assessment involves considering a number of different dimensions of change.

The business environment and business strategies

The UK engineering industry is at a particular turning point in a prolonged crisis. The competitive environment for engineering firms in the South East is not just that of market downturn during a recession. It is one in which a number of major changes coincide and interact: the global diffusion of new technological and organisational norms; the impact of European inte- gration; the end of the Cold War and defence procurement restructuring; and the pursuit of neo-liberal government policies in the UK. This is therefore a period of strategic change, in which the impacts of such major structural changes in the competitive environment tend to overwhelm the on-going processes of technological change, organisational evolution, and product change.

Company responses to change of course vary greatly, especially in such a complex and diffuse industry as engineering. Responses will depend on a number of specific key factors, including those outlined in Figure 6.5. This does not mean that change is random. Virtually all companies are aiming to enhance their competitiveness, cut unnecessary costs, and increase their profits. Strategies adopted to meet these aims vary, and a clear distinction is discernible between those companies merely reacting to change in order to survive, and those who are employing proactive changes in an attempt to meet desired objectives. In the former case, the danger is that in

Figure 6.4 Key tendencies characterising recent structural change in engineering

a return to the core business

new modes of integration of different functions and activities

application of new production technologies and modes of organisation of the work process – *flexible production systems*

the combination of intensive and extensive use of space – with simultaneous tendencies towards *globalisation* and *localisation*

Figure 6.5 Factors affecting the ways in which companies respond to strategic change

---

the specific environmental changes relevant to the company (these will vary according to sector, place in the production chain, etc.)

the resources that can be deployed in developing and implementing company strategy (aspects of organisational structure, skills composi- tion of the workforce, relationships to financial institutions, etc.)

decisions made by company leaders regarding the best direction for the company to go in

---

venturing into new areas without sufficient planning and research, companies approach or cross thresholds for commercial viability, so endangering the very existence of the company.

Plant closure, rationalisation and reorganisation

In the face of excess capacity, a drastic option is to resort to plant and site closure, either in whole or in part. The most dramatic element of this is the closure of large plants by big firms (such as Rolls-Royce near Watford or BAe at Kingston upon Thames, both in the early 1990s). Such major closures have particular significance both for the locality concerned and for the industry more widely, and are the most obvious way in which multi-plant companies can react strategically to changes in the competitive environment by reassessing their current geographical pattern of production and the logic of particular sites within wider company strategy. The impetus to close plants may be particularly strong when, as is the case with a number of large engineering companies, they are the result of past mergers and takeovers which have left a legacy of plants and sites which may owe more to past history than current needs.

Such major plant closures represent however only the tip of the iceberg of plant and site 'rationalisation'. Alongside plant closures are numerous instances of partial site closures by big- and medium-sized firms, often – but not always – through the relocation of certain operations to other sites elsewhere, while keeping other functions in situ (this 'outcome' is considered in more detail later). In other cases such rationalisation is part of wider 'downsizing' strategies involving the reduction of productive capacity. Alongside – and of course associated with – plant closure or

131

rationalisation by big firms, there was a high level of small firm closures in the South East in the early 1990s.

Internal organisational change and the division of labour

The most competitive business strategies in the engineering industry are closely associated with internal organisational changes, notably the four types of change outlined in Figure 6.6.

Internal reorganisation of the *division of labour* in the ways outlined in Figure 6.6 has been particularly characteristic of big firms, where corporate decisions to reform organisation have been a prominent element in business strategies, promoting management 'delayering' and flattening of hierarchies, and taking out layers of management to 'slim down' organisations. The drive for flexibility is best exemplified by the widespread shift from separate skilled craftsmen to multi-skilled technicians (such aspects of employment change are considered in greater detail later).

The same process of internal organisational change is much less evident in smaller firms. This may be because many such firms 'lag behind' in implementing new thinking about industrial organisation. However, it may also be a reflection of the fact that many SMEs already have some of the key features of organisational structure which big firms are now aiming at: notably, very 'lean' managements, very 'flexible' workers, and no trade unions. If this is the case, and small- and medium-sized enterprises are in the vanguard of current change, this has very significant implications for occupational and class structures, for trade unions, for skills and training, for the engineering industry in general, and for the South East region.

Technological change

In-depth discussions with engineering companies in the South East confirm that certain well-known trends, such as the increasing use of computer-controlled machinery, have continued in recent years. Many companies

Figure 6.6 Common aspects of internal organisational change

flatter management hierarchies

a drive for *flexibility*

a squeeze on support functions

reorganisation of production on a product/project 'cost centre' basis were not investing heavily in new equipment, however, for financial reasons. Indeed, many smaller companies were purchasing their equipment second-hand at auctions: 'taking advantage' of the rationalisation and closure of larger engineering companies/sites.

Within the engineering industry the interaction between product and process technology may have important consequences. For instance, the shift from electrical to electronic components, and from metal to plastic products, are resulting in major process changes. These include a reduction in the significance of manufacturing itself within the overall production process. This opens up the possibility of changes in the location of production (an issue explored in more detail below).

These same developments have important implications for skills development and training. Many of the skills for which employers reported 'shortages' and/or 'recruitment difficulties' were those related to new technologies or new ways of using existing technologies.

Employment change and implications for training

Despite reporting of (a relatively small number) of often very specific skills shortages, the main thrust of employers' human resource development strategies is the drive for flexibility.

In functional terms there is evidence for 'the galvanisation of employment' as traditional occupational divisions and demarcations become increasingly redundant. However, despite the increase in emphasis on 'intermediate' skills or 'technician' occupations, in many instances the strategy adopted to achieve functional flexibility involves the 'training up' of operatives to perform specific tasks previously undertaken by a skilled craftsman, rather than the provision of a more general training which might equip the individual with the full range of skills normally associated with the traditional engineering craftsman. Such a wide-ranging training may not be necessary in order to meet the narrower objective of enabling workers to undertake a variety of tasks, and to therefore achieve faster production response times.

In turn, in numerical terms there is evidence for the increasing use of fixed-term contracts, casual and temporary working, with many companies developing registers of workers to be called upon in accordance with production needs. Hence, for many of those working in the engineering industry, 'flexibility' means a deterioration in the quality of employment.

Although most engineering companies predicted no change in employment levels over the short and medium term, or predicted a continuation of job losses, there was a general recognition of the importance of continuing investment in *training* in order to maintain and enhance competitiveness. Training is most prevalent among large employers, so the demise of large engineering firms has significant implications for the numbers of individuals receiving training, and for the training infrastructure.

Although most engineering companies recognise the need for their workforce to have both '*flexibility* and *specialisms*', the reality is that many employers – particularly smaller employers – are interested in providing training only to meet company-specific needs. This may mean provision of specific on-the-job training, rather than more general off-the-job training which individuals could 'take away with them'.

In the South East, the defence industry has historically been the training 'power-house' of the region. With cut-backs in defence expenditure, and associated rationalisations and closures, the defence industry can no longer perform this role in the same way. What is needed is a co-operative, proactive, long-term approach – which is holistic in scope – designed to meet the needs of the engineering industry in the South East in the 1990s and beyond.

Inter-firm linkages

A dramatic change in important parts of the engineering industry has been the way in which firms relate to both customers and suppliers. In key defence-related sectors like aerospace and electronics, the relationship with clients is changing fundamentally, from a 'cost plus' contractual relationship with (government) clients, to a more commercial, cost-conscious approach. Allied to attempts to diversify out of defence markets, this is producing considerable instability – affecting both employment levels and locational decisions – in what were previously very stable large firms.

The more competitive environment also has its effect on subcontracting. This can take the form either of subcontracting work that was previously done in-house, so as to reduce costs, or of forcing internal departments to compete with external suppliers. Subcontracting is a complex phenomenon and there are many types of subcontracting relationships in engineering. All types of subcontractors, however, face pressures to compete on price, on quality, and on delivery times. The emphasis between these aspects varies, as does the impact on subcontracting firms. Many of those which survive and prosper are likely to do so through improved quality and efficiency.

The changing firm structure of the engineering industry

The combination of a number of the trends discussed above is tending to produce a marked change in the firm structure of the engineering industry, as both big firms, and weaker small firms, have experienced serious problems. Processes of decentralisation are taking place both within big firms, and from big firms to suppliers, in order to offload or spread risk, while the weaker small firms are going to the wall.

While medium-sized firms are themselves not exempt from the pressures of a more competitive environment, there is a discernible tendency for the characteristic unit of production to become the medium-sized enterprise or the autonomous division of a bigger firm. This has interesting implications for the future of the engineering industry, because it entails a weakening of the hegemonic role previously played by a relatively small number of very large firms. Strategic decision making in the industry may be becoming more diffused among wider and weaker policy networks (this issue is explored in greater detail in the final part of the chapter).

The changing geography of the engineering industry

The various trends examined above lead to some important hypotheses about the changing role of the South East region in the spatial division of labour within engineering in the UK. In the first place, it is important to note the pervasiveness of structural change, which means that there is uncertainty about the permanence of plants of all types and sizes throughout the region. However, there is some evidence -- and particularly several prominent examples, including Rolls-Royce, BAe, and GEC – that multinational and multi-site companies are taking advantage of their locational flexibility to rationalise manufacturing on to sites outside the South East. The closure of Rolls Royce's helicopter engine plant at Watford, for example, resulted in the shifting of work to other plants in the South West, the Midlands, and Scotland. In some cases, this coincides with an overall reduction of manufacturing activities, but in other cases it is a question of corporate reorganisation without a significant decline in business. The result is a decline in engineering manufacturing capacity in the region which, particularly in certain locations, is reducing the 'critical mass' of activity and the skills base. This in turn has implications for the survival of remaining firms, since the local engineering infrastructure on which they depend is being eroded.

On the other hand, the erosion of the manufacturing capacity of the region does not currently appear to pose a threat to R&D and administrative activity. Firms continue to see advantages in keeping R&D and administrative functions in the region, and believe that any problems of distance to manufacturing plants can be overcome. In particular, the 'lifestyle' characteristics of the South East are viewed as advantageous by companies in attracting and retaining their research and managerial staff, but other regions are not perceived as possessing the same attributes, although appearing stronger in terms of the survival of a 'manufacturing culture'.

The decline of 'manufacturing functions' (as opposed to research, design, maintenance, and servicing functions) in the engineering industry in the South East is likely to have some limited knock-on effects on manufacturing suppliers. However, such effects are likely to be restricted as there is only very limited evidence that the diffusion of a 'just-in-time' approach is associated with any geographical concentration of suppliers around manufacturers/assemblers. On the other hand, the decline of manufact- uring may well have serious implications for another category of suppliers: those providing 'site and services' subcontracting (e.g., cleaning, building maintenance, delivery, etc.) to manufacturing plants. Such supplies are frequently obtained locally and the impact on them is likely to be the chief knock-on effect if the reduction in the region's manufacturing capacity continues.

High-tech by default? The role of the South East in the engineering spatial division of labour

The South East has long been home to industries associated with high-technology manufacturing, as well as to the R&D activities related to that manufacturing. In this sense engineering in the South East has long possessed a high-technology aspect and image. Now that so much manufacturing activity is being relocated from the South East to other regions, the South East may be becoming an even more 'high-tech' region, statistically speaking – but only by default – as manufacturing activities close down but R&D stays. Forecasts suggest that a growing proportion of the workforce will be employed as professional engineers and scientists, engaged in R&D activities. On the surface this would seem to be a positive tendency. However, with the knowledge that it results from a process of virtual collapse of manufacturing activity that used to be located in the South East, the interpretation might be different. While a balanced local economy will benefit from the continued presence of R&D, the sudden disappearance of tens of thousands of jobs in manufacturing activities will be difficult indeed to counteract.

The indications are, then, of an emergent spatial division of labour within UK engineering in which previously integrated production sites in the South East lose their manufacturing capability to other regions of the country, but retain their R&D. That means that the R&D base of the South East would not appear to be threatened even as it undergoes substantial restructuring of its own, and that the South East should continue to play a vital R&D role in the engineering industry's national spatial division of labour.

A LOCAL ECONOMIC DEVELOPMENT STRATEGY FOR A HEALTHY ENGINEERING INDUSTRY

The need for an industrial strategy

The engineering industry is a key part of the UK and the South East economies. However, at a time of major structural change throughout all sectors of engineering, the nature and scale of the industry's future contribution to the national and the regional economy is in question. The mid-1990s are likely to be critical for the UK engineering industry. The early 1990s were characterised by deep recession, retrenchment, and job losses. Employment decline is forecast to continue for the mid-1990s, in the context of intensified international competition. However, the 'crisis' in the industry at the start of the 1990s has stimulated new strategic thinking about the industrial policy context necessary for recovery and sustained growth.

The National Economic Development Council (NEDC, 1992) identified a number of strategic issues facing the industry (see Figure 6.7).

Central to the NEDC's analysis is a recognition that a high proportion of the industry depends, directly or indirectly, on three principal customer sectors: motor vehicles, aerospace/defence, and capital plant. The NEDC suggest that key elements of a strategy for the engineering industry should be constructed around these sectors. In particular, attention is drawn to the opportunities to meet the needs of a rejuvenated motor industry driven towards higher quality by the arrival of Japanese manufacturers in the UK. Benefiting from this opportunity will require higher quality standards and better strategic management in automotive supply firms. In the case of aerospace and defence, the NEDC identifies problems of surplus capacity, diversification, and re-deployment of capital, skills, and management resulting from falling defence budgets, more open markets, and intensified international competition and calls for more effective government action to assist the positive restructuring of this sector. In the capital plant sector, the NEDC identifies the privatisation of utilities and the impact of the SEM as major factors exposing UK firms to a more competitive environment.

Similar points have been made by the Engineering Employers' Federation (EEF, 1992). A recent policy statement places emphasis on education, training, and an orientation to the needs of the final consumer applied right through the supply chain. The EEF also argues strongly for a more strategic approach on the part of both the industry and government. Employers are urged to develop strategic thinking, to look for organic

Figure 6.7 Strategic issues facing the engineering industry

the development of more effective supply chain relationships

the need to address skills gaps

improving management competence and encouraging 'learning businesses' growth rather than acquisitions, and to review investment practices in order to remove any bias against longer-term projects. Meanwhile, government is urged to take both immediate and long-term action. Immediate priorities should include extended capital allowances for plant and machinery, encouragement of internationally mobile investment to locate and remain in the UK, and increased funding for the Training and Enterprise Councils (TECs). Longer term, the EEF calls for a stronger and more applied technology policy, the use of central and local government purchasing to stimulate strategic industries and businesses, infrastructure investment, export support, and greater regulation of prices in the telecommunications, energy, and transport industries with the interests of customers and suppliers in mind.

Trade unions have also called for a more active leadership role by government in uniting industrialists, the financial sector, and the trade unions to create a consensus to revive manufacturing. The MSF Union has called for a 'Manufacturing Forum' to shape such a consensus to revive the manufacturing base.

One important factor behind calls such as that of the EEF and MSF for improved government industry dialogue and a more explicit industrial strategy has been the increasing awareness of the alternative approaches to industrial policy pursued by some of the UK's major competitors within the European Union. Increasingly, UK industrial questions must now be situated within a European context.

The regional dimension of an industrial strategy

As indicated above, the nature and scale of the engineering industry's future contribution to the regional economy of South East England is in question. An increasingly powerful view has developed that supply-side policies, such as those influencing labour supply through training, are not by themselves sufficient to ensure a 'quality' future for the engineering industry.

The role of local and regional public agencies in economic and industrial development policies in the UK – and particularly in the South East – remains relatively underdeveloped compared with other parts of Europe. Nevertheless, local agencies do make a major contribution to the economic and social infrastructure, particularly in respect of those functions listed in Figure 6.8.

In recent years the framework for local policy has changed substantially, with TECs having a strategic role in local training and economic development policy, and many local authorities recognising the need to play an 'enabling' role in the local economy. However, there is a need for more active local and regional policy initiatives in relation to the engineering industry on a number of fronts (see Figure 6.9).

Many of the issues concerning technological innovation and *diversification* are most appropriately dealt with by firms themselves or by national

Figure 6.8 Key functions of local agencies

education and training

land, industrial policy, and the transport system

advice and assistance to businesses, especially smaller firms

Figure 6.9 Areas of potential for local and regional policy initiatives

technological change, product development, and diversification

industrial linkages and supply chains

inward investment

small firms

employment and training

land, planning, and the environment

transport infrastructure

or European initiatives. There is, however, an important role for more local initiatives to respond to problems experienced by companies in financing new development, research, and production; to help diffuse innovation within the local economy; and to promote positive adjustment within the local labour and property markets which meet the needs of firms and promote growth and employment in the local economy. In particular, local government, along with trade unions, TECs, and others, has been active in promoting positive local strategies for defence conversion. It may often be most productive to address defence diversification issues within a broad engineering industry perspective, promoting innovation within the local and regional economy, not just the firm.

With regard to industrial linkages and supply chains, it has been suggested that firms perceive the South East as a strong R&D location but less as a manufacturing location. Local and regional policies building on competitive advantage would seek to strengthen R&D linkages and infrastructure. Manufacturing supply chains may be developed more effectively around key firms rather than localities. Local networks of site and services suppliers should however be an important focus of specifically local action.

Inward investment policies will play to the region's strengths if they market the high skill, high technology, R&D base of the engineering industry, rather than the cost of labour or the strength in depth of 'manufacturing functions'. Such policies could be most effectively promoted by a single South East Development Agency.

Local and regional policies for small firms in the engineering sector need to be selective, identifying and supporting key categories of small firms which contribute to the strengths and dynamism of the regional economy and which can provide good quality employment.

In the training field, many different agencies currently play a partial role in the evolution of the engineering skills and training base. There is a need for a more overarching and strategic view of employment and training needs than exists at present. This might involve consideration of the establishment of 'centres of excellence' in key areas of engineering training; targeting engineering firms on a town-by-town basis with regard to training provision; and establishing an inter-agency working group on the employment of women in engineering, in order to promote equal opportunities and encourage optimal use of human resources.

With regard to land, planning, and environment, local and regional policies should seek to ensure the re-use of large sites vacated by firms to provide a spatial focus for the consolidation and rebuilding of the industry in the region, and promote the availability of modern flexible small business accommodation as part of targeted broader policy packages for smaller engineering firms. Achievement of these objectives would be aided by closer links between planning authorities, firms, and industrial property agents and developers.

Continued enhancement of the local and regional transport infrastructure, and more effective liaison over, and resourcing of, local public service provision in some areas, are important issues.

The South East Engineering Forum

The need for a co-ordinated policy initiative on the engineering industry in the South East has now been recognised by the establishment in early 1994 of the South East Engineering Forum (SEEF). The industry already has a range of policy forums locally, nationally, and Europe wide. But the specific value of SEEF is to bring together all the main stakeholders in the future of the industry (with the exception of government) at a regional level. SEEF membership is open to individual companies and industry associations, trade unions, TECs, local government, and other agencies concerned with the industry in the region. It already numbers among its members the Engineering Employers Federation, the MSF, the AEEU, seven Training and Enterprise Councils, and twelve local authorities.

SEEF has two main objectives: disseminating good practice and promoting the industry. Its aim is to work through and for its members and existing organisations, highlighting innovative schemes by TECs or local authorities; promoting exchange visits between big and small firms, and between local authorities, TECs and trade unions; disseminating information on EC policy and funding; and publicising school–industry links. It will interact with existing national and local networks to shape future policy for the region and lobby government, MPs and MEPs, and other agencies.

The willingness of a range of key interests to join SEEF is indicative of two things: the continuing importance of manufacturing to the UK economy, including that of the South East, and the recognition of the need for collaboration as well as competition between stakeholders in the industry. The question is whether initiatives such as SEEF are too little and too late to rescue an industry which sometimes seems headed for terminal decline, or are just in time to save the employment, skills, and prosperity which it has long provided.

NOTE

1 The research was undertaken by the authors with Andrew Mair (then at the Local Government Centre) and Chris Hasluck of the Institute for Employment Research. We acknowledge their contribution to the arguments advanced here, in particular by Chris Hasluck on industrial trends and forecasts, and Andrew Mair on company strategies and linkages. The research was sponsored by the SEEDS (South East Economic Development Strategy) association of local authorities and funded by SEEDS with other local authorities and TECs. The research report *The Engineering Industry in South East England* is obtainable from SEEDS, c/o Economic Development Unit, Harlow Council, Latton Bush Centre, Southern Way, Harlow, Essex CM18 7BL.

REFERENCES

Engineering Employers Federation (1992) *Industrial Strategy: Proposals for Recovery and Sustained Growth*, London: EEF.

Lipietz, A. (1986) 'New Tendencies in the International Division of Labour: Regimes of Accumulation and Modes of Regulation', in Scott, A.J. and Storper, R. (eds) *Production, Work, Territory*, Boston: Allen and Unwin.

Moulaert, F. and Demaziere, C. (1994) 'Local Development in Western Europe: A Survey'. Paper to conference on Cities, Enterprises and Society at the Eve of the XXIst century, Lille, CNRS/University of Lille.

National Economic Development Council (1992) *Engineering at the Crossroads*, London: NEDO.

Wilson, R.A. (1992) *Review of the Economy and Employment 1992*, University of Warwick: IER.

Wilson, R.A. (1994) *Review of the Economy and Employment 1994*, University of Warwick, IER.

7

THE TRANSFORMATION OF THE MOTOR INDUSTRY IN THE UK

Garel Rhys

There is a renaissance in the affairs of the car industry in Britain. Whether this will apply also to the UK components and commercial vehicle producers remains to be seen. The car industry is set for major expansion but the position facing the commercial vehicle sector is less certain, while the component industry still faces restructuring.

This transformation in the British motor industry has seen the ownership and control of large and small car makers, commercial vehicle firms, and most of the 100 largest component firms transferred abroad. New foreign investment – be it Japanese, US, European, or from elsewhere abroad – reinforces this. As a result the motor industry in the UK has become truly part of the global industry. So the rise and then decline of the British-owned motor industry is being followed by the emergence of a motor industry stronger and more efficient than anything that went before. However, we can no longer talk about a *British* motor industry but rather a motor industry in the UK. The purchase of Rover by BMW in 1994 virtually completed the process of the transfer of ownership abroad. How did the UK motor industry come to this state of affairs?

RISE AND DECLINE

In the pre-First World War years the British motor industry was slow to develop compared with the German, French, and especially the US industries. However, and as today where the Japanese are the mentors, the UK industry absorbed much of what was then world best practice and became a major force in the inter-war years. Of course protectionism abounded and, as elsewhere, high tariffs protected the industry against imports, especially those from the USA. What exports there were mainly went to markets where the UK had an advantage through imperial preference.

Although the first decade after the Second World War was one of excess demand for vehicles, until the early 1960s UK productivity was the equal of any in the European motor industry. However the seeds of decline were already there. The government's use of the motor industry to spearhead the post-war export drive did not go so far as to allocate sufficient foreign exchange to establish efficient overseas sales and service networks to look after the customers properly. In the plants, workforce militancy was bought off, rather than solved and countered, while a number of companies had weak product lines and insufficient sales to reach optimum size. Too many people have tried to find a single cause for the decline of the British motor industry. In fact, the industry was laid low by the unholy trinity of poor management and control, dreadful industrial relations, and harmful government policies. No other traditional centre of vehicle manufacturing faced such a combination of adverse factors in such quantity. Although some weaknesses in the structure of the UK industry were evident as early as the late 1930s, these need not have been serious if the industry had not faced the problems it did in the 1950s and 1960s. The creation of British Leyland in 1968 combined almost all the British-owned vehicle industry in one company. The decline of British Leyland became the effective end of the British owned motor industry. It might be argued that (Church, 1994: 124) government involvement in British Leyland in 1975 was too late to save it as a major force in the European motor industry. This need not have been so. If the injections of public money had been made conditional on demonstrable improvements in labour relations, and if the medium-class cars of the early 1980s had been 'winners', there was just time to put British Leyland on course.

Current position

Despite the huge upheaval in the structure of the UK motor industry it is still a major component of the UK economy. Directly and indirectly it accounts for about 4 per cent of UK gross domestic product, and remains a keystone of manufacturing industry in the UK.

Without car manufacture, much of the rest of UK industry would not exist in its present form. Although there were specialist makers in terms of output, the commercial vehicle industry largely grew from the car industry. The car and components industries grew up together.

Without a core of domestic car production, many component producers would not be able to continue making parts for the industry, as their turnover in this sector would be so small that their unit costs would be uncompetitive. Without UK sub-assembly and component manufacture, there would be no true manufacture of commercial vehicles, although some might be assembled here from imported parts.

Eight companies – Ford, Jaguar, Nissan, Peugeot Talbot, Rover, Vauxhall, Honda, and Toyota – currently account for some 99 per cent of total car production in the UK: that is, nearly all UK production is made by 'foreign' firms.

Most of the remaining car manufacturers tend to specialise in the high quality or high performance market segments, where the demand is too limited to justify volume production methods or, alternatively, where they are able to benefit from an established market. The outstanding example is, of course, Rolls Royce Motors Limited. Others include Lotus, taken over by General Motors in 1986, and then sold to Bugatti; Aston-Martin Lagonda which became part of Ford in 1987; TVR, based in Blackpool; and the family firm of Morgan, located in Malvern, Worcestershire.

Iveco Ford, Leyland, ERF, Foden (part of Paccar of America), Seddon Atkinson (owned by the Iveco Ford group), IBC (Isuzu Bedford Corporation) were the leading commercial vehicle makers in the early 1990s, accounting for almost all British production of these vehicles.

In the commercial field, small independent manufacturing companies also survive through specialisation. The British company ERF has concentrated on the heavy end of the market, and Dennis on fire engines and buses. While ERF accounted for less than 2 per cent of total commercial vehicle production, it produces almost 30 per cent of trucks over 20 tonnes gross vehicle weight. Dennis is the UK's leading bus manufacturer. In the van sector, Ford produces Transit vans in Southampton, and LDV continues to make medium and heavy vans in Birmingham. The Bedford commercial vehicle arm of Vauxhall entered a joint venture with the Japanese company Isuzu in 1986 to produce vans in Luton, Bedfordshire.

Rover Group continues to produce Land Rovers at Solihull in the Midlands. The Range Rover, made at Solihull since the early 1970s, was not launched in the USA until 1988 but has successfully established itself there. In 1994 Rover was bought by BMW. The German company recognised the transformation of Rover under Honda's guidance and saw it as a major commercial opportunity.

The car manufacturing sector is fairly homogeneous, but the component sector is characterised by a multiplicity of companies of different sizes and functions. Thousands of companies supply the motor vehicle manufacturers or other component makers, or specialise in producing replacement parts for the aftermarket. The car producers each take supplies of goods and services from between 1,000 and 5,000 small businesses. It is difficult even to arrive at a definition of the component sector as many companies supply identical materials to the motor industry and to other industry sectors, for example, steel, paints, and general engineering goods.

In addition, many companies do not consider the motor industry to be their main customer. In government statistics, the motor industry definition (Standard Industrial Classification 35) excludes the manufacture of tyres, electrical equipment, instruments, glass, and various other items. Indeed, the employment in the industry as officially defined, and as indicated below as 215,000 in 1993, understates total employment by around 65,000.

The major production inputs to any car assembly plant include:

- chassis and transmission parts
- engine parts and units
- electrical and electronic components
- steel
- presswork
- castings and forgings
- rubber tyres
- glass, paint, trim, and carpets
- plastics, injection-mouldings, and moulded-foam
- seat belts, mirrors, and other miscellaneous items.

The list of inputs for commercial vehicle production is similar but includes, for example, major sub-assemblies like cabs, engines, and gearboxes.

The three biggest companies in the component field are GKN (forgings, castings, pressings, chassis, body, and transmission parts), Lucas (braking systems, diesel engine parts, shock absorbers, filters, etc.), and T&N (Turner and Newall – producing brake linings, pistons, gaskets, and con-rods).

It is estimated that about 50 per cent of the output of the component sector goes to vehicle manufacturers, 30 per cent is exported directly, and 20 per cent is sold as replacement or aftermarket items.

PRODUCTION SITES

The traditional homes of the British motor industry have been the South East and the West Midlands, which respectively account for more than 40 per cent and 33 per cent of motor vehicle and component manufacture.

In the South East, Ford's main car plant is located in Dagenham, Essex and Vauxhall's is in Luton, Bedfordshire. Rover has major plants in Cowley, Oxford and in Longbridge, Birmingham. Vauxhall's IBC van plant is situated in Luton and nearby, at Dunstable, Renault Truck Industries assembled commercial vehicles until early 1993. Iveco Ford's truck operations are at Langley near London. Ford produces Transit vans at Southampton and Escort vans and cars at Halewood on Merseyside. Vauxhall also operates on Merseyside making cars and vans.

Production in the West Midlands comes from Rover with plants in Longbridge, Solihull, and Canley near Coventry, from Peugeot Talbot Carbodies, and Jaguar all in Coventry. Ford has a large parts distribution centre at Daventry, Northamptonshire.

Wales is fast becoming a major area of component making, particularly engine manufacture, into which Ford announced in 1988 one of its biggest single investments anywhere: a £500 million plant at Bridgend, mid-Glamorgan. This makes South Wales the main supplier of engines to Ford's

European plants. A Toyota engine plant was built in North Wales. The motor industry is now the largest single manufacturing sector in Wales employing 27,000 people in over 160 facilities.

In 1984, Nissan Motor Manufacturing of Japan selected Sunderland as a 'greenfield' site for car production, initially producing the Bluebird. In 1988 Nissan produced 55,000 cars. By the early 1990s, 100,000 cars a year had been reached and, with the introduction of a second model, the Micra, output should exceed 300,000 a year by 1996.

Toyota, another Japanese company, announced in April 1989 that it would set up a new car manufacturing plant at Burnaston, near Derby in the East Midlands, with initial production of the Carina starting in late 1992. Shortly afterwards, and as indicated, the company decided to build an engine plant at Shotton in North Wales to supply the Derby factory.

In July 1989 Honda, which had a long collaboration with Rover Group, announced expansion plans at Swindon, Wiltshire, which include the manufacture of 100,000 cars by the mid-1990s and an extra model for the Rover range. The company also started engine production in 1989 at Swindon. In 1994 it announced a further expansion to 150,000 cars a year.

The mergers which took place in the industry in the 1960s and 1970s, and also in more recent times, resulted in companies acquiring plants in widely dispersed locations. This was far from ideal for the rationalised production on which improved productivity in the industry depended.

The forced dispersal of plants owned by the same company had become more pronounced in the 1960s when the government would not allow companies to expand their capacity next to existing facilities. Instead, companies had to set up new plants in the development areas in order to increase employment in those regions. Thus a Ford plant was built at Halewood, when Ford was based at Dagenham, and a Vauxhall plant at Ellesmere Port, also on Merseyside, when Vauxhall's 'home' was at Luton. Rootes built a factory at Linwood, near Glasgow, while its base was near Coventry. That was closed in 1981. Leyland had a factory at Bathgate, near Glasgow which closed in 1985. The only vestige of motor manufacturing in Scotland in the mid-1990s is the Albion axle plant and a limited number of component firms.

The wide dispersal of any one company's activities has resulted in different plants being used for either production of specific components and sub-assemblies, or for the final assembly of the vehicles. Therefore it is difficult to identify with precision the contribution to final output by individual areas.

The major centres of the motor industry are still the West Midlands and South East. However, the North West (Merseyside) has become a major centre of car making, and Wales in component making. The Japanese have also established themselves in non-traditional areas, such as Derbyshire and the North East of England.

The success of the Japanese plants, and the emergence of Wales as a motor industry centre demonstrates that successful operations in non-traditional areas was possible. This required careful groundwork and planning, something not done in the 1960s. In fact it was not until the 1990s that the assembly plants left from those built in the 1960s began to operate fully efficiently.

EMPLOYMENT CHANGE

There has been dramatic contraction of employment in the vehicle and parts industry since the 1970s. From 505,000 in 1971, numbers fell to 361,000 in 1981, 222,000 in 1991, and to 215,000 in 1993. (More widely defined, the industry employs about 280,000 of which 50 per cent are in the component sector.) Since the mid-1980s, the ebb and flow of overall employment change has presented a more varied and hopeful picture. The many changes which have transformed the industry and helped to more than double productivity per person have made the remaining jobs more secure. Moreover, there are and continue to be significant new investments which are generating jobs. These developments are primarily focused on inward investment, but established companies are also playing major roles.

The fall in numbers employed and the increasingly varied roles they now play are the most vivid symbols of the deep restructuring that the UK industry has undergone. This restructuring must continue if the sector in the UK is to compete effectively and have a presence within Europe and throughout the world. This highly competitive world environment means that the main companies active in the UK vehicle sector clearly need to have European and international interests in siting, sourcing, and managing their operations. This will inevitably involve decisions which create or reduce jobs.

STRUCTURAL CHANGE

Evolutionary changes and developments in the quality of vehicles, the organisation of production, work processes and management are the main themes which have characterised the industry over the past decade. The production process has become more automated and the networks of suppliers to vehicle manufacturers have changed. Vehicles have become more sophisticated to match customers' aspirations. Increasingly sophisticated environmental and safety requirements have also been needed. The change and development continues. The co-ordination and harmonisation of the EC in the establishment of a Single European Market has also sharpened attention on the Europeanisation of national markets.

As a result of such demands, the days are gone when the UK vehicle sector could be viewed in national terms with car manufacturers and products being country specific. The production, sourcing, distribution, and marketing decisions of the industry are now firmly orientated to the European and world stage. Company structures and processes reflect this as they have become more complex. Few companies have the resources to tackle a multiplicity of markets on their own. Consequently, the need for co-operation in partnerships or joint ventures has changed the UK ownership and control structure. Viewed in this setting, the 'exporting of jobs' may be inappropriate to explain a complex set of circumstances. Automotive companies are seeking to balance a varied and complicated portfolio of interest.

To cope with tougher trading conditions, there is a need to react to the multifaceted demands of the market and to control costs. This has meant that the structure of, and processes used in, vehicle manufacturing have had to change. In essence, this new model emphasises the need to concentrate on core activities using an adaptable workforce. As a result, vehicle manufacturers concentrate much more on the final assembly of vehicles. More than ever components for this final activity are supplied from tiers of subcontractors.

This so-called 'lean production' system has meant rationalisation of all sources and modernisation of remaining facilities. Where companies have been able to build new plants on greenfield sites this has had positive advantages in introducing the new model and in establishing different working practices. Yet throughout the UK industry, the influence of such changes are clearly at work and some UK plants are approaching the best practices. Employees too have benefited from on-going training allied with the introduction of new technology and organisational changes associated with an emphasis on total quality. The relationships with networks of suppliers are vital so that the logistics of supply and emphasis on project management became key ingredients in this model. The technology embodied in the many components used in vehicles can be so complex that external sourcing needs to be spread throughout the world.

Production organised on these lines further emphasises the importance of a pan-European and world-wide scale of operations. Whether in terms of cost, quality, market presence, government assistance, or overall corporate development, some countries can offer the best business choice for development. This is not a straightforward import or export of UK jobs, it is more akin to a complex web of optimising international business operations. The UK industry's recent success in gaining such investments and the jobs it brings could equally be viewed as jobs lost to other potential host countries. This process will intensify as development takes place in Central and Eastern Europe.

THE ATTRACTIONS OF THE UK

The UK motor industry in particular, and the economy in general, is in an improved position to retain and attract foreign investment. There are a number of reasons for this:

- the UK actively welcomes foreign investment in the motor sector
- industrial relations have improved and the UK now has a low strike record
- total unit labour costs are comparatively low by European standards
- there is already considerable momentum in inward investment into the UK especially from Japan and the USA, but also from Europe, and the Japanese are strongly established in consumer electronics and in automotive manufacture
- the UK motor industry's recent record on productivity, performance, and quality has improved. It has developed some of the most cost-effective production sites in Europe and world-class automotive research, development, and design capacity.

The attraction of Japanese inward investment, and that from other countries in the automotive sector, was part of a general policy to attract investment to create and preserve jobs and generate exports and save imports. The government also saw this automotive investment as in some ways compensating for the decline in the size of British Leyland (Rover) and its influence on the UK economy.

There are, however, some qualifications to the attractions of the UK as a manufacturing base, notably that productivity, though improving, is still too low in many enterprises. This is especially so in the component sector. Moreover, other EC and European countries will respond effectively to the competitive challenge.

Automotive manufacture in the UK is becoming a varied, high quality and increasingly productive sector. In some instances, the industry is among the world leaders but the variations are too great and improvement still has to be made. The role of the foreign-owned or foreign-partner companies has been very important in this renaissance. It is anticipated that the UK will become a major production and exporting nation in the EC in the latter half of the 1990s producing over two million cars. This compares with the current record production of 1.90 million in 1972.

With its wide network of parts and component manufacturers, the sector needs an international outlook. Current organisation of the production process and the nature of its markets are geared to this end. To succeed in the global motor industry, motor manufacture in the UK must match world class efficiency. Initially this meant restructuring production by closing inefficient plants, and matching capacity to demand. Eventually the restructuring had to encompass improving work practices, management, systems, work organisation, and the quality of products. This process is incomplete.

CAPACITY RESTRUCTURING

In the period from 1978 to the mid-1980s, all the major UK car makers closed plants or reduced in scale. Most of the closures were undertaken by British Leyland (BL) as it abandoned its attempt to remain as a front line European mass producer and attacked the problem of low productivity. The latter was identified with plants of inefficient scale and configuration, and with archaic work practices allied to poor management. In 1978 British Leyland closed a car plant on Merseyside and postponed investment in its Bathgate truck plant. These were moves of great import. In the case of the car plant it was the first time that a major UK car company had closed a plant to reduce excess capacity. The truck plant decision demonstrated the willingness of the BL board to hold back investment where poor industrial relations meant no prospect of profitability.

In all BL closed twenty-five plants between 1978 and 1985. Other facilities were reduced in size and others re-organised to undertake new activities. In addition Peugeot, ERF, Atkinson, and Jensen closed plants, and Ford closed six major facilities (Rhys, 1992: 34). In the case of BL its workforce of 176,000 in 1977 was reduced to 82,000 by 1982. In 1994 the companies that had made up BL (Rover, Leyland, LDV, Jaguar, Alvis, etc.) employed no more than 50,000. This probably involved the loss of as many jobs again in the supplying industries. Ford, Vauxhall, and Peugeot shed 50,000 jobs in total between 1978 and 1992. However, increased efficiency in the UK motor industry resulted not only from job reductions but also from improvements in organisation and plant utilisation (Rhys, 1992).

UK EFFICIENCY: LONG TERM

Japanese firms such as Honda, Toyota, and Nissan are by many measures three of the most efficient firms in the world motor industry. Ford and GM are in the unique position of being the only non-Japanese firms with *major* shareholdings in Japanese firms. Although constraints exist this allows them unprecedented access to Japanese thinking, operations, and developments. This is borne out by the figures showing how the US industry has improved its efficiency over the last decade, and much more so than the West European motor industry (Table 7.1). The other company which has had similar access is Rover. Hence most of the firms that comprise the car industry in Britain are embracing Japanese, or world, best practice, ideas.

The Japanese presence in the UK will increase significantly by 2000. By then production could be over 800,000 million units (Table 7.2), contributing greatly to exports (Table 7.3). Production emanating from US, European, and Japanese-owned plants will be similar. Hence, the vehicle industry in Britain will consist of plants and companies wedded to minimising inputs of labour, capital, and time, while maximising outputs such as

Table 7.1 Productivity comparisons and changes

Hours needed to produce 'standard' vehicle in body and final assembly		
	1979	*1989*
Japan	25	18
USA	35	27
W. Europe	41	36*
UK Japan		19
US Europe		31

Source: Womack 1990; author's estimates.

Notes: 9 of the 18 hours difference with Japan was direct labour time on the final assembly tracks.

Table 7.2 The 'new' British producers

	1990 Output	*1995* Capacity	*2000* Capacity
Nissan	80,000	300,000	300,000+
Toyota	–	100,000	250,000+
Honda	26,000	100,000	200,000
IBC (GM)	–	40,000	80,000
	106,000	540,000	830,000

Table 7.3 Car export recovery in the UK

1989	339,006
1990	414,104
1991	605,076
Nissan	70% to be exported
Toyota & Honda	60% to be exported
IBC	85% to be exported
Year 2000. Total UK exports will be between 850,000 to 1,100,000 cars.	

quality and variety, as well as the vehicles themselves. This maximises economies of scale at the lowest possible absolute cost level, and is consistent with lean production.

EFFICIENCY IN EUROPE

Elsewhere in Europe the introduction of 'best practice' production features has been slower and less fulsome. In the case of France and Italy this has been due to a combination of factors. For instance: domestic production is dominated by national champions which have had very little direct contact with Japanese producers; no major Japanese investments have yet occurred in these countries; it was expected that the European Community would continue to limit Japanese imports severely, thereby reducing the incentive to improve efficiency; and there was a reliance on massive automation to replace labour by capital and thereby obtain 'Japanese' productivity levels by another route (for example, Fiat's Casino plant). The German industry had prided itself on its productivity and quality record, and at first was reluctant to admit that it had much to learn. Led by Ford and GM and followed by BMW, then VW, and finally Mercedes Benz, this is no longer the case. Even so, the German-owned companies are not finding it easy to come to terms with the precise requirements of lean production such as simultaneous operations, and team working.

The US multinationals in the UK, Germany, Spain, and Belgium are introducing lean production, albeit with individual and local variations on a theme. The German, Spanish, and Belgian plants had better physical productivity than some of those in the UK but not all, and the UK lower cost base often means that in terms of financial productivity UK plants top the list. Now the UK is closing the underlying productivity gap as well. The German producers, ever more fearful of their high cost base measured in Deutchmarks per hour, are eager to embrace methods which will eliminate this penalty. Clearly, then, the German industry will have some very lean firms by the end of the century. However, the internal structure of German firms and especially the key role given to the trade unions at supervisory board level could constrain the introduction of some of the required changes. In addition VW's massive investment in flexible high volume techniques will prevent the introduction of some of the benefits of a leaner system.

In the case of France and Italy the position is more problematic. The vehicle firms, apart from Renault Industrial Vehicles, are regional players. Up until recently they felt that their region would be protected from the full blast of Japanese competition. Hence the need to ape world best practice was less urgent. This is not now the case, but the vehicle firms involved were slow to introduce the changes required to obtain the benefits of lean production. On the other hand the French and Italian producers are starting from a higher productivity base than did the UK producers. For instance, in 1989, no traditional UK assembly plant took less than thirty-five hours to build a car; this was the European *average* for a volume assembly plant. Indeed, in France and Italy all the main plants operated in the range thirty to thirty-eight hours. So even if in 2000 the French and Italian makers do not achieve the degree of lean production existing in the UK, starting from a higher base their overall productivity may be similar.

In addition, the French and Italian firms face serious difficulties on the demand side of the equation. In terms of both their dependence on sales in their domestic markets (Table 7.4), and their dependence on protection from the Japanese in Western Europe (Table 7.5), the French and Italian firms tend to be the most vulnerable to increased competition.

IMPACT OF JAPAN

The Japanese companies so far have chosen the UK as the main location for their initial presence in Europe. As a result the competitiveness of the motor industry in Britain was greatly enhanced in the 1990s. Conversely, unless subsequent Japanese investments go elsewhere, the degree of learning from the demonstration effect of nearby Japanese plants will be unequal across Europe for vehicle firms and component producers alike. So whereas Holland and Spain have Japanese car plants, there is as yet little sign of such developments in Germany, France, and Italy. The balance of probability is that these countries will find it difficult to close the 'leanness gap' with the UK by 2000. Furthermore, despite attempts in the past, neither the French nor the Italians have significant joint ventures with the Japanese.

Table 7.4 Domestic market dependence 1990

Company	% total sales
Fiat Group	67
Renault	49
PSA	47
VAG	47
Ford Europe*	39 (UK)
GM Europe*	35
BMW	35
Mercedes Benz	48

Note: Assume 'domestic' market is their largest European market.

Table 7.5 Proportion of sales in markets most protected against the Japanese* (1990)

Company	%
Fiat Group	78
PSA	65
Renault	73
VAG	36
Ford	31
GM	22

Note: i.e., France, Italy and Spain..

This could change rapidly, and Renault may benefit indirectly from the Volvo-Mitsubishi venture in Holland. After all the GM-Toyota joint venture in the NUMMI plant was very important in changing attitudes in the USA. The Ford-Mazda links and those of Chrysler-Mitsubishi had a similar impact. The US firms in Europe, and Rover by its links with Honda, have benefited from this process. Interestingly, given the cost problems starting to affect car firms in Japan, the Japanese-owned firms abroad may be those setting the agenda for world best practice in future.

In short, the motor industry in Britain, with the two front rank US firms, three major Japanese players, plus Rover-BMW as one of the world's major specialist makers, could at the turn of the century be competing strongly with German-based manufacturers for the custom of the European car buyers. This was an unthinkable state of affairs in 1980. Indeed, Rover's utilised capacity by 2005 could be 1.25 million vehicles which together with BMW's 750,000 would give a world class operation of 2 million units a year. The French and Italians may find it very difficult to keep up. This could have serious implications for their major producers of components.

The renaissance of UK car making would have disappointing results if a major proportion of the value added was not sourced in the UK. The Japanese companies have all been ready to publish their plans for expenditure on components and materials in Europe. Toyota and Nissan talk in terms of £650 million to £700 million when production of 200,000 and 300,000 cars a year respectively is reached. Honda has stated a range of figures from £600–800 m, which seems to indicate that they too will produce 200,000 cars in the UK, together with a similar number of engines.

Initially components and materials were to be bought from 150 European suppliers in the case of Nissan, 136 in the case of Honda, and 167 in Toyota's case. Then, with the introduction of a second model, the Nissan total in 1992 became 190. The British suppliers are 127, 89, and 82 respectively. As neither Toyota nor Honda received public funds to help their UK investment, unlike Nissan which obtained £125 m, they do not feel under the same obligation to 'Buy-British' as Nissan. In the fullness of time the three Japanese firms may increase local (i.e., European) content from the planned 80 per cent to nearer 90 per cent, and additionally Toyota, like Nissan already, is likely to increase car and engine production beyond the present objective of 250,000. Furthermore, IBC will produce around 90,000 vans and car-type four wheel drive vehicles. Extra production should also come from the traditional UK players including some of the ultra specialists (see Table 7.6).

JAPANESE COMPONENT MAKERS IN EUROPE

In an open, fair, rigorous, and time consuming competition, UK-based firms have done well in obtaining initial orders from the Japanese. So far only a small number of these (for example, NSK Bearing) are Japanese firms manufacturing in the UK. The purchase of components from 'local' Japanese firms has provoked considerable outrage and controversy in the USA, not least because of the local content issue. It is likely that the US problem will not be duplicated in Europe:

- MITI has been dissuading component producers from following the vehicle firms to Europe.
- Toyota in particular is not keen that its start-up plants should be supplied by other start-up plants.
- Experience in the USA has not been encouraging for the Japanese parts suppliers. Loss making continues and is endemic.
- The volume of Japanese car production, although significant, is marginal to support supply factories. The volumes per car maker may not be viable for a stand alone supply facility.
- The Japanese car makers are reasonably impressed by the quality, technology, and competitiveness of the European component makers because of their specialist high volume structure. This is very different to their attitude to US component firms.

Although greenfield investments by Japanese component firms may be relatively limited, this does not mean that there will be an insignificant Japanese supply infrastructure. A three-handed approach can be expected:

1 outright purchase of European component firms
2 joint ventures
3 technology licensing.

It must be said that options (1) and (2) are likely to be more numerous than (3). In other words, there is still a threat to the European and UK component sectors as presently constituted if they prove incapable of meeting the needs of their customers when in volume production. So what is the likelihood of this?

THE STRUCTURE OF EUROPEAN COMPONENT MAKING

Unlike the vehicle producing sectors of the motor industry there is no single universally accepted figure for the size and structure of the component sector. Estimates range from 1,500 'major' and 10,000 'minor' component firms. The usual estimate is that there are around 3,250. Although it is generally accepted that Bosch, Valeo, and Magneti Marelli rank one, two, and three in Europe, the consistency and ranking of the top twenty is disturbingly variable. However, the UK is well represented with something like six suppliers (Lucas Automotive, GKN, Pilkington, BBA, T&N, and BTR) identified. This compares with eight German firms, one of which is a joint venture with the USA. In other words the 'British' part of the motor industry is in the component sector, six of which are of a size to be genuine world players. On the other hand Germany accounts for over 45 per cent of European component production which implies that most of the major companies in the second rank of the top forty are German. In a tiered system of component supply, this should mean that German firms should be very well placed to win contracts from the top tier. Equally, if the UK loses its top companies for whatever reason the chances of second and third tier work coming to the UK would be further diminished. Top, or first, tier status refers to component manufacturers who supply direct to vehicle manufacturers. Second tier firms supply to first tier firms. Third tier firms supply to second tier. Some companies, of course, straddle all three tiers. The current tendency towards domestic purchasing will be reduced with:

- vehicle producers' purchasing reorganised on a European basis
- 'open frontiers' after 1992 aiding international transport
- improved communications infrastructure.

The main beneficiaries are likely to be the top tier suppliers. They in turn will tend to buy from suppliers local to them. On the other hand, just-in-time (JIT) sometimes favours close proximity of component firms to vehicle plants. Of the fifty Japanese component plants in Europe in 1990, almost 40 per cent were in the UK. The main factors in securing this high proportion were: concentration of Japanese vehicle firms; low labour costs; English language; stable labour relations recently; and positive central and local government attitudes.

COMPETITIVENESS

As regards competitiveness, the European component industry as a whole lags well behind Japan in productivity and efficiency. While the technology level of the European industry seems adequate, compared with Japan it is well behind in the speed of product development. So while Europe is excellent in some product areas (for example, electronics) Japanese component makers achieve:

- higher quality
- higher labour productivity
- better stock turns
- better variety
- faster cycles in delivery, design, and development
- lower product cost.

A very large number of EC component suppliers say they are using just-in-time. However, when stock turns are compared with Japanese practice perhaps less than 5 per cent are actually using JIT. So as well as poorer performance, the European industry suffers from a degree of wishful thinking. Perhaps the most worrying elements in comparing Japan with Europe is that because of the extra speed of product development in Japan, Europe could find its future competitiveness undermined. This is a Europeanwide problem, but what of the position in the UK?

Labour productivity and stock turns in the UK are behind those in France and Germany and, while the rate of change in improvement in the UK during the last three years has narrowed the gap with the rest of Europe, it has not closed it. As to be expected, the performance is patchy with some sectors doing better than others (see below), but the UK average performance is behind France, Germany, and Spain. However, given the present choice of suppliers by Honda, Toyota, and Nissan, and the improvements experienced by the latter since 1989, there is no reason to believe that UK-based assemblers will transfer their orders en masse to the Continent. On the other hand, further Japanese involvement in the UK supply chain must be expected, as must further inward investment by European firms in the wake of the example set by Bosch. The issues of proximity and JIT will encourage UK-based supply, but not necessarily from UK-owned firms. Many of the latter need to increase efficiency (Cardiff Business School and Arthur Andersen, 1993).

The number of European direct suppliers will fall from the present 800 to 900 supplying Renault and Fiat respectively, or the 1,700 each supplying VW and Ford to closer to the 150 to 300 level. This does not necessarily imply a radical reduction in the number of independent component producers, as many could survive as second or third tier suppliers. In practice, however, restructuring will occur as the top tier firms will obviously favour some firms in relation to others. In effect, the survival of many second or third tier suppliers in the UK will depend upon the maximum number of UK-based firms obtaining first tier status.

The UK value of cars made in the UK by Honda, Toyota, and Nissan will be 65–70 per cent. This means that about 50 per cent of the bought-in components and materials will be sourced in the UK. The products made by Peugeot and GM have about 60–65 per cent UK value, with Ford and Rover achieving figures of 70–80 per cent. Hence the Japanese are offering considerable incremental business to the UK supply infrastructure. Already foreign investment is being attracted by the potential this offers, especially as it may provide an opportunity to enter the supply chain of Japanese-based plants.

On the commercial vehicle front, and apart from light and medium vans, the future for production in the UK is uncertain. The UK content of vehicles is likely to drop further as continental designs displace products of British origin from the assembly lines. The opportunities for the supply infrastructure here will be limited.

In order to prosper in the competitive markets of the 1990s the UK component makers must introduce lean mass production or other approaches to world best practice. This allows plant and equipment to manufacture large volumes consisting of a variety of products. The lean element is important as it requires less inputs:

- it can use half the human effort in manufacturing
- investment in tooling can be halved
- time and effort in design can be halved
- inventories and defects can be halved
- product variety is increased, and so on.

This is the nature of the competitive gap with Japan, and to close it action is needed on a broad front.

First and foremost, attitudes must be right in the sense that it must be accepted that there is a problem. Once such awareness exists there must be a will to overcome that problem. Consequent to this an education programme can be implemented to point the way ahead. This can address the problem of uncompetitive cost, quality, and product development. However, another set of problems stem from buyer–supplier relations. This requires a mutual interest by both parties to reform their relationship which needs initiatives such as the dissemination of information and the establishment of supplier 'clubs' by the vehicle makers.

The adoption of modern manufacturing processes to speed up development and introduce more flexibility into the system requires the training of workforce and management. The vehicle makers should look to assist their suppliers, while the suppliers might consider that a joint venture with a Japanese company would be appropriate.

The structure of the component industry is likely to change both because of the need for fewer direct suppliers per vehicle maker, and also because of the introduction of a more tiered system among the suppliers. In some instances the vehicle firms will lead the restructuring, but it is in the hands of the component firms to take their own initiatives here. The creation of centres of excellence to offer the vehicle firms a full service, as well as the creation of vertically related supplier groups would put the participants in a good position when this whole process gathers pace.

The vehicle makers are looking for the best suppliers in terms of quality, cost, delivery, and technology. In addition the suppliers must be able to give the vehicle firm operational support, and will be judged on the stability of their management and their technical development capabilities. A commitment to, and an ability to offer, constant improvements to products in terms of cost, quality, technology, and other factors, and to reduce lead times in prototype and regular production, will be demanded by the vehicle makers.

In short, to become and remain competitive a supplier must effectively adopt modern, flexible manufacturing, and new product development processes. Alongside this, the whole structure of the components manufacturing industry will have to change. Given that many companies in

Europe are supplying similar products, an inevitable rationalisation will ensue which will mean that there will be fewer direct suppliers to vehicle manufacturers. These remaining direct suppliers will have enhanced capabilities, and there will be significant changes in the vehicle maker–supplier relationship. This radical re-organisation will present challenges to which many UK-owned component firms will find difficult to respond successfully.

THE UK IN THE 1990s

The UK car producing sector is in the process of renewal and expansion. This involves the traditional players as well as the Japanese companies. The UK car makers will be among the most efficient producers in Europe by 2000. The Japanese owned firms will force the other UK firms to emulate their performance if they wish to survive in a consumers' market. The car markets in the UK in the 1990s, as in the rest of Europe, should reach record levels. To prosper in these markets firms must not be deflected from their longer-term strategies.

The UK supply chain must improve to hold its own against European competition, and Japanese component makers pose a significant threat. As the performance of Japanese companies in the UK illustrates, given the right attitudes, action, and equipment, UK-based companies can prosper in the most demanding and competitive of markets. This must also be so of the UK supply infrastructure. Despite the vagaries of the UK market, the recovery in UK vehicle production will produce a market for components and material which, in the early years of the next century, may be second only in Europe to that in Germany. If UK-based firms prove incapable of supplying this growing domestic market it is difficult to see them prospering elsewhere. The opportunity exists for the leading UK component firms to consolidate their position as, or to become, global players.

The annual car markets in the UK in the 1990s will still be strong and in some years reach figures in excess of 2 million. Indeed towards the end of the century car markets in the region of 2.5 to 2.7 million are not impossible. In Western Europe the car market in 1990 reached a record of 13.6 million and, while this fell to 12.8 million in 1991, the 1990s will see years when markets of 14 million and even 15 million can be achieved. However, if UK car production remained at its present level of about 1,400,000, albeit the best since the early 1970s, then the size of the UK market would result in continuing and large balance of payments deficits in motor industry trade. It is clear, however, that car production in the UK is set for major growth.

So what precisely is the present capacity of the car sector of the British motor industry? More importantly, what is the likely production capability of the industry in the late 1990s, given the present investment intentions of the car producers currently based in the UK (Table 7.6)? Finally, by comparing these potential capacity figures with the likely level of car demand in the 1990s, what is the implication for the balance of trade in cars in the late 1990s?

The most dramatic incremental capacity increase is provided by new inward investment by Honda, Nissan, and Toyota. By December 1993, Nissan's investment increased capacity to at least 300,000 units of which more than 60 per cent will be exported. Japanese production expertise will ensure further annual production increases.

By the end of the century Nissan should be making over 300,000 vehicles a year in the UK, and exports would then be between 200,000 and 250,000 units. Toyota will be making at least 100,000 cars a year in the UK by 1994 and 200,000 by 1997, of which two-thirds will be exported.

Honda's new car assembly plant at Swindon means the manufacture of 100,000 cars a year in 1995 and 150,000 by 1997. Again, over two-thirds will be exported. These will have 80 per cent European content by the end of 1994. These three Japanese 'greenfield' developments include engine manufacturing plants which will help to achieve relatively high UK-content figures, by value, for the cars made.

In 1972 the UK produced more than 1.9 million cars, a record that has never been equalled. Of these about 350,000 were kits which had not been near an assembly plant. So the assembly of 2.1 million cars in, say, 1997 would be a record well beyond previous achievements. Furthermore, development in the late 1990s could take production to 2.3 million which could remove, or at least reduce, the balance of payments deficit in motor industry products. In addition, an output of 2.3 million would restore the UK to a position among the major vehicle producers and offer exciting possibilities to UK-based component firms.

Table 7.6 Car making capacity in the UK with future predictions

Company	Capacity per year 1988–9	Output 1992	Estimated 1994	Capacity per year 2000
Rover	725,000	378,800	600,000	850,000
Ford	470,000	302,000	550,000	550,000
Vauxhall/IBC	260,000	319,000	330,000	420,000
Nissan	60,000	179,000	300,000	300,000
Toyota	–	–	100,000	250,000
Honda	–	1,000	75,000	200,000
Peugeot	115,000	86,000	120,000	120,000
Jaguar	60,000	20,600	60,000	120,000
Others	10,000	5,500	10,000	10,000
Total:	1,700,000	1,291,900	2,145,000	2,700,000

COMPONENT SUPPLIERS IN THE UK

Extensive rationalisation and modernisation programmes have been undertaken within the component industry, to some extent reflecting the changes which have taken place in vehicle manufacturing. In recent years, several British-based component producers have established production facilities in continental Europe to be near centres of vehicle design and development.

Many multinational vehicle manufacturers and other vehicle makers operating in countries without a significant component industry of their own, such as Sweden, buy parts from Britain which may then be incorporated in vehicles sold here.

Exports of UK-manufactured automotive parts and accessories accounted for £4.77 bn of the motor industry's total exports of £10.72 bn in 1991. The economic contribution of the components sector is, therefore, substantial. Many other British-designed components are, of course, produced under licence or by joint-venture projects around the globe.

Diversification has been the objective in recent years and has been practised extensively by the larger component manufacturing groups such as GKN, Lucas Industries, and T&N, which have moved into hi-tech electronics, aerospace, property, finance, and a host of other activities in order to spread their financial interests. However, the improved efficiency of the UK component industry is patchy and much remains to be done if world class is to be achieved.

PERFORMANCE AND PRACTICE: THE CHALLENGE

A study published in 1993 into the manufacturing performance and management practice of eighteen vehicle component plants highlighted the challenge ahead facing this industrial sector (Cardiff Business School and Arthur Anderson, 1993). Nine of these plants were in Japan and nine in the UK. The study measured performance in the key areas of quality and productivity, and examined the management practices which supported world class performance. The main findings were:

- Some plants (subsequently designated the 'world class plants') are simultaneously able to achieve outstanding levels of productivity and quality.
- All the world class plants in the study were Japanese but not all Japanese plants are world class. Some UK plants have either high quality or high productivity, but none have both.
- The world class plants show a 2:1 productivity differential and a superiority in quality of 100:1.
- This superior performance was achieved despite high product variety and a rapidly changing line-up of products.

- The world class plants were more automated than the others, and had higher production volumes, but together these factors are estimated to account for less than 20 per cent of the performance gap.
- The world class plants engage in only one-third of the amount of rework and carry one seventh of the amount of inventory compared to the other plants.
- The world class plants have much more active structures for shopfloor problem solving and improvement; production team leaders play a particularly significant role in these plants.
- The supply chains in which the world class plants are embedded differ markedly from those of the other plants.
- The world class plants only carry one-quarter of the stock of finished goods compared to the other plants. They serve customers who operate active clubs for their suppliers and the variability of their schedules from their customers is low.
- The world class plants keep 75 per cent less stock of incoming parts, run clubs for their suppliers, and receive far fewer defective items from their suppliers – a 50:1 differential with the other plants.

The UK economy has a unique opportunity to learn from 'lean producers' such as Toyota, Nissan, and Honda, who have chosen to locate manufacturing operations in the UK. They could help to bring UK suppliers up to world class levels. However, to do this companies must first be willing and committed to learn, and then act accordingly. Understanding the relative performance of an operation against tangible performance measures creates the imperative for change. Hence to maintain its improvement the UK component firms must:

- find out how far behind world class they are
- use the resulting data to commit the firm to closing the gap
- recognise the gap can only be closed by building the knowledge and skills of all staff, working together in teams and communicating
- analyse all key processes to eliminate activities that add no value to the customer
- organise the firm around process flows and not functional departments
- find out what customers really require and try to only build to customer order, not for stock
- create opportunities to learn from world class customers or joint venture partners
- encourage teams to benchmark their activities and create examples of best practice
- build shared destiny relationship with suppliers – through establishing supplier clubs.

In this way, UK component firms will not only exceed the efficiency of other European firms but close the productivity gap with what is world best practice. The renaissance in UK car production could then spread to the component sector where half the employment in the motor industry exists. It is clear that world best practice *can* be achieved by non-Japanese firms: some world best practice companies have been found to be French, Spanish, or US enterprises (Cardiff Business School and Arthur Andersen, 1994).

In the mid-1980s the automotive components industry was a sector of industry where very little was known about the number of suppliers, the size of the sector in turnover, employment, and value added. Since the trail blazing report by the House of Common's Select Committee on Trade and Industry into the UK motor component industry (House of Commons Trade and Industry Committee, 1987), myriad reports have been issued on the UK and European supply sector. Much is now known about the nature and structure of the industry, and what is needed to be done to make the sector secure by achieving world class performance.

Ten years ago, vehicle manufactures were re-sourcing components outside the UK because of a lack of confidence in the competence of the suppliers. By 1994, the reverse was true. A recent internal study conducted by one of Europe's largest vehicle suppliers indicated that the UK in the early and mid-1990s is the most cost efficient location for manufacture in the EC. There is much to be done, however, before the UK industry can claim to be competitive in world class terms.

Many of the policy concepts and strategy options discussed in reports and articles, and sometimes professed by purchasing executives in the vehicle manufacturers, have yet to become realities. Suppliers are still wary of their customers' rhetoric, while the vehicle manufacturers speak privately and publicly of dissatisfaction with their component suppliers' performance (DTI and SMMT, 1994: 6). Typically, the vehicle manufacturers claim that they are moving towards:

- long-term relationships with suppliers
- single sourcing
- JIT deliveries
- Total Quality Management in supply chains
- 'open-book' costing
- greater (and earlier) involvement for suppliers in product technology
- systems design
- fewer direct suppliers
- tiered structures in supply bases
- supplier development

Discussions with suppliers indicate that some of these techniques are either not happening or are being used in an adversarial, counter-productive manner. Indeed the trust needed for establishing such a close and open system is absent.

The emergence of 'lean production' in 1990 brought with it the realisation that the Japanese vehicle manufacturers were obtaining significant competitive advantage from new forms of management and organisation. The supply system required for lean production is 'lean supply'.

Lean supply brings together many of the concepts previously addressed in a piecemeal fashion: it represents a comprehensive strategy for component suppliers and their automotive customers. In the same way that lean production has galvanised the automotive assembly industry, so lean supply presents major challenges to the purchasing operations of the vehicle manufacturers and the strategists in component firms. If this can be fully implemented in the UK, and in Europe, then the component sector can reach world class performance and share in the growth of UK car production (DTI and SMMT, 1994).

THE POSITION OF THE UK

In relative terms the German motor industry dominates the European scene. It accounts for 46 per cent of the value of European vehicle production and is equally dominant in the component sector (Table 7.7).

Between 1988 and 1992 the increase in component production in the UK and Germany outweighed productivity increases thereby increasing employment. In the case of the UK this was by a factor of 10 per cent. This illustrates the impact of increased car production in the UK from under 900,000 cars in 1982 to 1.4 million in 1994, and also the attractiveness of the UK as a supply base for Europe. The improved record of productivity, quality and continuity of production meant that the UK had become an efficient supply location.

The UK had become a low unit cost centre of production as low input costs were combined with improved productivity. The improvement in input costs is shown by data on total labour costs per hour in Table 7.8. Table 7.9 indicates the improvement in the financial cost of car production

Table 7.7 Percentage of total West European car production

	Production	*Value added*	*Employment*
Germany	47	53	46
France	19	15	15
UK	12	11	16
Italy	11	9	11
Spain	7	8	8
Others	4	4	4

Source: Boston Consultancy Group, 1993.

Table 7.8 Total labour costs (DM per hour)

Country	1980	1993
Germany	26.9	44.5
Sweden	28.6	45.4
France	19.9	26.4
UK	14.9	26.6
Japan	14.8	33.9
USA	24.8	35.1
Spain	12.6	17.8
Belgium	28.1	17.8

Source: Verband der Automobilindustrie e. V. (VDA), Frankfurt, 1994.

Table 7.9 Unit cost of car (index)

	1984	1994
UK	148	90
Germany	100	100
France	110	96
Italy	122	92

Source: Author's estimates.

in the UK. In 1984, car production was 48 per cent more expensive in the UK than in Germany. By 1994, car production in the UK was 10 per cent cheaper than in Germany.

In the case of car making the unit cost of car making in the UK was among the lowest in Europe. In 1984 the position was very different as can be seen in Table 7.9.

In the period 1984 to 1994 annual productivity in the UK motor industry rose by 9.1 per cent a year, France 5.8 per cent, Spain 5.7 per cent, Japan 4.8 per cent, Italy 3.8 per cent, USA 3.3 per cent, and Germany 1.9 per cent. The culmination of this over a decade has transformed the economics of car making in the UK. Consequently not only Nissan and Toyota have a cost advantage but also Rover, Vauxhall, and Ford. In the case of the Japanese companies the UK efficiency duplicates world best practice and this is a spur to the other UK-based producers to emulate this. In short, UK car making is using a world and not a European standard of excellence.

As the main growth of vehicle production in Western Europe is likely to be in the UK, the UK component sector has a major growth opportunity. This is why it is important for the industry to achieve world best standards.

165

Table 7.10 Component purchase (Ecu billion 1992)

	1992	1999 (Forecast)
Germany	39.4	35.5
France	15.9	16.8
UK	11.2	17.7
Italy	9.4	10.9
Spain	8.2	9.5
Others	4.7	6.1
TOTAL	88.8	96.4

Source: Boston Consultancy Group, 1993.

On average Japanese-based car firms have a basic productivity advantage over their European rivals of 30 per cent. However in 1993/4 this was eroded by exchange rate variations. In the case of components, on average the Japanese had a 250 per cent advantage although in some instances the gap was much less, perhaps as 'low' as 20–35 per cent. This meant that the 1993/4 exchange rate changes encouraged Japanese car firms to increase their local European sourcing where the productivity differences were less marked. To insure long-term competitiveness the European and UK component sector skill must increase productivity. If this is achieved UK firms will benefit from the growth in component purchase in the UK and increase sales abroad.

The UK component sector consists of about 2,500 firms. Of these around 250 are large firms, with the rest being small and medium enterprises. In the main the large firms will be the top tier suppliers with the others being second and third tier. In the UK and Europe the firms failing to address the need to perform at world class levels in the main come from the lower tiers. This is a European-wide problem, and at least the issue is recognised in the UK. The need for continuous improvement and attention to detail becomes relevant after the UK industry has reduced the immense gap in performance between itself and the world's best. If the latter is not secured, then to achieve world class the large UK component firms will source *their* supplies elsewhere, and the benefits of the impact of the growth in UK car production will be constrained.

CONCLUSION

The decline of the UK motor industry between 1975 and 1985 was costly to many parts of the economy. The knock-on effects to other parts of the economy of reduced vehicle production was considerable. One job lost in the motor industry meant one job lost in the rest of the economy. In addition a combination of decreased exports and increased imports meant a huge balance of payments deficit on motor industry trade. In 1989 this reached £6.5 bn, or 35 per cent of the deficit on all manufactured goods (Rhys, 1990). The taxpayer had to make a huge contribution to the rescue and restructuring of firms like British Leyland and Chrysler UK, as well as supplying investment funds to growth projects. An idea of the sums involved is given by the state expenditure on British Leyland alone between 1975 and 1988 of £3,450 million. However, from the early 1980s this industrial decline turned into a recovery. In 1982 car production was 888,000, while in 1994 a figure of almost 1.4 million was reached. Employment in car production has stabilised and increased marginally. A combination of inward investment by new entrants, and improved performance by existing producers, has transformed the prospects of the UK car. From being in terminal decline it has emerged as Europe's lowest cost producer.

Although the outlook for car production is promising, the component sector still needs to complete its transformation. In addition, the commercial vehicle sector faces dire problems, mainly because the industry has become marginalised in the European market. Apart from Ford, which through its van production accounts for over 60 per cent of UK commercial vehicle output (DTI and SMMT, 1994), the industry has no major European players. Most plants are owned by foreign firms, although specialists like ERF and Dennis have strong positions in niche markets. Heavy commercial vehicles and buses are highly complex and expensive pieces of capital equipment, and are a good measure of a country's manufacturing ingenuity and knowledge. If the UK becomes totally excluded from this market, it will not only have dire consequences for the balance of payments but will be a sad reflection on its wider, underlying, manufacturing capability.

During the last twenty years there has been a major restructuring of the motor industry in Britain. The UK no longer has a 'national champion' car maker contesting supremacy in the European car market. Instead, we have an industry consisting of car companies where ownership and control exists elsewhere. However, this has created an industry consisting of the world's major and most efficient car companies. The UK is a major base for their operations, and the motor industry in Britain is in the throes of major growth and expansion. The car industry has seen a major transformation from old to new, with the emergence of internationally competitive facilities quite unlike the moribund industry of old.

At the same time the UK component sector, just like the position in Europe as a whole, is still in the throes of change. It remains to be seen whether the sector can put in place the structure, organisation, and activities that will allow it to become world class and to benefit from the renaissance of UK car production and the transformation of the UK into a good 'home' for the manufacture of motor industry products.

A large question mark also hovers over the commercial vehicle sector.

Ford remains a major manufacturer of light and medium vans, but the UK plants of mainly foreign-owned companies look vulnerable. The re-emergence of Leyland as a separate UK-owned company, and the ability of LDV and ERF to successfully operate as an assembler of bought-in products, may give some hope that the UK can retain an interest in this part of the motor industry.

The success on the car side, but the problems in the component and commercial vehicle sectors, means that the UK motor industry as a whole has only partly transformed itself. There is growing confidence that the UK economy will survive as a major car maker, but what the British content of these vehicles will be in 20 years remains to be seen. The commercial vehicle sector may find survival more difficult except in a smaller and more truncated form.

REFERENCES

Boston Consultancy Group (1993) *The Evolving Competitive Challenge for the European Automotive Components Industry*, CEC, Bruxelles.

Cardiff Business School and Arthur Andersen Consulting (1993) *The Lean Enterprise Benchmark Profile*, London: Andersen Consulting.

Cardiff Business School and Arthur Andersen Consultancy (1994) *Worldwide Comparative Study on Manufacturing Competitiveness*, London: Andersen Consulting.

Church, R. (1994) *The Rise and Decline of the British Motor Industry*, London: Macmillan.

DTI and SMMT (1994) *A Review of the Relationship Between Vehicle Manufacturers and Suppliers*, London: DTI.

House of Commons Trade and Industry Committee (1987) *The UK Motor Component Industry*, London: HMSO.

Rhys, D.G. (1990) 'The Motor Industry and the Balance of Payments', *The Royal Bank of Scotland Review* 168, 11–27.

Rhys, D.G. (1992) *The Challenge of the External Environment: Car Industry Case Study*, Milton Keynes: Open University Press.

Verband der Automobilindustrie e. V. (VDA) (1994) Auto '93/94 Annual Report. VDA, Frankfurt.

Womack, J.P. (1990) *The Machine That Changed the World*, New York: Rawson Associates.

8

SYMBOLISM AND SUBSTANCE IN THE MODERNISATION OF A TRADITIONAL INDUSTRIAL ECONOMY

The case of Wearside

Ian Stone

'Well in *our* country', said Alice, still panting a little, 'You'd generally get somewhere else – if you ran very fast for a long time as we've been doing'.

'A slow sort of country!' said the Queen. 'Now, *here*, you see, it takes all the running *you* can do, to stay in the same place. If you want to get somewhere else, you must run at least twice as fast as that!'

Lewis Carroll, *Through the Looking Glass*

INTRODUCTION

Within the last five years, Wearside has seen the closure both of its last remaining shipyard and coal mine. The industries which were the staples of the Wearside economy since the last century have now gone. These decisive events are in one sense merely the culmination of a process of contraction affecting so-called 'sunset' industries over several decades; yet the *fact* of their disappearance, and the government's reluctance to act to save them, shocked and angered many in the area. In fact, to the government, the final disappearance of these industries is important symbolically. Tory governments since 1979 have re-cast the objectives and mechanisms of economic management, as they relate both to the national and regional economies. State support for industries which are uncompetitive has been withdrawn; supply-side policies have been introduced to support private enterprise and to increase the UK's attractiveness as a location for international production. Shipyards and coal mines – large subsidised state-owned plants, overmanned, with too-powerful unions and outdated labour practices – were regarded as synonymous with past policies and failure. In contrast, the emerging new industry based around Nissan's greenfield car assembly plant, was seen as offering a basis not just for

169

economic but cultural and political transformation within this old industrial area.

Reputedly the largest single Japanese investment in Europe, the new plant has been established by a company which is a renowned exponent of new manufacturing and personnel practices. Its decision to locate in Wearside – and the subsequent success of the factory operationally – has been exploited by those promoting the North East as testimony to the changed attitudes of labour in the region, particularly its willingness to embrace flexible work practices and new union roles. The availability of labour resulting from the massive 'shake-out' during the early 1980s, combined with the much-publicised adaptability of workers, has helped local development agencies to attract to the North East a relatively large share of the total investment into the UK from overseas. This has had an important impact in terms of diversifying and modernising the manufacturing base of the region, while also providing replacement jobs for those lost during the recession of the early 1980s (Peck and Stone, 1992). The region's success in relation to inward investment has given rise to the notion of a *new* North East – signifying a region that has thrown off the shackles and outlook of its smokestack past.

What, though, is the substance behind the claims of transformation? Specifically, what is the balance between decline of older industries and the emergence of new ones, both in relation to employment and the achievement of a modernised economy? The physical signs of renewal are everywhere to be seen and development agencies constantly stress positive achievements, but these are hardly reliable indicators of the true extent of economic conversion. Indeed, there is a body of opinion which questions the extent and significance of change in the recent period. Some writers have raised doubts about the scale of employment generation and the unevenness with which the benefits of growth have been distributed (e.g., Hudson, 1991; Robinson and Shaw, 1991). Others have disputed the dynamism imparted to the local production system by the developments of the 1980s (e.g., Garrahan and Stewart, 1992; Sadler, 1992; Amin and Tomaney, 1993). This chapter examines these issues through detailed analysis of the restructuring process in an old industrial district over two decades, and its outcomes in terms of employment and growth potential. It offers a unique insight into the components of change affecting industry, through drawing upon the author's industrial establishment data bases for Wearside (covering 1973 to 1990) and Northern Region foreign-owned companies (1972 to 1993). Additional material has been derived from interviews with managers of small firms and inward investors connected with research into Wearside, together with data drawn from the employment Department's Annual Census of Employment (ACE) and the Population Census.

The chapter begins by outlining the characteristics of the economy before deindustrialisation took hold, followed by a review of the business and policy environment relating to Wearside as it has evolved over the period. Within this framework, it examines the restructuring process in relation to the main sectors of the local economy, focusing particularly on its traditional core activity, manufacturing. This allows an assessment of the character and impact of deindustrialisation, and the relative achievements of efforts at reindustrialisation. The impact of restructuring in terms of size, sector, ownership, and location are outlined, followed by a section showing the link between the restructuring process and the Wearside labour market and the ways in which it has adjusted to massive change. Finally, recognising that the process of economic renewal is still underway, an analysis of the better-performing sectors is undertaken with a view to determining the extent to which the modernisation process has succeeded in establishing a basis for continued growth and employment generation.

ECONOMIC AND POLICY CONTEXT

Background

Wearside is part of the metropolitan area of Tyne and Wear in North East England. It is synonymous with the area of Sunderland Borough – elevated in 1992 to City status – diversely made up of the older urban settlement of Sunderland itself (population 191,000), the more recently established Washington New Town (60,000), and the mainly rural former coalfield zone to the south consisting of Hetton-le-Hole and Houghton-le-Spring (population 45,000) (see Figure 8.1: Map). Although the local authority area is officially Sunderland, the term 'Wearside' will be used throughout, with 'Sunderland' used when referring to the old urban core itself.

The core of the old Borough, the industrial urban centre of Sunderland, developed originally on the basis of a coalfield port shipping coal to the Thames Estuary. The nineteenth century saw the emergence of a range of industries linked initially to the production, shipment, or use of coal, principally shipbuilding, heavy engineering, and glass manufacture. The overspecialisation of the economy gave rise to severe local problems in the interwar period, and attempts at diversification date from that period. Development Area status, for purposes of qualifying for regional aid, helped the old Borough capture a share of the substantial amount of mobile investment from the 1950s to the early 1970s. New generation industries had largely grown up in the West Midlands and the South East, but major companies in these industries responded to regional capital grants, infrastructural investments, and the availability of a pool of labour released from contracting traditional industries by setting up branch factories in the area. The earlier branch plant investments located on the trading estates created in Wearside's older industrial zones; subsequently the focus for such

Figure 8.1 Map of Wearside showing location of significant investments and disinvestments

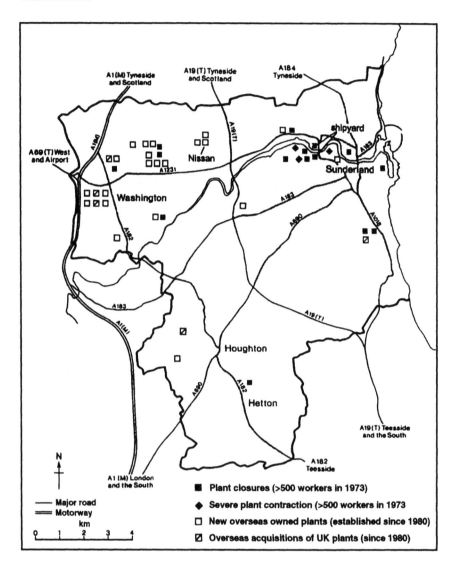

investment shifted outwards to the industrial estates developed on the edges of the urban area, and, from the late 1960s, to those being developed in and around Washington New Town. Diversifying investments also began to take place in new industrial estates in the coalfield area of Wearside – something which had long been discouraged by the National Coal Board in an effort to prevent competition for local male labour (Hudson, quoted in Massey, 1984).

The basic sectoral pattern – a substantial remnant of traditional industry alongside an implanted branch plant sector – characterised all the UK peripheral coalfield areas in the early 1970s. Wearside's industrial economy was thus representative of the North East in general although, with nearly 50 per cent of the workforce engaged in manufacturing and mining, the degree of dependence on industry was greater (by some eight percentage points) than in the region as a whole. This was the period when the old heavy industries and the new light engineering branch activities were alike organised predominantly in large production units belonging to companies with headquarters elsewhere in the UK. The establishment of branch plants by non-local companies combined with company takeover and merger activity to increase external control over the post-war period. In 1973 over 80 per cent of manufacturing employees worked in externally owned establishments. In spite of the spatial dispersal of new manufacturing investment the (then) town of Sunderland still had an overwhelmingly dominant share of the Borough's manufacturing employment.

The new industries were also significant in that they opened up employment opportunities for women in an economy where the traditional heavy industries had relied overwhelmingly upon male labour. Women increasingly entered the labour market in this period, both through the semi-skilled assembly line employment provided by branch factories and the gradual expansion of service sector employment – including the growing public sector. The latter activities were also initially very much centred upon Sunderland itself, and limited in extent and type by the overshadowing effect of nearby Newcastle. In the early 1970s, for example, the share of service sector employment in Wearside was several percentage points below the average for the region (and almost nine below the UK figure).

Policy framework

Industrial restructuring of any urban centre is a reflection of interactions between external forces and local conditions. Government policies, at different spatial scales, have interacted with the business and technological environment to create the context in which industrial change has occurred. Prominent among these external factors since the early 1970s are internationalisation of business, technological change, the growing emphasis on flexibility within production, and the enhanced competition to which UK manufacturers have been exposed by the increasing openness of the economy (exacerbated by shocks such as oil price hikes and periodic overvaluation of the currency).

Government policy for most of the 1960s and 1970s was interventionist (utilising, for instance, planning, wage fixing, incomes policies, and nationalisation) and the deployment of Keynesian demand management to maintain employment levels was prominent. Since the late 1970s, there has been a radical shift in the role played by the state in relation to the economy, including a move towards using monetary rather than fiscal control mechanisms and targeting inflation rather than employment. Within this framework, measures to improve the supply-side of the economy and to ensure market determination of economic outcomes have been dominant (Stone, 1994a). Thus, the 1980s were marked by attempts to make the labour market more responsive to price signals (including legislation to restrict union power), increased support for innovation and small businesses, and privatisation of state enterprises coupled with an unwillingness to support loss-making activities. Government has resisted arguments that it should be more interventionist in relation to industry; indeed, in the 1980s it showed scant concern for the needs of manufacturers where these conflicted with other priorities, particularly control of inflation. Regional policy underwent radical revisions during the 1980s: subsidies and coverage have been reduced sharply; aid has been made more discretionary with employment a key criteria; and greater emphasis than previously has been placed on service industries and the development of indigenous potential. In relation to industrial regeneration, much reliance – nationally and regionally – has been placed upon attracting inward investment. Central government's resistance of EC attempts to establish common policies on employment has meshed with its labour market reforms to make the UK the prime European location for foreign capital in the 1980s (Thomsen and Woolcock, 1993).

Within the confines of this external environment, changes in Wearside have been conditioned by local factors. The extent and pattern of rationalisation affecting the stock of establishments existing in the early 1970s has reflected characteristics such as ownership, age of plant, on-site functions, labour relations, products, and markets. The process of industrial renewal, whether through modernisation of existing plants, incoming greenfield investments, or new start-ups, is similarly influenced by Wearside's industrial past and its experience of restructuring. Deindustrialisation and reindustrialisation are not discrete processes, but ones which are linked in a complex way. Earlier waves of investment in Wearside combined to give rise to particular forms of social and economic structure, which in turn have conditioned the nature of subsequent waves. In the manner described by Massey (1984), the emerging character of Wearside's manufacturing sector, particularly the investments since the mid-1980s, cannot be understood without reference to the specific history of the locality in terms of its industrial structure and related labour market characteristics (see also Hudson, 1988). These are important in determining the role the area plays in the broader spatial division of labour, not just in relation to industry but also, increasingly, to 'footloose' tertiary activity.

In Wearside, as elsewhere, the yawning gap which opened between the rate of job loss and that of job creation in the late 1970s and early 1980s, prompted the development of an increasingly elaborate set of agencies and initiatives designed to foster local economic regeneration. These efforts have focused on the achievement of growth through *exogenous* sources (e.g., inward investment) together with the development of a range of support measures for the *indigenous* sector, previously the Cinderella of development policy. This attempt has been developed principally through a strategy for reindustrialisation. A pool of unemployed skilled manufacturing workers swollen by the collapse of large sections of industry, together with an established supplier base, available industrial sites, and good communications to Europe for exporters, suggested a strategy of reindustrialisation rather than one founded upon service-related activities. Local policy makers accordingly seized upon inward investment successes in the 1980s to promote Wearside as 'the region's advanced manufacturing centre', exhorting investors to 'Make it in Wearside'. Increasing availability of resources for site redevelopment and environmental improvement of industrial wasteland allowed the reindustrialisation strategy to be supplemented by attempts to generate jobs through the development of tourism, offices, and business services, all of which were relatively underdeveloped in Wearside as a result of its past industrial specialisation and the proximity of Newcastle, the regional capital.

Attracting inward investment to the region has primarily been the responsibility of the Northern Development Company (NDC); the local council, through its Economic Development Office, works with local agencies like the Tyne and Wear Economic Development Company and Tyne and Wear Development Corporation (TWDC) to develop appropriate sites and conditions in Wearside, and to market to prospective investors the area's locational advantages. To assist recovery from the shipyard closure, The Wearside Opportunity (TWO) was formed as a joint public/private sector initiative to market the area as a centre for advanced manufacturing and to coordinate the provision of sites for incoming industry. Sunderland's designation as a Development Area makes it eligible for maximum levels of government regional policy assistance. Like the rest of the conurbation it qualifies for Regional Selective Assistance, which offers grants on fixed asset costs of up to 30 per cent to manufacturing and to service activities which trade in non-local markets, depending upon the amount of employment created or safeguarded. Part of Wearside is also designated an enterprise zone. Established in the wake of the shipyard closure, it applies to sites along the banks of the Wear in Sunderland, and to part of the outlying Doxford International Park, recently developed alongside the A19 arterial roadway. The zone, the currency of which extends to the year 2000, offers 100 per cent capital allowances on buildings, exemption from local taxes, and a simplified planning regime to companies locating within its boundaries.

These initiatives, ultimately funded largely through central government and the EC, offer significant levels of subsidy on private investments in capital equipment, property and human capital formation as well as operating to renew and develop local social overhead capital, especially communications. They aim to divert investment projects into the various target areas, and to impart a competitive advantage to existing or expanding local establishments. The *scale* of the effort is important, since achieving a momentum of change is an important underpinning to promotional activity. At a very local level, the intensity of effort will only be applied for so long, however. The flood of redundancies in the 1980s, culminating in the closure of the shipyards, focused attention on Wearside and precipitated the build-up of regeneration structures. Most of the initiatives, including the enterprise zone are time limited – for example, TWO has already ceased to operate, TWDC has only a few years to run – and it is only a matter of time before the focus of effort in local conversion activity is redirected elsewhere.

Indigenous development is fostered through a plethora of initiatives introduced in the 1980s supporting independent and small businesses. Regional policy instruments now include grants supporting investment and innovation-related spending by firms with fewer than twenty-five employees (Regional Enterprise Grants); and provide up to two-thirds of the cost of business consultants for small and medium independent firms (the Enterprise Initiative). Local authorities have a more central role in relation to developing local business, although here too the tendency has been for them to work in partnership, both with development agencies and the private sector. Sunderland council has offered a variety of loans and grants to local businesses since the early 1980s. Currently these include rent relief grants, interest relief grants on capital investment loans, relocation and exhibition grants. It has also been active (since 1975) in the provision of nursery and workshop units, and in operating numerous small business advice schemes. It is assisted in this by access to EC programmes, including IDOP, RENAVAL, and RECHAR, which support the conversion of older industrial regions. The TWDC offers financial assistance ('Business Boost') to help firms offset start-up and property costs; the Wearside TEC provides grant payments to unemployed people starting a business, and skills training grants for people new to business; Entrust offers advice and low cost loans to small and new firms; British Coal Enterprise Ltd advances low cost loans for new or expanding businesses locating in this coalfield area, while also co-operating jointly with the DTI and European Community in 'Recharge North East', an initiative to provide management and marketing expertise to manufacturers and firms providing services to manufacturers. Central government, through such initiatives as the Loan Guarantee Scheme (designed to encourage bank lending to small businesses), is also part of this extensive support framework.

The initiatives are designed to overcome barriers restricting enterprise, through reducing the costs of start-up and expansion, and assist businesses to expand or develop in other ways through subsidising inputs of specialist knowledge. The provision of subsidies and information should have the effect, at the margin, of overcoming individuals' reluctance to set up or expand a business. The effectiveness of all this support activity is difficult to gauge; there are many who question the quality and appropriateness of available assistance. What cannot be doubted is the *extent* of the effort to generate new and growing businesses; it would be hard to find another sub-regional economy with a more elaborate and pervasive structure of regeneration initiatives.

ECONOMIC RESTRUCTURING SINCE THE EARLY 1970S

This section examines the structural changes which the Wearside economy has undergone since the early 1970s, analysing the processes underlying the change in each of the major sectors of the economy. Table 8.1, which relates to numbers in employment in Wearside, shows the huge structural

Table 8.1 Changing employment structure in Wearside, selected years (percentage of total for respective years)

SIC div/sector	1973	1981	1991
0 Agriculture and fishing	219	125	200
	(0.2)	(0.1)	(0.2)
1 Mining and utilities	10,965	5,807	2,767
	(9.8)	(6.0)	(2.8)
2–4 Manufacturing	42,231	25,447	25,064
	(37.7)	(26.5)	(25.5)
5 Construction	7,975	4,563	5,148
	(7.1)	(4.7)	(5.2)
6–9 Services	50,593	60,124	64,905
	(45.2)	(62.5)	(66.2)
Total employees	111,983	96,191	98,084

shift occurring between 1973 and 1991. Leaving aside agriculture and fishing, which are tiny, the main sectors have changed markedly. In particular, the production sectors (manufacturing, mining, and utilities) have contracted dramatically in absolute and relative terms, while the significant increase in service employment has not been sufficient to outweigh employment contraction in the former staple industries.

Manufacturing

Overall change

Deindustrialisation, whereby an economy experiences an absolute and proportional decline in industrial employment (Caslin, 1987), is central to any analysis of the process of industrial change affecting urban areas since 1970. As far as manufacturing itself is concerned (i.e., leaving aside contraction in the coal industry), the phenomenon has only been of significance in this region since the early 1970s, even though UK manufacturing employment began to contract after 1966. The redistribution – through regional policy inducements and controls – of the new jobs generated within the country favoured assisted areas like the North East, allowing the region to more or less hold its employment level up to the early 1970s, in spite of the contraction in traditional manufacturing (Northern Region Strategy Team, 1977). The period of the 1970s and first half of the 1980s was marked by an adverse structural shift in the balance of employment turnover resulting from a combination of enhanced levels of contraction and closure and a dramatic fall in the number of mobile industrial investment projects. It is thus only since the early 1970s that job generation via the attraction and development of industry has implied an attempt at *re*industrialisation, in the sense of *reversing* the proportional and absolute decline in manufacturing employment. Prior to that, regional policy operated to ensure an inflow of investment – mainly new branch plants, supplemented by government office relocation – which would maintain a flow of new job opportunities to replace those in dying staples.

In overall terms, manufacturing employment in Wearside declined dramatically over the period 1973 to 1990, falling by 43 per cent from 43,150 to 24,580 (author's Wearside industrial database). This fall is less marked than that affecting the rest of Tyne and Wear (down by 55 per cent), but above that for the UK (down by one-third). The largest losses occurred during the recession of the early 1980s, when 11,000 manufacturing jobs (equivalent to 30 per cent of the total) disappeared between 1979 and 1983 alone. Manufacturing employment's slow recovery from its 1986 low of just below 24,000 jobs was interrupted in the late 1980s by the closure of the remaining shipyards. Largely because of this labour market shock, there was virtually no improvement in the level of employment in manufacturing during the boom of the late 1980s, and Wearside's factories actually employed *fewer* people in 1990 than they had in 1983. The new jobs being created by inward investment and small firms were outweighed by those being lost in the older plants, even at a time when, notwithstanding closure of the shipyards, the overall pace of deindustrialisation had slackened markedly. In net terms, therefore, forces for industrial contraction were such that, even in the boom period of the 1980s, reindustrialisation was not taking place.

Using components of change analysis it is possible to identify more precisely the respective contributions of job loss and job generation to the net reduction of manufacturing employment (for details see, Stone, 1994b). Closures played a particularly prominent part in the restructuring: of the 1973 stock of 329 establishments, over half (178) had closed by 1987, resulting in the loss of 19,250 jobs. Further employment loss, amounting to 6,600 jobs, resulted from net *in situ* change: the sixty-five survivors which contracted recorded a loss of 9,700 jobs, outweighing by far the 3,000 job gains among the seventy-three expanding establishments. New creations – new firm formations or investments originating from outside Wearside – were the chief source of jobs to replace those lost through closures and contractions. Although there were no fewer than 293 new units, their small average employment size meant that they contributed only 7,400 new jobs at the end of the period. Thus, while the 1973 stock of manufacturing establishments experienced a net decline of almost 26,000 in its workforce over the period to 1987, the inflow from new creations amounted to little more than a quarter of that total. The net fall in manufacturing employment over the period was just under 18,500, nearly two-thirds of which occurred during the period since 1979, mainly during the recession years of the early 1980s.

The scale of the contraction in manufacturing employment, which research shows is in line with that found in other industrial districts in northern conurbations (Champion and Townsend, 1990), meant that Wearside's unambiguous specialisation in manufacturing (38 per cent of employment in 1973) compared with the national average (32 per cent) had virtually disappeared by the early 1991 (25 and 24 per cent respectively). Within this overall change, dramatic structural shifts have occurred in the manufacturing sector over the past two decades (detailed in Stone, 1994b). The main element in the contraction has been the collapse of the externally owned UK sector (i.e., plants with UK headquarters outside Wearside), employment in which fell by two-thirds (from over 28,000 to under 9,800) during 1973 to 1990. This dramatic fall is largely a reflection of the general failure of British manufacturing since the 1970s, exacerbated, in the case of Wearside, by the specific character of the local plants and the role they played in relation to the company overall (see below). The decline of the externally owned UK plants (down from 65 to under 39 per cent of total manufacturing employment over 1973 to 1990) has had the effect of increasing dramatically the proportional significance in today's Wearside of both the indigenous and foreign-owned sectors (see below). The employment contraction has been greatest among large plants: just twenty-four plants of over 500 workers employed a total of over 28,500 in 1973; by 1990 there were only eight such plants with a combined workforce of 7,900. The decline in big plants, combined with the large expansion in new firms in the lower size groupings, has resulted in an economy which is increasingly characterised by small establishments, reflected in the decrease in average employment size from 131 to 55.

Restructuring has also embraced a huge locational shift in manufacturing employment from the older urban centre of Sunderland to Washington (see Figure 8.1: Map). This trend is consistent with wider experience which shows that New Towns have performed comparatively well in manufacturing terms alongside other urban centres (Champion and Townsend, 1990; Lever, 1991). In 1973, some 80 per cent of manufacturing employment was located in Sunderland itself, compared to 14 per cent in Washington New Town. The respective figures for 1990 (56 and 35 per cent), arguably understate the extent of the spatial shift, since the Nissan factory and part of its supply complex is only classified to Sunderland rather than Washington by virtue of an anomalous postcode designation. Crediting the Nissan-related jobs to the New Town would significantly alter the balance, and imply that in the early 1990s Washington in employment terms became the prime manufacturing centre of Wearside. This is a reflection of the concentration of large closures and significant contractions in the old urban centre, the tendency for new investors to locate in the New Town, and the significantly better performance of the latter in terms of generating new firms.

The following sections examine the process of change as it relates to vital elements in the anatomy of the Wearside manufacturing economy, indicating the contribution of each to the structural shifts identified above.

Shipbuilding and marine engineering

At the heart of the 'traditional' sector of Wearside manufacturing was shipbuilding and marine engineering. This integrated complex, which included the most successful post-war UK builder of merchant vessels, Austin and Pickersgill (A&P), in the 1960s accounted directly for over 13,000 Wearside jobs. The vast majority of these were full-time and for males; they were also mainly skilled jobs in terms of technical and manual occupations involved and the companies were heavily committed to training through apprenticeship schemes. Even in the early 1970s, when direct employment had come down to around 9,000, Wearside could still boast a fully comprehensive shipbuilding capacity consisting of five shipbuilding yards (two of which were about to undergo wholesale modernisation with covered building facilities), a repair and refit yard, two marine engine building facilities, a marine electrical installation, a propshaft and propeller service unit, and a specialist marine coatings factory. Numerous small firms specialised in supplying castings and components for the vessel construction and outfitting activities clustered along the banks of the lower Wear. Although the key firms in this sector had, by the early 1970s, been acquired by companies headquartered elsewhere in the UK, these establishments continued to operate with considerable local autonomy and a wide range of on-site operational functions, including design capability.

This industry virtually disappeared during the period under review. The Wearside yards were always builders of merchant rather than naval ships, the market for which tended to be less cyclical and the profits more assured. The rise of new shipbuilding nations and the drawn-out recession in merchant shipbuilding – from the mid-1970s through to the late 1980s – thus put these yards under great financial pressure, making them vulnerable to rationalisation and closure, in spite of falling real wages and significant changes in work practices. Nationalisation in 1977 by the Labour government was seen as a means by which the industry could be rationalised, consolidated, and strengthened; in the event, under an incoming Conservative government seeking to withdraw from its involvement in industry, it became a vehicle for rationalising the industry virtually out of existence. British shipbuilders' restructuring, which began with a reduction in the number of berths on the Wear, led to the creation of North East Shipbuilders Ltd (NESL) in 1986, involving the cessation of shipbuilding on the Tees and the amalgamation of the two modernised Wearside yards, Sunderland Shipbuilders and A&P (Stone, 1989). When an orders crisis emerged shortly afterwards, attempts to find a private buyer became enmeshed in the financial arrangements associated with the sale of the Govan shipyard on the Clyde to a foreign buyer and EC rules on subsidies, culminating – after a prolonged campaign to save the yard – in NESL's closure in 1989, with the loss of the remaining 2,000 shipyard jobs (Hinde, 1993). In a Community seeking to reduce European shipbuilding capacity, approval for an enterprise zone covering the affected area was conditional upon shipbuilding not being allowed to resume while the regeneration measure was in force.

The contraction of the core business locally and throughout the UK led to rationalisation among other subsidiaries in the local complex. Unlike the branch plant sector, the establishments of which have tended to be relatively isolated within the local economy, the contraction of the shipbuilding core gave rise to decline throughout the whole complex of associated activities (Raby, 1977; Stone and Stevens, 1986). Only the smaller, less specialised or less dependent suppliers have been able to survive relatively unscathed through diversification into other markets. In contrast to the situation on the River Tyne, where shipbuilding skills and facilities have been converted in some degree to offshore construction for the oil and gas fields, the physical constraints of the River Wear has made this option a much more limited one, and only marginal activity of this kind has developed. Research into the placement into jobs of former shipyard workers shows that, of those actually finding work, in nearly two-thirds of the cases this was located outside Wearside (Hinde, 1993).

The branch plant sector

Mobile investments attracted to Wearside in the post-war period up to 1973 as a group fared no better than the longer-established factories, in spite of the fact that they represented relatively recent investments in non-traditional industries. The paucity of local supply linkages, limited range of functions, and simple semi-skilled assembly operations which characterised many of these plants made them cheap to close and thus vulnerable in company rationalisations (Watts, 1981). Closures affecting just eight plants, combined with a dramatic contraction in a ninth (which subsequently closed altogether), resulted in the loss of over 11,000 jobs in the period 1973 to 1987. Of the surviving plants, many had their workforce sharply thinned down during the 1980s, as labour intensification measures were applied. Only two of these closures (involving 1,000 jobs) were of foreign-owned plants; it was branch factories of UK companies that proved especially susceptible to recession.

In some cases closures resulted from consolidation of production at sites elsewhere due to market contraction (e.g., TI Tubes and Cape Insulation). In many cases, however, it reflects product obsolescence. Examples include Plessey (electro-mechanical telephone exchange equipment), Hepworth and Jackson the Tailor (both made-to-measure suits), and Thorn-EMI (TV and radio components); all of them significant employers of females (for details, see Stone and Stevens, 1986). These branch plants were typical of many established in the 1960s and 1970s in lacking the capacity to develop their own new products (and markets), and being dependent on corporate decisions made outside the region for new product lines and modernising investment. A number of sizeable plants still survive – Rolls Royce, Associated Engineering and David Brown Gears (engineering), and Dewhirsts (clothing) – but the adverse shifts in the business environment facing manufacturing in the UK seriously exposed the development weaknesses of the previous regional policy regime.

Inward investment from overseas

Inward investment, for a region, in a technical sense includes acquisitions and new projects undertaken by UK as well as overseas companies. In manufacturing, however, the flow of inward investment into Wearside from elsewhere within the UK has been relatively limited in the period under review; the main contribution has been from overseas sources. As a result of recent (i.e., post-1985) new investment, employment in the overseas-owned sector in aggregate recorded a substantial increase over the period 1973 to 1993, rising from 6,800 to just under 10,000 (author's Northern FDI Database). This reflects 'genuine' employment growth based on the establishment of greenfield plants, rather than inward investment via takeovers of UK-owned plants, which has been central to the growth in the size of the foreign-owned sector in the region as a whole (Smith and Stone, 1989).

Since 1973 there has been a near doubling in the number of foreign-owned factories in Wearside, with twenty of the thirty-eight establishments in 1990 being set up in the 1980s. The influx of new plants has thus more than compensated for job losses since 1973 arising out of closures (notably Timex, RCA Records, and Domtar papermill) and contractions (for example Philips Components and Corning's glassworks) of foreign-owned plants. By 1993, with many of the recent investments still in their expansionary stage, the foreign plants together accounted for well over a third of Wearside's manufacturing employment (up from 15 per cent in 1973). This is considerably above the current equivalent figure for the Northern Region (22 per cent), and strikingly in excess of that for the UK (6.5 per cent in 1989). It indicates a high degree of concentration of Wearside's manufacturing employment in foreign plants.

The bulk of recent overseas investment in Wearside has gone towards the creation of an entirely new industrial activity. The integrated production system built around the new Nissan car assembly plant (which itself employed over 4,000 in 1993) bears some similarity to the pre-1980s agglomeration centred on shipbuilding. The developing network of components suppliers has been encouraged by 'local content' agreements, and by the fact that production in the specialist vehicle supplier plants – e.g. Ikeda Hoover (seats), Calsonic (exhausts), Nissan-Yamato (pressings), TRW (two plants, valves and switches), Marley Kansei (instrument panels), and R-tek (trim) – is synchronised with that of Nissan on the basis of frequent deliveries through the day (Peck, 1990). While a proportion of the parts are being supplied from producers elsewhere in the UK and Europe via a (part Japanese-owned) local transport/warehousing intermediary, the requirements of synchronised production, combined with expanding demand for components as Nissan's output rises, will continue to draw suppliers to the area.

Because of the particular focus on vehicles, a large majority of the jobs created in Wearside by recent foreign investments have been full-time, skilled, and for males. This is important in that the jobs so generated nominally replace those lost in the shipyards and coal mines. Not surprisingly, however, given the fact that new inward investment has been creating an entirely new industry in Wearside and the surrounding area, specialist skill requirements mean that a substantial proportion of the new jobs have been filled from outside Wearside's boundaries. The new industry, in that sense, is less embedded in the Wearside local economy than was shipbuilding, the vast majority of employment in which was for Wearsiders. The specific labour force requirements of a major new employer like Nissan – for example, its preference for recruiting relatively young workers – has by no means matched the profile of workers released from the shipyards and mines and many local firms have had to cope with the problems caused by the loss of their skilled workers to the incoming plants (Peck and Stone, 1992).

The small firms sector

After experiencing contraction in the small firms sector in the 1970s, Wearside in the 1980s was relatively successful in terms of generating employment through the formation of new firms and expansion among small firms. This is consistent with expectations, not just because of the introduction since 1980 of national and local initiatives supporting small entrepreneurs, but also because of broader trends in the economy, including the tendency for larger establishments to contract out work formerly undertaken in house, the development of more flexible technology (for instance CNC machinery), the growth of opportunities in specialised niche markets, and the higher level of unemployment which has 'pushed' individuals made redundant by larger firms to seek to make use of their skills (and any redundancy money) by setting-up their own business.

Between 1973 and 1987 the local manufacturing economy, which started the period with a total of 329 establishments, saw the creation (including some short distance cross-boundary relocations) of 238 new surviving indigenous (i.e., Wearside-owned) firms, employing between them over 3,800 workers. A further 600 jobs were created through net expansion by indigenous firms operating throughout the period. Indeed, the small firms sector (under fifty employees) – overwhelmingly made up of indigenous firms – was the *only* size category within manufacturing to record net employment growth over the period 1973 to 1987. Surprisingly, given the relatively poor record of the Northern Region as a whole in terms of small firm growth, Wearside's small firms outperformed their counterparts in other local economies over 1986 to 1990, when employment growth in survivors grew at an annual rate of 11.4 per cent, compared with 7.7 per cent for Northern Ireland, 4.8 per cent for Leicestershire, and 3.0 per cent for the Republic of Ireland (NIERC, 1992).

Reflecting these trends, the contribution of new indigenous firms to the stock of manufacturing jobs has also improved. Storey (1982b) calculated that new jobs established in the county of Tyne and Wear over the period

1965 to 1978 amounted to 3.7 per cent of the total stock in manufacturing. Wearside data for 1973 to 1987 (relating to part of that county) suggest a figure of 15.5 per cent. Moreover, while the Northern Region in general has a much smaller proportion of manufacturing employees in companies employing fewer than 100 workers than nationally (22 per cent compared to 35), the recent performance of Wearside's small firms sector has pushed its figure to very near the national average (33 per cent in 1990).

It is important to view these new developments in their correct perspective. In line with research showing that small firms have notoriously high closure rates and that few achieve significant growth (Storey, 1982a), virtually half of the initial stock of indigenous Wearside firms (98 out of 206) had closed by 1987. This resulted in an employment loss of 3,250, almost cancelling out the gains made through new creations. The local indigenous sector may have shown an impressive growth in the number of units, but in terms of *net employment* it changed little from its 1973 level of 8,000, and only increased its share of Wearside's manufacturing employment (from 19 to 32 per cent) because of the fall in manufacturing employment overall. While the net transfer (through acquisitions) of some 1,500 jobs from indigenous to non-indigenous ownership means that the performance is somewhat understated in the above figures, it remains the case that the sector's growth has been less impressive absolutely than in relative terms.

Other sectors

Coal mining

Mining has traditionally been a key industry in and around Wearside, and as recently as 1960, over 18,000 Wearsiders found employment in NCB mines, nearly all of them males working full-time. The closure of the smaller and worked-out pits proceeded steadily through the 1960s as the Durham coalfield gradually shifted eastwards to focus on larger and more efficient units with substantial reserves of coal. The speed at which the industry was scaled down was controlled through subsidies on coal used for energy generation and a tax on oil; even so, the number of Wearside residents employed in mining was down to around 12,000 in the early 1970s. Of the ten working pits in 1979, most ceased production in the early 1980s, leaving just three mines with 4,400 employees in 1984. The only mine to survive into the 1990s – Wearmouth Colliery, one of a handful of North East 'superpits' reaching far out under the North Sea for their reserves – succumbed in 1993 to a combination of factors which dramatically reduced the demand for steam-raising coal, including the subsidisation of nuclear energy, and the preference of privatised electricity companies for generating power with North Sea gas. Opencast and imported coal supplies have also played an increasing role within the UK market because of the cheapness of these sources compared to that of domestically produced in deep mines.

Miners whose pits were closed in an earlier period, if they were not able to find work in surviving mines, frequently found alternative employment in the new branch factories being established in the region. Specific employment subsidies and re-training helped in the transition. The fall-off in mobile investment from the early 1970s, combined with the dramatically reduced size of the mining industry, has made it increasingly difficult for miners whose collieries are closed to find alternative employment opportunities.

The service sector

The only major Wearside sector to expand since the early 1970s has been services. While this is consistent with trends in the national economy, the growth performance of services in Wearside has been poor in comparison. As Table 8.1 shows, Wearside in 1973 had a comparatively small share (45 per cent) of its employed population engaged in services compared to the North (49 per cent) and the UK (over 54 per cent). The difference between Wearside and the UK in terms of percentage employment in services has narrowed (from nine percentage points to four), and between Wearside and the Northern Region disappeared altogether. However, this is more to do with the overall decline in Wearside's *total* employment, since the growth rates in service employment have been greater at the national level (35 per cent) than in Wearside, where the growth of 14,300 jobs since 1973 is equivalent to an increase of only 22 per cent. The sector is dominated by female employees, the proportion of females to total services employment (63 per cent) has not changed since 1973. Moreover, over half (53 per cent) the women in this sector are part-timers.

A large sector which has shown moderate growth at the national level, distribution (wholesale and retail), hotels and catering, has shrunk in employment terms from 22,300 to 21,000. This reflects the comparatively slow growth of local income, the growth of larger-scale more efficient retail operators, and the general unsuitability of Wearside to the significant development of tourism. New supermarkets and retail sheds for carpets, garden goods, and DIY have largely been developed outside Sunderland itself and have displaced many smaller establishments; like other establishments in retailing chains they have been active in the shift towards part-time working, particularly for young females.

Substantial growth has occurred in banking, insurance, and business services, with a rise from 2,300 to 7,300 over the period, which proportionately has exceeded the increase occurring nationally. However, because this has been from a low base, its share of employment (7 per cent)

– as in the region as a whole – remains well short of the national figure of 12 per cent. In terms of developing such activities, the region suffers from the dominant role played in the region's service economy by London and the South East, as well as from its small population base, peripheral location, lack of head offices, and 'branch plant' character of much of its industry and commerce (Richardson and Gentle, 1993). Wearside is further disadvantaged in that it is overshadowed by the North East's regional capital, Newcastle upon Tyne, and increasingly for the North of England as a whole, Leeds. Apart from the North of England building society, which has its head office in Wearside, all twenty of the banks, building societies and insurance companies operating there do so only through a branch office. This restricts both the size of the sector locally, since it is – like retailing – catering only for a local market and the type of employment it offers.

The growth of tradable services, which is an important way of generating employment in a local economy, has been limited in Wearside, in spite of one or two significant developments. Site availability has permitted the emergence of some warehousing/distribution facilities which serve ('export' to) the wider region and beyond. Mail order and mail promotion services companies have also developed their activities, taking advantage of low wage flexible female labour. New developments catering for non-local demand include an insurance telesales office, a European HQ and billing centre for a sportswear company, and a new hotel complex. These are likely to create over a thousand jobs, again, mainly for females with a significant part-time component. There has also been a proliferation of small businesses serving a wider market (for example, limited mail shots, product bar coding, and data entry). As with the above developments, these activities largely involve female workers and do not involve significant levels of skill. Further employment has been created in providing externally oriented services as a result of the expansion in higher education (University of Sunderland), and the establishment of a central government office (Tax Inspectorate), to go with an earlier office decentralisation (Child Benefits) which created over 2,000 jobs in Washington.

LABOUR MARKET ADJUSTMENT TO ECONOMIC RESTRUCTURING

Employment change

Reflecting the scale of economic restructuring in Wearside, the level and pattern of employment has shifted dramatically. ACE data for 1973 to 1991 (which slightly overstates the extent of contraction, since it relates only to *employees* and ignores self-employment, which has been growing) show a sharp overall fall in the demand for labour, from nearly 112,000 to 98,000

(–12.5 per cent). This reflects the loss of industrial jobs and the failure of employment in services to achieve compensatory growth. This contrasts with the experience of the national economy, where service sector growth over the period has been sufficient to maintain the overall level of demand for labour in crude terms. Deindustrialisation has hit male workers hard: with numbers employed falling by 17,700 (from 66,700 to 49,000). The fall in male full-time employment (from 65,150 to 46,100) is particularly noticeable; at 29 per cent it is proportionately half as great again as the fall in total employment, and significantly higher than that experienced at the national level (down by 19 per cent). The loss of these jobs is not in any way counterbalanced by an absolute rise of 1,300 in the number of male part-time employees.

Wearside's economy has exhibited the same bias as that found nationally in generating jobs for women rather than men. Female employment rose from 45,250 to 49,100 over the period, so that – in a city traditionally identified with male-dominated heavy industry – women are now marginally ahead of men in terms of numbers employed. However, the absolute gain made by females (3,800 or +8 per cent) is small in comparison with the situation nationally (+24 per cent), and falls well short of filling the gap left by the reduction in male employment. Full-time employment for women has actually *fallen* substantially (by over 14 per cent, compared to a rise of 5 per cent nationally), and the sharp rise in part-time employment among females (+56 per cent) has by no means matched that achieved nationally (+100 per cent).

Moreover, it must not be forgotten that the overall balance of change in employment numbers – both nationally and within Wearside – conceals a downward bias in terms of hours worked. Bearing this in mind, the virtually static position of aggregate employment in the UK in 1991 compared with 1973 is in reality a significant fall, as part-time working has risen by 2.1 million. From this perspective, the relatively substantial rise in part-time working among Wearside women (+8,200) barely outweighs the fall which has occurred in full-time employment among females (–4,400), let alone the collapse in male employment. This is because within the part-time definition of 30 hours or less per week, many part-time jobs involve only a few hours. Accepting the ratio used elsewhere (for example, by Townsend, 1985–86) of 2:1 as the appropriate fraction of full- to part-time, on a full-time equivalent basis, there is no case for arguing that female employment has increased at all.

Labour market adjustment

How has the supply-side of the Wearside labour market adjusted to changes in demand, and particularly the long-term contraction in job opportunities for males? The labour market adjustments can be identified using population census data for 1971 and 1991. The focus above was on jobs generated *within* Wearside's boundary, which, due to commuting, is not synonymous with the employment of Wearsiders; the attention here is on the local community and the labour market position of Wearside residents as it has changed over two decades. The population census-derived figure for those 'in employment' (including self-employed) fell from a total in 1971 of 116,870 to 103,850 in 1991. This fall of over 13,000 jobs (equivalent to 11.1 per cent) is consistent with the picture given above based on ACE data, allowing for some growth in self-employment and a small net outflow of commuters. With numbers in employment in the nearby Tyneside economy showing an even greater contraction (16 per cent), there has not been a significant source of alternative employment opportunities for Wearsiders faced with a contracting demand for labour.

While at a regional scale, people faced with worsening employment opportunities have shown a tendency to vote with their feet, net outmigration does not appear to have reduced the labour supply in Wearside. The North's positive balance of births over deaths has been more than outweighed by persistent net outmigration since the early 1970s, causing a net fall in population of 1.4 per cent over 1971 to 1991 when nationally it increased by almost 3 per cent. In spite of an even sharper contraction in Tyne and Wear as a whole (–6.7 per cent), Wearside has moved *against* the trend, growing by 1.1 per cent. This is a reflection of the doubling of Washington New Town's population, which has concealed large losses in Sunderland itself. The important point is that the adjustment to a contracting demand for labour in Wearside is not one of a net shrinkage of population; rather, this has risen, *ceteris paribus* increasing the pressure for labour market adjustment.

One possible labour market response in this situation is for there to be a decline in the numbers participating in the labour market. The activity rate – the proportion of residents of working age who are employed, self-employed, on a government training scheme, or seeking work – has remained surprisingly constant overall, showing only a slight reduction (from 73 to 72 per cent). The actual number of economically active people in Wearside has in fact increased by nearly 3,000 (from 124,270 to 127,010), reflecting the rise in both total population and the proportion of Wearside residents of working age. These figures conceal a large discrepancy between males and females. While the activity rate for Wearside males fell over the two decades (from over 92 to 81 per cent), the rate for women increased (from 53 to 62 per cent). For both sexes, current activity rates in Wearside are significantly below national levels of 87 and 68 per cent.

In absolute terms, the number of economically active males in Wearside contracted from 82,370 to 72,750 over the whole period. The fall has been particularly marked among those in the older age groups, a substantial proportion of which are 'discouraged workers' and have taken early

189

retirement or registered as 'permanently sick' (24.8 per cent of Wearside men aged forty-five to sixty-four are officially so classified, compared with 11 per cent nationally). Economically active females have increased in number from 45,280 to 54,260; the extent of the increase has been held back by a lack of job opportunities.

Overall, therefore, a rise in population, an increase in the proportion of Wearside residents of working age, and higher economic activity rates among women have outweighed the fall in male activity rates to bring about an expansion in the labour force over 1971 to 1991. In the context of a sharp fall in demand for labour, a substantial rise in unemployment is inevitable. Census figures for unemployment put the total in 1971 at just under 7,950 for males and 2,650 for females (9.8 and 6.2 per cent respectively). By 1991 these had risen to 13,500 and 5,400, representing 19.0 and 9.8 per cent of the male and female workforce – substantially above those in the region (14.5 and 7.8 per cent), and, for males in particular, exceeding even more markedly national figures (11.3 and 7.0 per cent). Furthermore, these figures take no account of government schemes (mainly work experience for younger age groups) the numbers of which have increased sharply in recent years (to nearly 3,000 for males and 1,350 for females, or 4.1 and 2.5 per cent of the 1991 labour force). Indeed, the proportion of the sixteen to twenty-four age group which is either un-employed or on a government scheme is higher in Wearside (32.5 per cent) than anywhere in Tyne and Wear (overall average 29.4 per cent) and, again, well above the national average of 19.6 per cent. The rates of unemployment would plainly be higher in Wearside but for the labour supply adjustment of 'discouraged workers' opting for early retirement or permanently sick status, particularly among males of forty-five and over.

POTENTIAL FOR GROWTH IN A RESTRUCTURED WEARSIDE

While there are prospects of further growth through service sector expan-sion, this should not be exaggerated, given Wearside's relative lack of comparative advantage in relation to this form of activity. Indeed, technical changes in relation to some office activities threatens some of the jobs previously created in the sector. Moreover, the *types* of employment likely to develop in tradable services – part-time, low skill jobs mainly for females – do not meet, except in the more immediate sense, the real employment needs of Wearside. Reindustrialisation is thus crucial to the future of Wearside, and this section examines the basis for future growth which has been established in the overseas-owned and small- to medium-enterprise (SME) sectors.

Overseas-owned sector

Investment from overseas was undoubtedly the economy's main 'engine of growth' in the second half of the 1980s, taking over the role performed in the 1970s by the services sector and in the 1960s by UK companies setting up branch plants. These investments are important, not just in terms of their contribution to employment, but also to the modernisation of the Wearside economy. This goes beyond the new products, technology, production methods, and export capacity embodied in the establishments themselves, to embrace the impact of incoming companies upon existing firms and institutions in the local economy. The potential for growth has thus to be assessed from a number of perspectives.

While the vehicles-related producers differ from past branch plant investments in that they are extensively interlinked, they by no means defy the 'rules' of functional differentiation by space generally associated with multi-plant enterprises. Thus, it is the manufacture of the less sophisticated components – although made using sophisticated *processes* – which are located in Wearside, with more complex inputs and components supplied from elsewhere (Nissan's European design and research, for instance, is principally located in the South East). The tendency to concentrate on items at the lower end of the production chain places limits on the potential for localised growth from spin-offs. While such considerations have led some researchers to take a cautious view of the direct and indirect impact of the vehicles complex upon local employment generation (for instance, Amin and Tomaney, 1991), experience from other old industrial areas (from example, Ford in Saarland, Germany) which have undergone conversion through developing from scratch a vehicles industry indicates that the process takes *decades* to achieve and employment generation proceeds through the gradual deepening and widening of the supplier support network. Thus, although the recent recession has temporarily slowed the process, there is considerable potential for further employment growth as the existing plants grow to full capacity and new ones are attracted by the cluster of vehicle production activity. Moreover, the integrated nature of this development and the scale and character of the investment taking place in plant and training should ensure this is a more enduring development than previous branch plant investments.

The overseas investors are playing a significant 'modernising' role in terms of manufacturing techniques and the labour process. Following the massive withdrawal of British capital, Wearside has been increasingly incorporated into the broader division of labour via foreign rather than domestic investment, and is having to conform, socially and politically, to the requirements of foreign capital to maintain its development impetus. The social aspects of local production are being altered by incoming companies bringing new managerial techniques and personnel practices, many of them involving changes in the status and role of trade unions. They have been aided in this by deindustrialisation, which has increased the pool of unemployed to an extent which has made local labour (and unions) much more acquiescent than formerly. The smaller new plants especially are likely to be operating as non-union workplaces, while some of the large plants have opted for single union agreements in which the union's role is very much circumscribed (Peck and Stone, 1992). The location of almost all of these plants outside 'old' Sunderland (see Figure 8.1: Map) is, in part, related to the attempt to socially distance these operations from the old institutions and practices which prevailed in the traditional core of Sunderland's manufacturing economy.

Research into this aspect of inward investment in the North East in general has shown that changes to the way production is organised have been extensive, though the degree of sophistication of new personnel practices varies according to factory size and complexity of the production process (Peck and Stone, 1992, 1993). The research also revealed that the process was not confined to new plants; managers in longer-established factories had taken advantage of the competitive pressures and threats to survival (and, in some cases, ownership change), in the early 1980s particularly, to introduce changes to industrial relations and incentive systems and to enhance labour flexibility. Philips Components is a prominent example of a Wearside plant which has introduced wholesale changes in the way its human resources are managed. Labour intensification associated with this process undoubtedly contributed both to the scale of job losses (*in situ* contraction) in the 1980s, although it had its benefits in terms of the relatively robust performance of such firms in the recent recession.

Although the impetus for such changes were normally found to emanate from corporate sources, local management have found that the presence of a high profile company such as Nissan – the new manufacturing and personnel practices of which are well publicised – has made it easier to introduce new methods and work practices within their own plants (Peck and Stone, 1993). The changes appear to be more extensive than in at least some other areas of the UK, for example, the limited shift towards increasing functional flexibility found by researchers in the Southampton area. The latter has been ascribed to the paucity of greenfield investments, plants under threats of closure, and changes in ownership in the 1980s – an environment which contrasts sharply with that in and around Wearside (Pinch *et al.*, 1991).

The extent to which this recent boost to the local economy's competitiveness based on a new greenfield plants and revitalised old ones translates into significant growth is still unclear. The flow of inward investment into the North East has slowed in recent years, reflecting domestic problems in source countries and increased competition for mobile international investment. As improved flexibility in production is introduced more generally, the competitive advantage of producers in this locality will be eroded, particularly given the fact that many of the surviving Wearside plants operate in low technology sectors. The surviving externally-owned UK plants, in particular, are generally in labour intensive sectors of limited technological sophistication, with mechanical engineering and clothing accounting for over half the employment.

The SME sector

While there is clear evidence of a relatively good performance by the small-to medium-sized local firms in the 1980s, the true *dynamism* of the indigenous sector and its capacity for further growth must be seriously questioned. It is not clear whether the expansion in small firms in the 1980s reflected a new long-term trend, based on a genuine flowering of an enterprise culture, or simply a largely once and for all structural adjustment in response to the collapse of the large employers. Whatever the case, urban economies like Wearside's are faced with the simple fact that, given the historical dominance of large employers, any growth in the SME sector derives from a small base, putting them at a disadvantage in relation to areas where such firms have traditionally played a significant role. The relative size and structural characteristics of the indigenous sector as a whole make it unrealistic to expect that it will significantly fill the gap arising from the employment collapse of externally owned UK plants.

A particular difficulty in generating significant numbers of jobs from new or existing small firms is their inability or lack of ambition to achieve significant expansion. Analysis of Wearside data showed that, of the thirty-nine firms established post-1973 and of at least ten years' standing, not one was found to have more than fifty employees in 1987. The Wearside economy, like that of the region as a whole, has proved unable to develop a sizeable core of small to medium-sized locally-controlled companies with significant growth potential (CURDS, 1992). Altogether, in 1990 there were thirty-three Wearside-owned firms (out of a total of 443 establishments) with fifty or more employees, accounting for just 17 per cent of manufacturing employment. Of these firms, just four had in excess of 250 employees. Apart from one firm (Berghaus, manufacturing mountain-wear) – which was actually acquired by a UK company in 1993 – even the larger indigenous firms are engaged in sectors (brewing, printing, and metal goods) largely sheltered from international competition. Moreover, the local economy, in fact, recently lost (through re-location to Tyneside) Bonas Machines, a medium-sized indigenous company manufacturing computer-controlled weaving equipment based on on-site design and development, which had a successful record in world markets.

There is a core of small indigenous businesses which have established

193

themselves producing products for niche markets beyond the region, including overseas (for example, specialist chemicals, medical diagnostic kits, and electronic random number generators for lotteries). Rationalisation at Corning's glassworks factory has given rise to the establishment by redundant skilled glass-blowers of numerous small businesses making quality glassware products, conceived and designed in-house, for national and foreign markets. The majority of indigenous firms, however, compete in a regional market, usually on a subcontract basis. This particularly applies to the numerous mechanical engineering, metal goods, and clothing firms. Where they have their 'own' products, they are largely to be found in markets sheltered from overseas competition and mainly in those where entry costs are comparatively low. It is no coincidence that the sectors spawning the most new enterprises (mechanical engineering, clothing, printing, and timber products) are ones where employment performance at the national level has been better than the average due, at least in part, to 'natural' protection from imports. Many of the firms, particularly those in mechanical engineering and metal goods, have introduced new process equipment over the last decade – as a means of improving efficiency and widening the range of subcontract services they can offer – but they remain reliant upon major firms for their orders, carry out no design function, and do little in the way of marketing.

CONCLUSIONS

This analysis of two decades of industrial restructuring in an old industrial sub-regional economy has shown the limitations to modernisation based on current policies. Ongoing research by the author shows that, proportionally, the inflow of inward investment was higher for the Northern Region during the 1980s than for any of the UK's assisted regions. Yet, even Wearside, the recipient of a large share of that influx of inward investment and which, moreover, performed relatively well in terms of indigenous manufacturing growth, proved barely able to bring a halt to the deindustrialisation process, still less reverse it. In spite of the boom conditions, no significant growth in manufacturing employment was achieved between 1984 and the beginning of the 1990s. The scale of decline in industrial employment has been further increased by a parallel (and now wholly irreversible) decline in coalmining. The depressed level of local spending as a result of the contraction in the main industries, and the failure to attract a larger number of investments in tradable service activities, has meant that the new employment generated in the services sector has lagged behind national rates, producing a significant overall contraction in employment opportunities, even before allowing for a rise in the proportion of part-time jobs in the total.

The chapter has drawn attention to the rapid and extensive structural change affecting the Wearside economy, and the extent of labour market adjustment necessitated by it – including a dramatic shift in respective labour market roles played by men and women, a trend towards part-time work, a sharp rise in unemployment and government training schemes, and extensive withdrawal from the labour market by males. These developments have been especially severe in the old urban centre of Sunderland, which has suffered from marked spatial restructuring of both manufacturing and services towards Washington New Town. The younger, physically more mobile, and occupationally more adaptable, elements of the population have been able to respond more readily to the restructuring; older age groups, particularly those with outdated skills and whose ability to move is constrained, have been literally left behind by this restructuring process. Thus, riverside wards like those of Southwick and Pallion – which respectively lost 96 and 79 per cent of their manufacturing employment over 1973 to 1990 – have plainly experienced particularly severe labour market adjustments. In such wards, activity rates for both sexes are noticeably lower than the average, unemployment for males is around 25 per cent – with a further 5 per cent on government schemes – and permanent sickness for the forty-five to sixt-four age group rises to as much as 36 per cent. In the New Town, in contrast, activity and unemployment rates are not far out of line with national figures.

The character and degree of modernisation which has occurred within the economy has endowed it with an improved growth capacity, but not one sufficient to fill the employment and income gap left by the demise of the old industries. Competitive gains arising out of new industries, changing attitudes, and the spread of modern management techniques and personnel practices have increased the prospects of achieving a significant degree of reindustrialisation over the longer-run. In Wearside, as nationally, these advantages have to be set against two vital considerations. First, in proportional terms, Wearside's manufacturing is now dramatically smaller as a source of employment than in 1973 (or, indeed, any time in the post-war period). The *extent* of reindustrialisation needed – given the high level of unemployment (and disguised unemployment) and qualitative and quantitative limitations to prospective employment generation in services on Wearside – is very substantial indeed. Secondly, Wearside's economy is still confined by its inherited resource base and the framework of policy at national level. The full exploitation of development opportunities arising out of the new industries is constrained by well-documented weaknesses in the local capacity relating to educational attainment, the generation of new firms producing sophisticated products and services, and the development and exploitation of innovations (see, for example, CURDS, 1992). The absence of a meaningful industrial strategy at a national level has contributed to this weakness.

Wearside, in manufacturing terms, is a microcosm not just of the region but of the British economy; 'leaner and fitter' than in the 1970s, but in a number of respects structurally deficient and too small to allow the generation of anything like full employment in the economy as a whole. While prospects for further significant deindustrialisation are undoubtedly reduced by the diminished weight of 'older' relative to recently established plants in the manufacturing sector as a whole, reindustrialisation will be, at best, a slow process. The national policy pendulum has recently swung towards giving higher priority to industry. For economies like Wearside's it is important that it shifts even further and that an effective long-term strategy for manufacturing growth is developed, since the opportunities for growth through expansion of business services are otherwise limited, and more income must be generated locally if non-exporting services are to expand. With the SME sector largely dependent for its growth upon the larger companies, the continuing weakness of British manufacturing is giving rise to an increasing reliance upon the foreign-owned manufacturing sector as the 'engine of growth' for the Wearside economy. There is nothing new – or particularly threatening – in this; Wearside has for most of the post-war decades relied for its main growth impulses upon externally controlled production. It is the glaring extent of decline (and ongoing weakness) of British-owned manufacturing establishments which is at the heart of the problem in Wearside; this is what has holed the economy below its waterline, and a better balance between foreign and national investment needs to be fostered.

From a broader perspective, Wearside's jobs crisis is just part of a problem affecting all mature industrial countries. British attempts to deal with unemployment through freeing-up the labour market has undoubtedly created jobs; the more regulated labour markets of other European economies have not only impaired job generation but diverted inward investors from outside Europe towards the UK, with its lower labour costs. The problem with freer markets, as USA experience shows, is that they tend to sharply widen income differentials and to push low wage workers towards poverty. This is the result of a fall in demand for unskilled labour related to developments in trade and technology, combined with the need to restrict unemployment and welfare benefits to make the labour market operate effectively. At some stage – and this is now being explored seriously at EC level – re-thinking of both tax incentives to employers and the question of how employment is shared among the population might gain acceptance as a viable alternative to running ever harder in an attempt to meet conventional job targets.

REFERENCES

Amin, A. and Tomaney, J. (1991) 'Creating an Enterprise Culture in the North East? The Impact of Urban and Regional Policies of the 1980s', *Regional Studies* 25, 5: 479–88.

Amin, A. and Tomaney, J. (1993) 'Illusions of Prosperity: The Political Economy of Urban and Regional Regeneration in North East England', in D. Fasenfest (ed.) *Community Economic Development: Policy Formation in the US and UK*, London: Macmillan.

Caslin, T. (1987) 'De-industrialisation in the UK', in H. Vane and T. Caslin (eds) *Current Controversies in Economics*, Oxford: Basil Blackwell.

Centre for Urban and Regional Development Studies (1992) *North East of England: Economic Assessment*. A study prepared for the Northern Regions Councils Association, Newcastle: University of Newcastle Upon Tyne.

Champion, A.G. and Townsend, A.R. (1990) *Contemporary Britain: A Geographical Perspective*, London: Edward Arnold.

Fothergill, S. and Gudgin, G. (1982) *Unequal Growth: Urban and Regional Employ-Ment Change in the UK*, London: Heinemann.

Garrahan, P. and Stewart, P. (1992) *The Nissan Enigma*, London: Mansell.

Hudson, R. (1988) 'Labour Market Changes and New Forms of Work in "Old" Industrial Regions', in D. Massey and J. Allen (eds) *Uneven Re-development: Cities and Regions in Transition*, London: Hodder & Stoughton.

Hudson, R. (1991) 'The North in the 1980s: New Times or Just More of the Same?', *Area*, March, 17–26.

Hinde, K. (1993) *Labour Market Experiences Following Plant Closure: The Case of Sunderland's Shipyard Workers*. Research Paper 3, Newcastle Economic Research Unit, Newcastle upon Tyne: University of Northumbria.

Lever, W. (1991) 'De-industrialisation and the Reality of the Post-industrial City', *Urban Studies* 28, 6, 983–99.

Massey, D. (1984) *Spatial Divisions of Labour: Social Structures and the Geography of Production*, London: Macmillan.

NIERC (1992) *LEDU Monitoring and Evaluation Report*, Belfast: Northern Ireland Economic Research Centre.

Northern Region Strategy Team (1977) *Strategic Plan for the Northern Region, Vol 2, Economic Development Policies*, London: HMSO.

Peck. F, (1990) 'Nissan in the North East: The Multiplier Effects', *Geography* 75, 4, 354–7.

Peck. F, and Stone, I. (1992) *New Inward Investment and the Northern Region Labour Market*, Research Series No. 6, Sheffield: Employment Department.

Peck, F. and Stone, I. (1993) 'Japanese Inward Investment in the North East of England: Re-assessing Japanisation', *Environment and Planning C: Government and Policy* 11, 1, 55–67.

Pinch, S., Mason, C., and Witt, S. (1991) 'Flexible Employment Strategies in British Industry: Evidence From the UK "Sunbelt"', *Regional Studies* 25, 3, 207–18

Raby, G. (1977) 'Contraction Poles: An Exploratory Study of Traditional Industry Decline Within a Regional Industrial Complex', CURDS discussion paper, Newcastle: University of Newcastle upon Tyne.

Richardson, R. and Gentle, C. (1993) 'Tradeable Services and the Northern Economy', *Business Review North* 5, 2, 16–23.

Robinson, F. and Shaw, K. (1991) 'In Search of the Great North', *Town and Country Planning*, October, 279–83.

Rowthorn, B. (1986) 'De-industrialization in Britain', in R. Martin and B. Rowthorn (eds) *The Geography of De-industrialisation*, London: Macmillan.

Sadler, D. (1992) *The Global Region: Production, State Policies And Uneven Development*, Oxford: Pergamon.

Smith, I. and Stone, I. (1989) 'Foreign Investment in the North: Distinguishing Fact from Hype', *Northern Economic Review* 18, 50–61.

Stone, I. (1989) *Shipbuilding on Wearside: Reviewing the Prospects*. Report for Sunderland Borough Council, Sunderland: Sunderland MBC.

Stone, I. (1994a) 'The UK Economy', in F. Somers (ed.) *European Economies: A Comparative Study*, London: Pitman.

Stone, I. (1994b) 'Wearside in the "New" North East: Longer-term Perspectives on Industrial Restructuring', in P. Garrahan and P. Stewart (eds) *Urban Change and Renewal: The Paradox of Place*, Aldershot: Avebury Press.

Stone, I. and Stevens, J. (1986) 'Employment on Wearside: Trends and Prospects', *Northern Economic Review* 12, 39–56.

Storey, D. (1982a) *Entrepreneurship and the New Firm*, London: Croom Helm.

Storey, D. (1982b) *Manufacturing Employment Change in Tyne and Wear Since 1965*, CURDS, Newcastle upon Tyne: University of Newcastle.

Thomsen, S. and Woolcock, S. (1993) *Direct Investment and European Integration: Competition Among Firms and Governments*, London: Pinter.

Townsend, A. (1985–86) 'Part-time Employment in the North', *Northern Economic Review* 12, 2–15.

Tyne and Wear Research and Intelligence Unit (1994) *1991 Census Topic Report: Economic Activity and Employment*, Newcastle upon Tyne.

Watts, D. (1981) *The Branch Plant Economy: A Study of External Control*, Harlow: Longman.

9

FROM WORKSHOP TO MEETING PLACE?

The Birmingham economy in transition

Steve Martin

Birmingham's recent economic performance illustrates many of the problems facing old, industrial cities undergoing economic transition. The city's economy, and that of the rest of the West Midlands region, has traditionally been heavily concentrated on manufacturing. Unlike most other industrial regions of the UK, this 'manufacturing heartland' did not, however, suffer noticeable decline in the 1960s and early 1970s. However, a series of major economic shocks from the late 1970s onwards laid bare the structural weaknesses of the region's economy, and Birmingham's fortunes went into 'free-fall' as companies struggled to survive in the teeth of deep recession. Unemployment rose rapidly to unprecedented levels. In response the city council built up one of the largest and best resourced economic development departments in the country and embarked on an ambitious strategy to promote the regeneration of the local economy.

The 'Birmingham story' is, therefore, noteworthy both because of the suddenness and severity of the economic decline which it suffered and because of the cultivation by local policy makers of a range of imaginative strategies designed to enable it to meet the challenges involved in making the transition to a post-industrial economy. This chapter first investigates the nature and causes of Birmingham's decline. It then examines the role which the city council played in promoting local economic regeneration, exploring in particular its involvement in public–private partnerships, the use of EC funding, the encouragement given to new service activities and the concerted effort to promote a new image for the city. It concludes with an assessment of the outcomes of this strategy, examining the available evidence regarding the scale of the benefits which have resulted, who has had access to them, and the lessons which can be learned from the 'Birmingham approach' about the capacity of industrial city regions to adapt to the decline of manufacturing.

CONTEXT: THE ANATOMY OF INDUSTRIAL DECLINE

Birmingham's economy developed rapidly in the nineteenth century, based on mining, metal products, and engineering, and benefiting from the influence of its powerful city councillors who played an increasingly interventionist role in its development. Municipal enterprises, pioneered by Joseph Chamberlain in the late 1800s, laid the foundation of the city's success in attracting and retaining the growth sectors of the early decades of the twentieth century (Chandler and Lawless, 1985), and gave Birmingham a tradition of local economic intervention which has been maintained by recent city council initiatives. Until the mid 1960s, therefore, Birmingham perceived itself, with some justification, as the engine room of national economic growth and prosperity and its growth was fuelled by the global post-war boom from which it 'prospered more brilliantly than any other major British city outside London' (Sutcliffe, 1986).

However, by the 1970s, it had become increasingly clear that much of the city's fixed capital was redundant. Moreover, its once highly diversified, manufacturing base was increasingly concentrated on the automotive sector and this, as well as other areas of manufacturing, had been starved of investment and was becoming uncompetitive. The structural weaknesses of the economy of the 'city of 1,000 trades' became all too evident during the recessions of the 1970s and early 1980s (Spencer *et al.*, 1986) and were exacerbated by mounting international competition and growing import penetration. The city's fortunes plunged from the high water mark of the mid-1960s into a precipitous decline which gathered pace in the late 1970s and early 1980s, inflicting a series of major economic shocks which severely undermined the confidence of the city's business people, policy makers, and residents.

Decline was reflected in massive job losses. In 1961 the city had enjoyed virtually full employment. By 1971 unemployment had reached 6.1 per cent and, following the catastrophic decline of the late 1970s, it peaked in September 1982 at almost 22 per cent (more than 100,000 people). A total of 119,000 jobs disappeared from the city between 1971 and 1981, almost twice the scale of the job losses experienced in Scotland and Wales combined. A further 191,000 were lost between 1979 and 1983, primarily from manufacturing (which experienced net losses of 167,000) and, whereas manufacturing had contributed almost half of the city's jobs in 1974, by the mid 1980s less than one-third of its workforce was employed in this sector. The city's decline was mirrored in the West Midlands region where output per head fell from being 5 per cent above the national average in 1971 (second only to the South East region) to 13 per cent below it (second lowest after Northern Ireland).

Economic decline had a particularly severe impact on inner city wards where unemployment reached 30 per cent and led to growing social deprivation. By the early 1980s, the city had developed some of the worst urban problems in the European Community (Cheshire *et al.*, 1986) and contained the largest and most severe concentration of deprivation in the country, with half of the population of the inner core being among the most deprived 2.5 per cent in England and Wales. Thus, in less than a quarter of a century, Birmingham's fortunes had declined from a position of economic strength, located at the heart of the UK's second fastest growing region, to the point where the city became a by-word for deindustrialisation and was seen by at least one commentator as 'a sprawling, blighted, industrial zoo whose citizens sported a collective inferiority complex' (Lister, 1991).

However, benefiting from the national economic upturn, the city's manufacturing decline at last began to decelerate and, by 1987, the Birmingham business community had started to regain some of its former confidence. The region's GDP grew again and unemployment in Birmingham fell to less than 13 per cent by the beginning of 1989. The number of confirmed redundancies in the city fell to just over 500, compared to almost 10,000 in 1985 and more than 20,000 in 1981, and the level of vacancies was also increasing. There was, it seemed, tangible evidence to support the city council's Economic Development Department's motif, which proclaimed that 'the investment is working'. The 1989 economic development strategy explained that there were 'many indications that Birmingham is regaining its competitive edge in many of the manufacturing sectors in which it was previously world famous' (Birmingham City Council, 1989). The profitability and turnover of local companies was increasing, office rentals in the city centre reached £20 per square feet, skills shortages were increasing, as was acquisition and reclamation of derelict industrial sites by the private sector. By June 1990 unemployment had fallen to below 11 per cent for the first time in more than a decade and the city council's 'up-beat' pronouncements sought to exploit this revival in the economy's fortunes to attract inward investment.

Just as the catastrophic decline of manufacturing had plunged the city's economy into crisis in the late 1970s, the revival of manufacturing industry seemed to be leading it out of recession. Manufacturing output within the city grew by 6 per cent in both 1987 and 1988, led by a boom in the construction sector which experienced 8 per cent growth in 1987 alone. A significant growth in self-employment, particularly in the construction industry, also contributed to economic recovery, as did rapid growth in the level of employment in services (although the picture was complicated by an increase in contracting out and thus re-classification of jobs in wholesale redistribution and a range of other activities which had previously been performed in-house by manufacturers).

However, detailed analyses of the city's economic prospects demonstrated that recovery remained fragile in many sectors and the deep seated confidence which had existed two decades before had yet to return.

Forecasts by the West Midlands Enterprise Board suggested that the performance of the West Midlands economy would be close to the national average in the early 1990s. This represented a significant improvement on the experiences of the early 1980s when the region had declined far more rapidly than the UK economy as a whole. However, Birmingham's economy was not expected to be able to maintain the advances of the late 1980s because of the anticipated national downturn and because, on the basis of past experience, it was likely to perform less well than the region as a whole.

In fact the depth and duration of the recession of the early 1990s meant that it had a far more devastating impact than had been predicted. From 1990 onwards the Chamber of Commerce's Business Surveys began to indicate a sharp decline in the number of local companies working at full capacity. Confirmed redundancies in the city increased sharply – reaching 7,554 in 1991, with engineering and construction again being particularly severely affected. Between January 1991 and December 1992 manufacturing employment within the region declined by almost 16 per cent (compared to the national average of 11 per cent), and from 1990 to 1993 unemployment in the West Midlands increased more rapidly than in almost any other UK region. The number of jobs in Birmingham declined by 10 per cent between 1989 and 1992. One fifth of the city's manufacturing jobs and 5 per cent of its service jobs disappeared between 1989 and 1993, with the latter constituting a much greater proportion (30 per cent) of total redundancies than in the recession of the later 1970s and early 1980s (when they had accounted for just 5 per cent of all the city's jobs losses).

By the end of 1992 unemployment had reached 18.7 per cent, the highest in any major UK city except for Manchester and Liverpool and almost 50 per cent above the national average. The unemployed to job centre vacancy ratio increased from 14 to 51 between June 1990 and December 1992. Moreover, the 1991 census demonstrated that there were 10,000 additional jobless people (mostly women) in the city who were not eligible for benefit and had not, therefore, registered as unemployed. Reflecting the fact that construction and manufacturing were the earliest and hardest hit sectors, the largest number of job losses was among skilled manual workers, and male unemployment increased from 14.8 per cent to 25.6 per cent between 1990 and 1992 (compared to the West Midlands average of 21.4 per cent and the national average of 15.1 per cent). Inner city wards again bore the brunt of the downturn with unemployment rates reaching 40 per cent (nearly three times the national average) in Aston and over 30 per cent in four other wards by the end of 1992. Long term unemployment also exceeded the national average – 43 per cent of the unemployed in Birmingham had been out of work for at least a year (the national average was 34 per cent) and 20 per cent for more than two years (the national average was 14 per cent). Almost two-thirds of the unemployed were aged under thirty-five and a third were under twenty-five years old, and the Asian and Afro-Caribbean communities had unemployment rates of 27 per cent and 22 per cent respectively, compared to just 12 per cent among the white ethnic groups.

THE PROBLEM: CAUSES OF DECLINE

Birmingham's economic plight was the result of a combination of factors. The largest single influence on the city's economy was (and still is) the health of the UK economy as a whole. It is estimated that up to 75 per cent of job losses in Birmingham's manufacturing sector were linked to national trends, including underinvestment, exchange rate policies, and increased productivity leading to reductions in the demand for labour (Birmingham City Council, 1992a). These were, however, compounded by the city's 'manufacturing specialism' and the preponderance of producer services, which rendered it particularly susceptible to national economic cycles. Structural problems were also compounded by the virtual absence of attractive sites and premises and the West Midlands' ineligibility in the 1960s and 1970s for regional policy, with the result that new manufacturing investment may have been diverted away from the city, depriving it of a generation of investment in new product lines and processes. Indigenous businesses were also slow to invest in new technologies and few moved into high technology sectors or new markets.

Birmingham's decline was also a reflection of the overcapacity of the European car and truck market and the city's heavy dependence on vehicle manufacture either directly or as a provider of components. Massive redundancies at the Leyland (later Rover) site at Longbridge and the Leyland DAF plant in Washwood Heath, were magnified by knock-on impacts on their suppliers and, in the late 1980s and early 1990s, the decline of the UK coal industry also had a marked impact, with eleven of the twenty-nine Birmingham companies which supplied British Coal expecting their contracts to be delayed or cancelled (Birmingham City Council, 1992b).

The social problems resulting from economic decline were exacerbated by the outward migration of relatively affluent residents who, nevertheless, retained and commuted to jobs in the city. The result was that the proportion of the city's jobs which were filled by local residents fell from 82 per cent in 1961 to 69 per cent by 1981. This contributed to an erosion of the city's tax base without reducing significantly demand on Birmingham's public services and exacerbated the polarisation between inner city and suburbs.

THE RESPONSE: BIRMINGHAM'S ECONOMIC STRATEGY

The unexpectedly steep downturn of the late 1970s and early 1980s, combined with the prospect of losing the West Midlands County Council, prompted the city council to take an increasingly pro-active approach to economic regeneration. Its first comprehensive strategy, published in April 1985, reflected the increasing importance which was attached to economic development by the new Labour administration. Resources were devoted, for the first time, to an Economic Development Unit (which became a full Department in 1988) designed to bring together the existing, largely unco-ordinated initiatives and programmes scattered across the authority's Planning and Environmental Services Department.

The main concern in 1985 was the plight of the 116,000 residents who were registered as unemployed. The city council aimed to address this through 'locally based strategies and programmes which bring together existing public and private initiatives' (Birmingham City Council, 1985). It stressed the importance of 'basic industries with a high export content', nearly all of which were in manufacturing, upon which other jobs, particularly in the service sector, depended. A mixed portfolio of initiatives aimed at strengthening and retaining indigenous companies and attracting inward investment was therefore adopted. The city council aimed to develop a closer relationship with the private sector, assisting it with training, premises, and development sites, and encouraging the forging of better links between major companies and their local component suppliers in order to improve the latter's R&D capabilities, quality control systems, and investment in new product lines. The strategy also highlighted the need to address the 'dire shortage of good quality industrial land', noting that almost a quarter of the empty factory floorspace in the city was unlettable.

The city council's main priorities in the mid-1980s were therefore to:

- create of a variety of industrial sites for all types of potential investment in the city
- establish a co-ordinated approach to economic initiatives across the city council, including a 'one stop shop' within the EDU so that companies had easy access to sources of assistance
- close the gap between training needs and training provision
- develop 'high technology' initiatives for the city.

The objectives specified in the second (1989) strategy document were little changed. The newly formed Economic Development Department aimed to promote:

- employment support, including training for unemployed and disadvantaged
- business investment and enterprise including financial support,

204

consultancy, training to businesses, enterprise development, marketing and promotion to lead to inward investment, diversification and expansion of existing and new businesses

- the physical regeneration of key areas such as Heartlands and the Jewellery Quarter.

The approach outlined in successive economic development strategy statements represented one of the widest ranging and best resourced local authority attempts to foster local economic regeneration in the last decade and was differentiated from the strategies adopted in many other areas by four elements that were, at the time, seen as being particularly innovative. These were:

- the early and consistent emphasis on partnership with the private sector
- the extensive use made of EC assistance to fund economic regeneration initiatives
- the early and explicit acknowledgement of the need to promote services as alternative sources of economic activity and new jobs in order to alleviate unemployment resulting from the decline of manufacturing
- the strong emphasis enhancing the city's 'image' and securing an 'international identity' and 'influence'.

Partnership

The city council's long tradition of co-operation with the private sector meant that it was able to embrace an 'enabling' role much earlier than many other local authorities. It was realised that, because of resource constraints, the city council's role in economic regeneration had to be that of catalyst and 'prime mover' for new initiatives undertaken jointly with a wide range of other public and private sector partners. It therefore promoted a bewildering array of regeneration initiatives with private sector involvement (Carley, 1991), the most important of which have been the National Exhibition Centre (NEC), the Heartlands initiative, and the Aston Science Park.

The importance of the NEC was threefold. First, it established the city council's credentials in undertaking joint ventures with the private sector. Secondly, it demonstrated the potential of attempts to diversity the economy. Thirdly, it provided the collateral for the later development of the International Convention Centre (ICC). NEC Ltd. was established by the city council and the Birmingham Chamber of Commerce and Industry in 1970 to oversee the construction, marketing, and management of a large conference and exhibition complex on the eastern edge of the city. The original plan was to provide a show-case for West Midlands companies, thus boosting business with the rest of the UK. The idea was greeted with some scepticism when the NEC was opened in 1976, but within a few years was being acknowledged as a considerable success. By the early 1990s, when the NEC made an annual profit of more than £14 million and attracted 4 million visitors (Birmingham Convention and Visitor Bureau, 1991), it had become the largest exhibition facility in the UK, the tenth largest in Europe, covered an area of 130,000 metres, accounted for half of all UK exhibition business, and hosted a series of major international events (Cheesewright, 1992).

Birmingham Heartlands Ltd. was set up in 1988 by the city council (which owned 35 per cent of the company and provided four board members), in partnership with the chamber of commerce and five major developers (which owned 65 per cent and provided seven members of the board). It was conceived partly because of the local authority's desire to avoid the imposition, by central government, of an Urban Development Corporation and was operated as a non-statutory development agency. Although it did not engage directly in development schemes, it developed a strategic framework for the regeneration of more than 2,000 acres just to the east of the inner ring road, and provided a mechanism for a more equal partnership between developers and the local authority and greater scope for community involvement than was possible in many of the Urban Development Corporations established by central government in other major cities (Salmon, 1992). Although it eventually foundered in the wake of the recession of the early 1990s, the victim of depressed property values, it can be seen as a forerunner of the City Challenge initiative and is an important example of the pro-active approach adopted by the city council to stimulate regeneration.

The Aston Science Park was opened in 1983 with the aim of attracting high technology companies. Birmingham Technology Ltd. (owned jointly by Lloyds Bank, the city council and Aston University), provides premises, management support, and equity capital to firms and is designed to overcome the reluctance of London-based financial institutions to invest outside of the South East (Massey et al., 1992). This combination of measures has led to the attraction of a higher than average number of independently owned, start-up companies than other UK science parks and is an approach which has subsequently been emulated by other areas (Massey and Wield, 1992).

Other important public–private ventures include the upgrading of the International Airport (an important part of the attempt to enhance the city's and region's accessibility) and a number of city centre developments including the £30 million Hyatt Regency hotel and attempts to establish broader links with local employers through an 'Economic Forum'. Most recently the city council has been a key player (with the TEC and Chamber of Commerce) in the Birmingham Economic Development Partnership (BEDP), a legal entity formed in April 1993 to bring together a wide range, of existing, informal partnerships including the Small Business Development

Partnership (formed by the city council, the chamber, the Midland Productivity Group, the West Midlands Engineering Employers Federation, the University of Central England, and funded largely by the TEC) and the 'First Step Shop' (a partnership including the city council, the DTI, the chamber, Midland Bank, and the City Action Team). The BEDP is credited with having provided a model for the development of the Department of Trade and Industry's (DTI) Business Link initiative and not surprisingly, therefore, Birmingham was one of the first three pilots sponsored by the DTI's national One Stop Shop/Business Link initiative which was launched in 1993.

European Community assistance

A second important feature of the 'Birmingham approach' was that it was among the first UK local authorities to look to the European Community for funding for economic regeneration. The city council had enjoyed a good working relationship with central government over many years. Local politicians from both major parties have generally adopted a pragmatic and flexible approach, and officials, both in Whitehall and Regional Offices, perceived Birmingham as a fairly moderate authority which 'could be trusted'. As a result the city benefited from the rapid expansion of central government urban initiatives in the 1980s, being one of the first Urban Programme Partnerships areas (PSMRC, 1985) and gaining more than almost any other area from the Urban Development Grant programme (Martin, 1989). The more imaginative search for EC funding, however, led to a shift from its traditional UK-orientated outlook to an increasingly 'international' perspective both on the city's economic problems and their solutions.

The need to seek EC assistance arose from the limits imposed on the local authority's finances by central government and the fact that, in the early 1980s, it did not qualify for domestic regional policy assistance. The city council's response to these constraints was a typically 'entrepreneurial' approach to the European Commission for economic assistance. Initial consultations met with a sympathetic response from the Commission. However, Birmingham's lack of Assisted Area status meant that it was not eligible for finance from the European Regional Development Fund (ERDF). The city council was already seeking eligibility for regional policy assistance from the Department of Trade and Industry (DTI) in recognition of the severity of its economic decline since the late 1970s. In the meantime it lobbied the Commission for EC funding on the basis that the UK government had designated it as an Urban Programme Partnership authority. To this end it built up a comprehensive networks of contacts both within the Commission and the European Parliament, partly through one of the first local authority offices to be opened in Brussels.

The designation by the DTI in November 1984 of the city and parts of the surrounding region as an Assisted Area unlocked a variety of EC assistance. The local authority moved quickly to secure funding packages and there followed a plethora of council-led initiatives which attracted support from the ERDF, the European Social Fund (ESF) and the European Investment Bank. By 1987 the city had received £78 million from the ERDF and this was followed by a major injection of funding in the form of the first Integrated Development Operation Programme to be approved in the UK (in July 1988), and the designation, in 1989, of much of the West Midlands as an 'Objective 2' (declining industrial) region. The IDOP provided a total package of approximately £200 million between 1988 and 1991, including £128 million form the ERDF, £44 million from the ESF, and £44 million in loans (Martin and Pearce, 1992). With the matching funding which EC assistance attracted from national government, the private sector, and a variety of other sources, the city, therefore, acquired a multi-year programme in excess of £400 million, and by the early 1990s, Birmingham was being acknowledged as the British local authority which (with the possible exception of Strathclyde Regional Council) had benefited earliest and most spectacularly from EC assistance.

Business tourism

The city council acknowledged relatively early on that even a spectacular recovery in the competitiveness of the city's manufacturing base would not enable it to regain former levels of employment. As a result, it sought to stimulate new kinds of economic activity and EC assistance was channelled into a series of high profile developments just to the west of the city centre that were designed to promote business tourism. Public opinion, which tended to cling to the need for what were referred to as 'real jobs' (highly paid, manufacturing jobs, normally for men), lagged some way behind the policy makers' awareness of the need to promote employment in services, many of which seemed quite alien. However, the identification of business tourism as an area with potential for development in Birmingham stemmed directly from the success of the NEC which had alerted local businesses and policy makers to a potential 'growth' sector which the city might seek to exploit in its attempts to diversify the local economy and lessen its dependence on manufacturing. The city council's strategy promoted the creation of additional exhibition and conference facilities to attract visitors. Some of the newly acquired EC assistance was devoted to a 30,000 square feet extension of the NEC, but much was used to ensure that visitors stayed in the city centre in order to encourage spending on local accommodation, meals, and other entertainment. There was major investment in new hotels (some of which received assistance from national government programmes such as City Grant and its predecessor Urban Development Grant), a range of 'cultural' and sporting facilities and the strategy's centre-piece – the

International Convention Centre (ICC) which comprised eleven meeting halls and a new symphony hall. Built at a total cost of approximately £150 million, it can be seen as a potent symbol of the promotion, by the city council, of business tourism as a major source of future employment and wealth generation. Thus, whereas the NEC had been intended to enhance the profitability of local manufacturing industry, the backing given to the ICC signalled that the promotion of business tourism and a host of service-based activities, which were unrelated to the city's industrial past, were now key priorities for the city council.

Image

The fourth notable element of Birmingham's strategy in the 1980s was the emphasis placed on enhancing the city's image and influence. The 1989 economic development strategy added to the three major roles, which the city council had fulfilled during the mid and late 1980s, a new responsibility for 'improving the image of the city'. This was to involve more publicity for 'the many major business success stories', improvements to the environment (particularly to major traffic routes and the city centre), and 'special efforts' to ensure that new buildings in prominent locations were attractively designed. The city council also undertook to act as an 'advocate' for the city by promoting the interests of Birmingham's businesses and their employees to national and EC policy makers. To some extent this was a formal recognition of the local authority's long-standing and very pro-active approach to 'selling the city'. The desire to shed the old industrial legacy and the 'smoke-stack' image which accompanied it was, however, given added importance by the imminent opening of the ICC and the opportunity this offered to attract additional visitors. The fact that the *International* Convention Centre was funded in part by £49 million of EC assistance and the choice of its name were symptomatic of the significant broadening of Birmingham's horizons since the mid-1970s, contrasting with the designation of *National Exhibition Centre* fifteen years before. There was now an acknowledgement, and indeed a welcoming, of the fact that Birmingham was part of Europe, and a strong desire to acquire a role on the international stage. The city council claimed that it was now less interested in Birmingham's status as Britain's 'Second City' and much more concerned to secure its place as a 'leading European centre' (Fetter, 1990).

The growing emphasis on promoting the city's image spawned a range of attempts to upgrade the city's attractions to relatively affluent business tourists in order to reduce the perceived risk that visitors might meet in the city but choose to stay overnight elsewhere. Cultural attractions, leisure facilities, a pleasant physical environment, and good communications were increasingly seen as pre-requisites to economic regeneration, because of their importance in attracting visitors, retaining existing employers, and promoting inward investment (Confederation of British Industry, 1989). The city council, therefore, backed a wide range of improvements to cultural facilities and the physical appearance of the city centre and a major public relations campaign was enacted through the local press, TV and radio, 'glossy' promotional materials, and a series of public arts programmes. Major new initiatives to boost the quality of life offered by Birmingham and its image included cultural and sporting initiatives such as the city's bid to stage the 1992 Olympic Games, the construction of the National Indoor Arena – then the UK's largest indoor sporting arena with a capacity of 10,000 seats – the new symphony hall, financial support for the city's symphony orchestra, the launch of a new TV and Film festival, the attraction of the former Sadlers Wells (now re-named Birmingham) Royal Ballet Company and the D'Oyly Carte Opera company (both from bases in London), and the designation of Birmingham as the '1992 City of Music' involving a heavily subsidised, year-long music festival entitled 'Sounds Like Birmingham'.

These were accompanied by major improvements to the physical environment of the city centre which the Birmingham Unitary Development Plan highlighted as being fundamental to economic revitalisation and to improving the quality of life for the city's residents (Pearce and Waterston, 1994). Key environmental investments included the ambitious 'Highbury Initiative', the creation of a new 'Centenary Square' in front of the ICC, the pedestrianisation of parts of the city centre, and the installation of new statues and water features. In addition a series of major investments were undertaken to build upon the city's tourism potential, including canal improvements (using the Urban Programme and ERDF), and the renewal and promotion as a visitor attraction of the historically important Jewellery Quarter (funded under Industrial Improvement legislation, Urban Development Grant and City Grant) (Pearce, 1993).

Along with the concern with image there have been attempts to increase the city's political influence in Europe by tapping into networks involving other major European cities to influence national and European Union policies. In 1986 the city council joined Barcelona, Frankfurt, Milan, Lyons and Rotterdam in setting up what became the 'Association of Eurocities'. This is an important lobbying mechanism on behalf of more than thirty 'leading European cities' with a permanent secretariat in Brussels served by a full time 'Euro-cities' officer. Senior Commission officials have attended Euro-cities conferences and the Association has been consulted on key Commission policy statements such as its Green Paper on the Environment and the Europe 2000 document on European urban policy. This has enabled the Association to press DGXVI, and other Commission directorates, to put in place regional and urban policies which respond to the needs of the major industrial city regions. Birmingham has also been a key player in a number of other local authority networks both within the UK and Europe including, for example, the Motor Industry Local Authority Network (Firth, 1992), and has been actively involved in a range of international exchanges of experience which have enabled it to learn from European counterparts.

ACHIEVEMENTS AND PERSISTENT PROBLEMS

While it is too early to reach definitive judgements, there is only limited evidence that the city council's attempts to alleviate the negative impacts of economic transition have been able to arrest the city's chronic decline or enhance its long-term competitiveness. Persistent structural weaknesses mean that the economy remains very vulnerable to national and international recession. Manufacturing is likely to continue to be a declining source of jobs and the local economy is still dominated by engineering sectors which have relatively poor long-term growth prospects. The local economy continues to have a low share of industries which have experienced rapid expansion, particularly pharmaceuticals and electronics. Partly as a result of the over-representation of family-owned SMEs, which are generally slower to adopt new technologies, net capital investment per worker in manufacturing remained between 10 per cent and 20 per cent below the national average throughout the 1980s. Moreover, the service sector continues to be dominated by producer services and is thus heavily dependent upon local manufacturing companies. Future strategies cannot, therefore, be based on a simple substitution of manufacturing with jobs in existing producer services and there is a continuing need to revitalise the former while simultaneously diversifying into new sectors and products.

There are, however, some signs that the economy is now somewhat better placed than ten years ago. Some indigenous firms, notably Lucas, have relocated functions to other parts of the world in order to tap into international markets, but there has also been significant inward investment, and more than 100 overseas companies (including GKN, Cadbury, Foseco, and Rover) are now based in Birmingham. These major firms survived the recession of early 1990s better than that of the 1980s, (with less than half the level of job losses and only five major business failures). This suggests that the city's businesses are now more efficient than a decade ago, having adopted a range of new managerial methods, more flexible labour practices and increased automation. This improved efficiency is reflected in the city council forecasts that 'the local economy has the potential to grow at an annual average rate of 3.8 per cent between 1994 and 1997 and by 3.4 per cent from 1997 to 2005' (Birmingham Economic Information Centre, 1994). There are hopes that local motor vehicle components suppliers will benefit from Britain's position as Europe's prime motor manufacturer and the strong links they have developed with the UK based Honda and Toyota operations. However, major problems with third and fourth tier suppliers persist, with many continuing to struggle to meet the new standards required by the larger automotive companies.

There are opportunities for growth in other sectors. Financial services are, for example, becoming increasingly important and, according to city council estimates, may employ up to 30,000 local people. There are now more than twenty international banks in the city including a large number of regional headquarters and some national facilities, for example, TSB's retailing centre, and the operations centres of both Mercury and Birmingham Cable (which will be the largest Cable franchise in Europe) are based in the city. The most rapid (non-public sector) growth sector is, however, likely to result from spending by visitors. Birmingham's position as the regional capital for the West Midlands, located within an hour's drive for 3 million people, gives it an important domestic catchment area to draw upon and its staging of a 'Special Summit' of EC heads of government in October 1992 is seen as having been an important step towards securing a new role as a leading European city and international 'meeting place'. However, even if output growth in manufacturing is achieved, it will be accompanied by continuing decline in manufacturing employment – expected to amount to losses of at least 16,500 jobs over the next ten years (Birmingham Economic Information Centre, 1994). Thus, net increases in employment will not exceed 1.4 per cent per annum. A return to the employment levels of the late 1980s is, therefore, 'unlikely until well into the next century and relatively high levels of unemployment, leading to serious social and economic deprivation in some parts of the City, are likely to persist for many years to come'. This raises two key questions – how many jobs can be created in labour intensive service industries, particularly tourism and leisure, and who will benefit from this employment growth?

To date there has been very little empirical research into the employment impacts of the policies pursued by the city council and its partners. A preliminary survey of direct employment creation by the three largest developments – the NEC, NIA, and ICC – based on data derived from NEC Ltd's employment records, demonstrated that in 1992 the three venues employed a total of 1,063 permanent staff (comprising 1,017 full time equivalent jobs); 60 per cent of whom were employed by the NEC, 29 per cent by the ICC, and 11 per cent by the NIA (Martin, 1993). In addition the three venues provided approximately 360 FTE temporary jobs at any one time, for 'casual' employees working in catering, security, and as exhibition staff. The study noted that the planned expansion of the NEC meant that this 'snap-shot' underrepresented its medium-term impacts and that the ICC and NIA were expected to employ directly approximately 350 and 130 permanent staff respectively by the late 1990s. Moreover, the indirect employment impacts derived from increased visitor spending in local restaurants and hotels, as well as the positive impacts of supplier, employment, and income multipliers associated with all three developments are likely to far outweigh the direct benefits identified above. A study of the wider benefits of the NEC (Peat Marwick, 1989) estimated that it supported 11,000 jobs in the West Midlands economy and the city council expects that, on a pro rata basis, the ICC will support about 5,000 local jobs by 1996/1997. A further study commissioned by NEC Ltd, and based on surveys of visitors, exhibitors, local hoteliers, contractors, organisers, and promoters, estimated that activities taking place in the ICC in 1993 generated £28 million of 'retained regional income and 2,700 associated jobs', that the NIA 'created £17 million worth of retained regional income and 1,900 associated jobs' and the NEC £135 million of 'retained regional income and 12,200 associated jobs' (KPMG Peat Marwick, 1993). Estimates of the scale of indirect employment impacts are, however, notoriously inexact (Storey, 1990; Gregory and Martin, 1994), and definitive judgements of the long-term economic benefits will require much more detailed, longitudinal analyses.

The question of who has benefited, and who is likely to benefit in the future, from Birmingham's regeneration strategy has come under increasing scrutiny. Critics of the city's investment in high profile, 'prestige projects' and 'cultural industries' see it as an ill-advised import from US cities where such policies have, it is claimed, exacerbated the plight of the underclass and fuelled unrest (Law, 1993). Loftman and Nevin (1994), for example, believe that the city council has greatly exaggerated the potential job creation and private sector leverage associated with the ICC and related city centre projects, and that the benefits have accrued to 'better-off residents and workers at the expense of deprived inner urban areas and services on which the poor depend'. Similar criticisms of the way in which the resources for the new developments were allegedly diverted from education and other budgets were made by a former Secretary of State for Education and attempts to enhance the city's image have also been questioned. The latter can, it is claimed, be seen as a flawed attempt to remould civic pride by spinning together a false mythology of the individual 'Brummie' genius, pioneers of the industrial revolution with a futuristic townscape and new cultural identity which is quite alien to local residents (Hall, 1994).

Such criticisms have evoked a sharp response from senior council officers and elected members. There have been a series of 'up-beat' accounts of the council's achievements (see, for example, Bore, 1992), as well as more carefully argued replies from senior officers. It has been claimed that since the European Commission had no legal 'competence' to intervene in member states' education or social service systems, the choice facing the city in the mid 1980s was not between using EC finance for 'economic' projects or to improve its social infrastructure, but whether it wished to receive assistance for the former or nothing at all. Furthermore, it is claimed that the city council's overriding objective was to put in place an 'economic infrastructure' which facilitated future growth in the dramatically altered economic circumstances which Birmingham found itself in the early 1980s (Wenban-Smith, 1992). Direct job creation was not the *raison d'être* but a 'bonus', and attempts to judge the effectiveness of the new investment in terms of the level of direct, short-term job generation are, therefore, misguided. Proper assessments can only be made in the long term when the full benefits, including, most importantly, the transformation of the city's image, will be apparent.

However, these disclaimers seem to contradict a series of claims made by the city council in the local press, and contradict publicity materials (for example the ICC Induction Pack) that new jobs in the ICC would benefit local people living in neighbouring wards. They may also overlook the fact that EC assistance for 'prestige projects' could have been complemented by greater efforts to equip local people and the long-term employed to benefit from employment generation. The only independent research undertaken to date suggests that, while a relatively high proportion of those employed by the NEC, ICC, and NIA were unemployed when they were recruited, few of the best-paid jobs have gone to those living in the immediate vicinity of the three developments. Nevertheless, people living close to the NEC have gained more than half of the part-time/temporary jobs it provides and a quarter of ICC's part-time/temporary staff live in the Ladywood ward where it is located (Martin, 1993). However, the lack of a comprehensive, long-term, evaluation of who has gained access to the new jobs in prestige developments continues to cloud the debate, depriving policy makers and their critics of reliable evidence of the real extent of 'trickle-down'.

CONCLUSION

While definitive judgements about the final outcomes of the strategy adopted in Birmingham would be premature, the indications are that, while city centre developments have improved its physical appearance and external image and perhaps 'taken the edge off' economic decline, it has probably done little to address the severe problems faced by the long-term unemployed living in the poorest inner city wards. The 1994 DOE survey of inner city deprivation suggests that social conditions in parts of Birmingham are currently the fifth worst in the country and recent changes within the Labour controlling group on Birmingham City Council have led to a new emphasis on meeting the needs of the poorest sections of the community and working with local groups to safeguard the interests of those who may lose out if 'trickle-down' fails to materialise.

However, the difficulties faced by the city's policy makers are not unique to Birmingham. Recent studies suggest that central government's massive inner city programme has been unable to make significant inroads into the problems experienced in core inner city areas (Robson *et al.*, 1994) and the failure of economic development initiatives to benefit all sections of the community has emerged as one of the key dilemmas of regeneration policies on both sides of the Atlantic (Bovaird, 1994). Cities across the UK are witnessing increasing polarisation associated with the 'co-existence of increasing prosperity and expanding poverty' manifested in a 'growing band of people who gain no benefit from the regeneration of city centres' (Henley Centre, 1994). In this respect Birmingham is, therefore, typical of many old industrial areas beset by problems associated with a legacy of outdated infrastructure, peripherality within Europe, a workforce which is ill-equipped for employment in new growth sectors, chronic under-investment and continuing deindustrialisation and counter-urbanisation. The ability of such cities, with all of their industrial baggage, to respond to the constant re-ordering of market opportunities must be limited, particularly in the present, resource constrained environment. However, in the absence of a comprehensive industrial strategy to manage economic change at a national level, local agencies are likely to be the only source of properly targeted measures to safeguard the interests of the poorer sections of the community whose economic prospects, both during and after the transition to a post-industrial economy, remain bleak.

ACKNOWLEDGEMENTS

The author acknowledges with gratitude the provision of economic data by staff at the Birmingham Economic Information Centre, and comments by Graham Pearce on an earlier draft of this chapter.

REFERENCES

Birmingham City Council (1985) *An Economic Strategy for Birmingham*, Birmingham: City Council Planning Department.

Birmingham City Council (1989) *Birmingham Economic Strategy*, Birmingham: City Council Economic Development Department.

Birmingham City Council (1992a) *Annual Review 1992: Economic Prospects for 1993/1994 and Outlook to 2005*, Birmingham: City Council Economic Development Department.

Birmingham City Council (1992b) *Economic Development Strategy for Birmingham 1993/1994*, Birmingham: City Council Economic Development Department.

Birmingham Economic Information Centre (1994) *The Birmingham Economy Review and Prospects*, Birmingham: City Council Economic Development Department and Birmingham TEC.

Birmingham Convention and Visitor Bureau (1991) *Birmingham Tourism Statistics*, Birmingham: BCVB.

Bore, A. (1992) 'Economic Development Initiatives in Birmingham', *Public Money and Management* 12, 3, 67–8.

Bovaird, A.G. (1994) 'Managing Urban Economic Development: Learning to Change or the Marketing of Failure?' *Urban Studies* 31, 4/5, 573–603.

Carley, M. (1991) 'Business in Urban Regeneration Partnerships: A Case Study in Birmingham' *Local Economy* 6, 2, 100–15.

Chandler, J.A. and Lawless, P. (1985) *Local Authorities and the Creation of Employment*, Aldershot: Gower.

Cheesewright, P. (1992) 'Trade Fairs Wooed', *Financial Times Survey: Conferences and Exhibitions*, 25 February.

Confederation of British Industry (1989) *Regeneration of the Region: Change and Challenge in the West Midlands*, Birmingham: CBI.

Cheshire, P., Carbonara, G. and Hay, D. (1986) 'Problems of Urban Decline and Growth in EEC Countries: or Measuring Degrees of Elephantness', *Urban Studies* 25, 131–49.

Fetter, A. (1990) 'Marketing a City in Transition'. Paper presented to the *IBG Annual Conference*, University of Glasgow.

Firth, C. (1992) 'Restructuring in the Motor Industry: The Role of Local and Regional Authorities in the UK and Europe', in M. Geddes and J. Benington (eds) *Restructuring the local economy*, Harlow: Longman.

Gregory, D.G. and Martin, S.J. (1994) 'Crafting Evaluation Research: Reconciling Rigour and Relevance', *British Journal of Management* 5, Special issue, 43–52.

Hall, P. (1987) 'The anatomy of Job Creation: Nations, Regions and Cities in the 1960s and 1970s', *Regional Studies* 21, 2, 95–106.

Hall, T.R. (1994) 'Collage City: The Media of Urban Regeneration and Emergent Civic Identities in Birmingham'. Paper presented to the *18th Annual Conference of Institute of British Geographers*, January, Nottingham.

Henley Centre (1994) *Local Futures 94*, London: The Henley Centre.

KPMG Peat Marwick (1993) *The Economic Impact of the International Convention Centre, the NIA and the NEC on Birmingham and the West Midlands*, Birmingham: KPMG Peat Marwick.

Law, C.M. (1993) *Urban Tourism: Attracting Visitors to Large Cities*, London: Mansell.

Lister, D. (1991) 'The Transformation of a City: Birmingham', in M. Fisher and O. Owen (eds) *Whose cities?*, Harmondsworth: Penguin.

Loftman, P. and Nevin, B. (1994) 'Prestige Project Developments: Economic Renaissance or Economic Myth? A Case Study of Birmingham', *Local Economy* 8, 4, 307–25.

Martin, S.J. (1989) 'New Jobs in the Inner City: An Evaluation of the Employment Effects of Projects Assisted Under the Urban Development Grant Programme', *Urban Studies* 26, 627–38.

Martin, S.J. (1993) 'Economic Regeneration and the Hospitality Industry: No Jobs for Locals?' Paper presented to the *IBG/ESG Conference on The Geography of the British Hospitality Industry*, Birkbeck College, 16 September 1993.

Martin, S.J. and Pearce, G.R.A. (1992) 'The Internationalisation of Local Authority Economic Development Strategies: Birmingham in the 1980s', *Regional Studies* 26, 5, 499–503.

Massey, D. and Wield, D. (1992) 'Evaluating Science Parks', *Local Economy* 7, 1, 10–26.

Massey, D., Qunitas, P. and Wield, D. (1992) *High Tech Fantasies: Science Parks in Society, Science and Space*, London: Routledge.

Pearce, G.R.A. (1993) 'Conservation as a Component of Urban Conservation', *Regional Studies* 28, 1, 88–93.

Pearce, G.R.A. and Waterson, P. (1994) 'Strategic Planning Guidance: Review of the Content of the Unitary Development Plans in the West Midlands and Their Conformity with Strategic Planning Guidance', *Working Paper 28*, Birmingham: PSMRC, Aston Business School.

Peat Marwick (1989) *The National Exhibition Centre: Economic Impact Study*, Birmingham City Council.

PSMRC (1985) *Five Year Review of the Birmingham Inner City Partnership*, London: DOE Research Series.

Robson, B., Bradford. M., Deas, I., Hall, E., Harrison, E., Parkinson, M., Evans, R., Garside, P. Harding, A., and Robinson, F. (1994) *Assessing the Impact of Urban Policy*, London: HMSO.

Salmon, H. (1992) 'Urban Regeneration and the Community: Birmingham Heartlands: Mid-term Report', *Local Economy* 7, 1, 26–38.

Spencer, K., Taylor, A., Smith, B., Mawson, J., Flynn, N., and Batley, R. (1986) *Crisis in the Industrial Heartland: A Study of the West Midlands*, Oxford: Clarendon Press.

Storey, D. (1990) 'Evaluation of Policies and Measures to Create Local Employment', *Urban Studies* 27, 669–84.

Sutcliffe, A. (1986) 'The Midlands Metropolis: Birmingham 1890-1980', in G. Gordon (ed.) *Regional Cities 1890–1980*, London: Harper and Row.

Wenban-Smith, A. (1992) 'New Economic Role for the Centre'. Letter to editor, *Planning*, 907.

10

ECONOMIC REGENERATION IN SHEFFIELD

Urban modernisation or the management of decline?

Gordon Dabinett

The industrial city of the late nineteenth and early twentieth centuries will rapidly become an artefact from the past, to be visited in the form of an open-air museum . . . while our lives become increasingly dependent upon information technologies.'

John Brotchie *et al.*, *Cities of the 21st Century*

INTRODUCTION

All urban areas in Great Britain have had to face new challenges over the last three decades. The continued loss of employment and population, the flight of manufacturing and the rise in social and environmental problems have posed major enigmas for urban managers and those who seek to shape and influence the country's cities (Hausner, 1986). The complexity and apparent intractability of the difficulties have been matched by an array of policy initiatives, programmes, and projects pursued by a plethora of agencies and actors (Audit Commission, 1989). In the UK, the role of the city has become questioned for the first time since their rapid growth during the industrial revolution. At the heart of this reassessment are two issues. First, the unique spatial characteristics of urban areas are being threatened as modern capitalist society enjoys greater levels of personal mobility and distances are reduced as a result of innovations in telecommunications. Secondly, there is a debate about the nature of local versus global forces and the scope of specific localities to shape or determine modernising forces which seem so overwhelmingly predominant.

This chapter describes and reflects on the experiences of one city, Sheffield. Sheffield is the major centre of the South Yorkshire sub-region. This area does not form a cohesive conurbation in geographical terms, but in the past was united by the traditional industries of deep coal mining, steel making, and engineering. During the post-war years Sheffield was regarded as an area of relative prosperity in this region. Like all other urban areas it had a number of people that suffered social, economic, and physical inequality, but in relative terms these groups were small.

It can be argued that Sheffield only became strongly associated with depression and urban decline after 1981 (Lawless and Ramsden, 1990). At this time confidence in the city was very low since there was little new investment, housing and land markets were stagnant, employment was falling, and unemployment rising. A symptomatic and symbolic change was the way in which the main area of manufacturing employment in the city, the Lower Don Valley, was becoming a wasteland of vacant buildings and derelict sites as jobs were lost in the traditional industries. The city's position changed rapidly and relatively later than other cities, a state linked explicitly to the condition of the local economy.

ECONOMIC CHANGE IN SHEFFIELD

A decade of employment crises

Historically, Sheffield has been strongly associated with making things. This position was maintained in 1971 when nearly half of the jobs in the city were related to manufacturing. It was able to maintain a position as one of Britain's most important and prosperous industrial areas as a result of producing an internationally competitive product, specialised steels, and having strong linkages between this and other industries in the city such as cutlery and hand tools. The urban area contained a whole network of inter-linked activities, including subcontracting, forging, pressing, precision engineering, and specialist services such as non-destructive testing and scrap metal. While the city was also a service centre, containing universities, hospitals, centres of public administration, and cultural facilities, it never performed the same regional capital functions such as those associated with Leeds and Manchester.

From the mid-1970s a number of factors caused a severe reduction in manufacturing output and employment in the city. Various accounts have been given of this change (Gibbon, 1989; Sheffield City Council, 1984 and 1987; Watts, 1991), but the outcome was a rise in unemployment from 4 per cent in 1978, below the national average of 6 per cent, to 18 per cent by 1984, above the national rate of 13 per cent. Table 10.1 shows changes in the levels of employment during the period 1981 to 1991. The data clearly illustrate the process of deindustrialisation and restructuring, as manufacturing employment levels fell rapidly, reducing the absolute and relative importance of this sector to Sheffield's economy. By 1991, only 23 per cent of employment was in manufacturing, although this was still above the national average of 21 per cent. At the same time, service sector employment grew in relative and absolute terms, but not at a sufficient rate or scale to off-set industrial job losses.

Table 10.1 Employment change in Sheffield 1981–91

Division (1980 Class) Change	Total Employment			
	1981	1991	Change	%
Agriculture/energy	6,400	3,300	–3,100	–48.4
Extract/manufactured metals	27,100	7,300	–19,800	–73.0
Metal goods/vehicles	42,500	28,800	–13,700	–32.3
Other manufacture	16,200	13,100	–3,100	–19.1
Construction	11,200	9,700	–2,500	–13.3
Distribution/hotels	44,500	44,500	–30	–0.1
Transport/communication	13,600	12,900	–700	–4.9
Finance/business	15,900	22,100	6,200	39.1
Other services	64,200	69,900	5,700	8.9
Total	241,700	211,800	–29,900	–12.4

Sources: Census of Employment/NOMIS.

Note: Figures are rounded.

The changes in the composition of industrial employment are shown in detail in Table 10.1 which highlights the loss of 33,469 jobs in the metals and engineering sectors. This table also unmasks some of the features of the expansion in service employment, since the financial and business services sector grew by 39 per cent and gained 6,200 jobs, whereas other service activities also created additional jobs (5,700) but at a much slower rate (a gain of 9 per cent). The increase in service employment over this period was, to some extent, caused by the relocating to the city of certain functions by three large organisations: the Headquarters of the Manpower Services Commission and various functions of the Employment Department moved from London at different points of time after 1977; the Midland Bank relocated some of its national functions in a series of phased moves after 1976; and the Norwich Union relocated part of its financial advice and marketing back-office functions between 1990 and 1994.

The historical context of change in Sheffield is further illustrated by looking in detail at the remaining activities that made up manufacturing employment in 1991. The most critical feature was the remaining dominance of metal and metal related products in the 1991 employment profile. In 1991, some 32,300 jobs were in this category, two-thirds of all manufacturing employment in the city. The various elements of this sector and their inter-relationships are shown in Figure 10.1. The manufacture of steel and the first downstream processes of drawing, rolling, forming, forging, pressing, and stamping still accounted for 9,100 jobs in the city. Further downstream activities involved with manufacturing metal-based products contributed another 23,200 jobs, half of which were related to craft products such as hand tools, cutlery, engineers tools, medical appliances, and jewellery. Therefore, while the city still contained basic metal-bashing activities in 1991, the majority of employment depended on the manufacture of various value-added goods. This represented a shift in the relationship between these activities, since in 1981 there were 24,000 people in basic metal manufacture, 38 per cent of all metals-related employment, compared to 9,100 (28 per cent) in 1991.

Of the other main manufacturing sectors in Sheffield in 1991, two were associated with the metals industries, that is refractory products and

Figure 10.1 Metal industries in Sheffield 1991

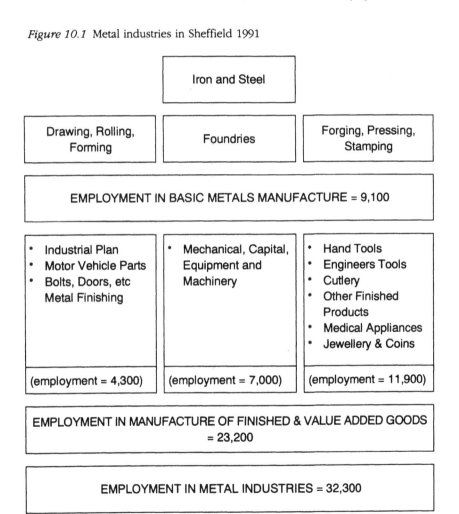

Source: NOMIS/Employment Department.
Note: All figures rounded.

electrical equipment. The other contained industries such as food manufacture, clothing, and shopfitting, which either provided products for the mass urban market or were able to take advantage of the labour available in urban areas and the communications networks associated with major conurbations. These activities accounted for approximately a quarter of the manufacturing sector, but there was no tangible evidence of diversification away from the traditional industries, nor any indications of a dynamic and growing new sector which might offset the more general loss of employment in manufacturing.

The rise and fall of an industrial district?

The loss of manufacturing employment since the 1970s can be attributed to complex and inter-related processes. The main thrust of change has been driven by the behaviour of major multinational corporations, although there has been an increasing role for small enterprises. Recent analyses of manufacturing performance within the context of regional development have predominantly addressed the concepts of globalisation and flexible specialisation (Ernst and Meier, 1992). It has been suggested that, insofar as the marketing and production of certain products increasingly require a global strategy, then local economies are forced to interact and network beyond their regional and national boundaries (CEST, 1992). At the local level, this has resulted in significance being given to the concept of the industrial district. The industrial district has become to be considered the most important micro-regulatory institutional framework of the flexible specialisation model, although there is little agreement on how to define it (Amin and Robins, 1991). But does the clear success of some local economies represent a re-emergence of the agglomeration economies which helped to create urban areas as major manufacturing centres?

A traditional perception of Sheffield is that of a locally integrated economy, with basic steel manufacture interacting with the craft industries in the city (Binfield *et al.*, 1993). The local relationships between companies have been put forward as an explanation for the successful development and expansion of the urban economy, with final markets which were often international in scope. For example, the Sheffield economy benefited from a major share of world markets in stainless steel; products of high quality and repute sold globally, often within the old British Empire; and technology expertise and plant/equipment were sold to newly industrialised countries.

These global markets have changed dramatically in more recent times, as a result of greater competition and shifts in world trade (Sheffield City Council, 1987). In addition, one of the main markets for many Sheffield products was capital goods for other industries such as construction, process plant, and the automotive and aerospace industries. Many of these have become increasingly global in scope and operations. As a result, those companies and activities which competed or were linked into such global markets became more competitive or modernised, rationalised, or closed (Gibbon, 1989). The local economy has come to operate much as any other open economy, and will increasingly need to compete in European and international markets to maintain market shares or to expand. There will be specific companies trading and subcontracting with other local firms but their role would seem less significant than in the past. These long trends would suggest that Sheffield has become far less territorially integrated, but this may not be a weakness.

Over the last ten years, medium-sized companies have sought to maintain or expand turnover by the combination of organic growth and diversification, or organic growth and acquisition of other small companies (Gibbon, 1989). As a consequence, the Sheffield manufacturing base in 1994 can be broadly divided into four groups of establishment:

1 Traditional, mature, family-owned companies, largely in the metals sector. Many of these are small businesses, but others have expanded through acquisition of other local companies. Advantages that may occur from local control are offset by the consequent lack of new investment and failure to introduce innovative business strategies.
2 A significant number of companies which have some degree of local ownership or control but are characterised by joint ventures with non-local companies or joint ownership patterns, often involving European partners.
3 A diverse small firms sector which contains some companies exhibiting strong growth. No sectoral patterns dominate but there are some indications that such companies are established on the basis of skills or markets associated with the traditional sectors of the city, for example, subcontract engineering, computer software, electronic systems, and plastics.
4 A small number of branch plants linked to motorway accessibility and distribution networks. Manufacturing inward investment to the city has been at a very low level compared to other steel closure areas such as Consett, Shotton, and Corby, and major foreign-owned projects have tended to go to adjoining areas in South and West Yorkshire (Lawless and Dalgleish, 1992). Therefore, while there are strong indicators of local control in much of the Sheffield manufacturing base, there is no evidence to suggest this has any degree of autonomy or creates a locally owned or managed industrial district.

Finally, do activities in the city represent the milieu used to describe successful industrial districts? Such networks or inter-relationships do not generally exist Sheffield-wide, but two institutional forms do reflect old and new patterns of co-operation: company associations and city partnerships. Old patterns of formal co-operation between private companies were usually based on common products or markets. A number of such associations are located in the city, reflecting traditional activities. In the past such organisations might have played a role in ensuring the success and development of the local economy by providing an institutional network to exchange best practice and to secure economies of agglomeration. However, the reduction in these industries has left such organisations under resourced and unable to play a wider role. Some still promote research and have secured links with higher education, but groupings not involved in such activities would appear to be more concerned with defending traditional markets and trade practices. Their potential to promote a successful district would appear to be limited.

New public/private partnerships have, however, attempted to address a city wide agenda (Lawless and Ramsden, 1990). The development of such partnerships within Sheffield can be seen to take one of three forms:

- private commercial interests and development agencies seeking to attract more visitors, trade, and investment to the city
- organisational frameworks and strategies designed to provide an opportunity for all major actors to be consulted on strategic development plans and policies
- specific projects where management boards have representation from the various interests in the city.

Evidence, albeit anecdotal, suggests that these institutional arrangements do not support any territorial integration thesis nor suggest that Sheffield is still or is being modernised as an industrial district.

THE RESPONSES TO ECONOMIC COLLAPSE

Conflict and urban employment policies in the early 1980s

In 1981, amidst the economic catastrophe, the city council became one of the first local authorities to make a clear step to address the crises arising in urban economies. While the concept of an economic response was beginning to emerge at this stage, the statements and proposals were a clear political response to rising unemployment, and were essentially an employment-based programme rather than a coherent industrial or re-generation strategy (Bennington, 1986).

> Sheffield City Council cannot stand idly by while this happens. We have established an Employment Committee and an Employment Department to ensure that the Council raises its voice against the absurdity of keeping over 40,000 people on the dole while there is a crying need for jobs to be done, products to be made and services to be provided. Our aims are necessarily modest. We have resources

only to undertake a limited number of tasks. Our intention is to show that there is an alternative to unemployment – and to argue positively that this alternative should be pursued.

(Sheffield City Council, 1982: 6)

During this period the situation was fuelled by the conflict between central government and the city council about local government funding and local taxation. With David Blunkett as leader of the council, Sheffield was at the forefront of the national campaigns to maintain local authority services and employment levels. Although Sheffield was declared a Programme Authority under the Urban Programme in the period 1979 to 1980, it was not given full regional assisted area status. The local authority refused to become involved in the deregulation experiments of enterprise zones and did not receive special status through other urban policy initiatives of this period. Conflict and division grew between private capital interests in the city and the controlling labour nexus of the council, the local Labour Party, and the trade unions (Duncan and Goodwin, 1988; Seyd, 1990, 1993).

The policies of this period have been widely discussed, and although defensive towards employment and the role of municipal socialism within the city, they did attempt to create a new economic order in the light of the broader global forces at play (Cochrane, 1988). The conflict arose with the particular policies of the incumbent Thatcher Conservative government to deal with the problems occurring in specific localities and to create a new macro-economic and political order. The local council continued to fight to change national policies towards the steel industry, but accepted that the past could not be recreated.

Thus, the leading advocates of this approach argued that:

in any regeneration of the economic and industrial life of the country, local initiatives in themselves will only play a small part. But they can make a wider political impact, not only committing people to new kinds of work experience but winning them over to a vision of a very different kind of society.

(Blunkett and Green, 1983: 7)

The approach was based on campaigning, municipal enterprise to protect public service employment and to improve the quality of jobs in the private sector, and exemplary economic development projects. The last sought to create new (or modern) employment through technology-based companies, workers' co-operatives, and small businesses created by the unemployed. Emphasis was placed solely on projects which were funded by public investment.

Urban regeneration goals in the mid-1980s

During the 1980s, Sheffield remained an area where local policy responses dominated and central government urban and regional initiatives were marginal, unlike their policies towards public expenditure, privatisation, and industry which were each to have significant impacts on the city over time (Dabinett, 1990). The local political situation was to change in the mid-1980s as a further Conservative government was elected and the council leadership also changed. The period became distinguished by attempts to achieve wider urban regeneration goals and the establishment of various partnerships to replace the old style corporatism and industrial bargaining relationships (Lawless and Ramsden, 1990). The period was to end when one of the main instruments of central government urban policy was imposed on the city with the declaration of an urban development corporation (UDC).

It can be argued that 1986 saw a paradigm shift in local policy. The council was forced to concede that private sector investment would be necessary to meet the shortfall between available public resources and the investment needed to complete agreed projects for regeneration. It was acknowledged that in order to secure such investment a new development strategy and agency were required. The agency was seen to be a public/private partnership which could change the anti-business image of the council, representing a significant shift away from municipal socialism. This turned out to be the Sheffield Economic Regeneration Committee (SERC) which oversaw the development of a strategy which was intrinsically linked with European Commission and Urban Programme project funding, rather than the injection of new funding, public or private.

The strategy claimed that the city council should have a central role in planning the economic future of the city (Sheffield Economic Regeneration Committee, 1989). It did not consist of a fixed plan but projects linked to a vision of urban regeneration said to be shared by all groups in Sheffield. Projects were linked to one of five programmes: physical and environmental improvement; business and technology support; training; city promotion; infrastructure development. Totterdill (1989) has argued that such an approach reverted to a simple project-based form of intervention, grounded in an unformulated trust in market-led development. Several reasons for the emergence of project-based, and often property-based renewal can be cited. The failure to develop clear sectoral analyses for key industries (other than steel making and the cultural industries) allowed planners to offer what were tangible, though economically superficial, models of regeneration based upon projects and property (Dabinett, 1991). The absence of statutory powers, almost total lack of Department of Industry intervention, combined with the resources available to support environmental and physical projects through Urban Programme and EC

226

structural funds certainly contributed to this imbalance. Crucial perhaps, was the perception of the city council as anti-business, a view which prevented necessary dialogue in the city.

During this period, the council developed its strategy to a relatively high level of political sophistication. But the events that followed were determined by a series of decisions largely outside the control of the city which were certainly part of the wider processes of modernisation occurring. Another Conservative government was elected, bringing with it a new priority towards the inner cities which was to lead to the establishment of an urban development corporation in the city in 1988. The city council approved the proposal to build a regional out-of-town retail and leisure centre (Meadowhall) 5 km from the city centre in the Lower Don Valley, once the centre of steel making. Finally, the council submitted a bid to host the World Student Games (WSG) in 1991, and won.

The WSG was to become the most controversial of the initiatives undertaken in the city. New construction amounting to some £147 million included the provision of two new swimming pools, a new athletics stadium, and an indoor arena. In addition, a cultural festival was also held with the Lyceum Theatre being renovated at a cost of £12 million. Very little sponsorship, advertising, or private capital was attracted to either the investment in the facilities or the holding of the Games. Projects attracted some grant funding, but the operation of the Games also left the city council with a further debt to pay. Consequently, opponents pointed out the cost to the city tax-payer, the concurrent closure or reduction in other public facilities in the city, and the elitist nature of the facilities. Others claimed benefits to Sheffield in terms of morale boosting, image creation, and the new activities and events attracted to the city with subsequent expenditure and potential visitor income.

While the WSG facilities represent the coming of the modern leisure society, Meadowhall represented the ultimate development of the consumer society championed by the Thatcher government during the 1980s and riled against by the previous city council ideology which sought to 'challenge the principle of production through the private market mechanism geared primarily to individual consumption' (Bennington, 1986: 23). Meadowhall was a clear example of the North American model of consumer choice and personal mobility being transposed to an environment where £250 million of private capital could lead to the regeneration of a vast area of derelict land. The scheme, adjacent to the M1 motorway but fully integrated with local public transport facilities, was granted permission by the city council in 1987 and was included in the UDC area and became a flagship of this agency's strategy to regenerate the Lower Don Valley.

On 7 March 1988, the government announced the proposed establishment of a UDC to be located in the Lower Don Valley. The area covered 810 hectares of land of which 35 per cent was derelict or vacant at declaration. It included some 800 firms employing 18,500 people mainly in metals related industries (Kirkham, 1990). The declaration and operation of Sheffield Development Corporation (SDC) represented a significant development in terms of the scale of new funding and the new organisational arrangements associated with a quango. The SDC formulated its regeneration plans through its own corporate structure and the publication of planning frameworks (Sheffield Development Corporation, 1989). These were based on the flagship approach, with many schemes already proposed in SERC documents, such as Meadowhall, a city airport and redevelopment of a major waterside area. While the SDC increased land allocated for industry and expressed concern for the future of activities vital to the steel industry such as metals recycling, it adopted a style of urban regeneration dependent on the much criticised trickle-down effect and a strategy based on the operation of the local property and land markets (Dabinett and Ramsden, 1993).

Thus, the mid-1980s saw a major shift in the way in which the crisis facing the local economy was managed. The defence of employment rights and public sector employment became marginalised as agendas addressed urban regeneration objectives. The need to address unemployment and employment creation appeared to lose priority in the light of efforts to secure investment and economic growth. This was a philosophy based more on inter-urban competition, major physical projects, and a role for private capital. These elements *might* be seen as requisites to a modern economy based on new infrastructure, new leisure and consumer activities, and the consequent patterns of new service employment and new labour structures. Attempts to establish partnerships in the city were city council dominated and led to the creation of embryonic but fragmented arrangements. These adopted the common aims of urban regeneration, but involved a disparate set of projects, players, and agendas.

Reforging partnerships in the 1990s

The 1990s saw the urban regeneration process being continued in the efforts made to stimulate new and additional economic activity in the city. The particular feature of this period was the increasing dominance of central government policy in the city. This expressed itself in two ways. First, partnerships in the city were reformulated to incorporate and give more importance to the SDC and the Sheffield Training and Enterprise Council (TEC), set up by central government in 1990. Secondly, the allocation of resources to regeneration was based more and more on competition. As a result, attempts were made to overcome internal agendas in the city to raise competitiveness in respect to other urban areas, and to secure funds on the basis of potential success and value for money rather than a fixed strategy.

The decade began with the publication of a new strategy, Sheffield 2000, by the partnership forum of SERC (Sheffield Economic Regeneration Committee, 1990). This represented an evolution in thinking and approaches from earlier strategies and represented more of a corporate working plan than an alternative employment, economic, or social policy for Sheffield. The strategy sought to provide a long-term view, a clear, co-ordinated framework, a vision. However, the need to search for new and additional funding to implement projects was well illustrated by the two bids for City Challenge funds in 1991 and 1992. Spatial targeting and specific project-based strategies were again features of these bids, both of which were to fail.

Apart from Meadowhall, investment at this time was being attracted to the city primarily through major public works: the WSG facilities opened in 1991; the South Yorkshire Supertram was given government approval and grant aid; the SDC began to invest in the Lower Don Valley through road construction and the preparation of sites. Other major investments in the city were undertaken by the two Universities, Sheffield Combined Heat and Power (CHP), Yorkshire Cable, and a limited number of major commercial property developments were mainly occupied by Norwich Union and the Employment Department.

The partnerships within the city also became reforged as another Conservative government was elected, but with a new leadership which began to recast urban and regional policies. The reforging of partnerships in the city could also have been triggered by the change in council leadership, or the preoccupation in the local authority with internal management and budgeting crises, or the new institutional environment created by setting up the TEC and SDC, or the failure of City Challenge bids. The new body, the Sheffield Liaison Group came together in late 1992 and published its Way Ahead Strategy in 1994 (Sheffield City Liaison Group, 1994). Previous partnerships and strategies were acknowledged, but the need to move forward was recognised: 'our emphasis is on action – action to create jobs through the generation of wealth' (Sheffield City Liaison Group, 1994: 4). Many of the programmes were the same as before, but there was some shift to small-scale projects and more consideration was given to the industrial structure in the city within the Business Link and Regional Technopole proposals. The individuals within the Group were also similar to previous partnership groupings, although greater importance was perhaps given to the role of central government agencies, the universities and further business involvement in the form of The Cutlers Company as well as the Chamber of Commerce.

The Way Ahead and Sheffield 2000 strategies shared a number of emerging areas of interest that were apparent in all regeneration efforts, but were perhaps given different priority:

- technology support, now focusing on the Technopole but also on the development of telecommunications
- inward investment and changing the image of Sheffield
- a concern for the environment, both in terms of industrial activity but also infrastructure such as CHP and Supertram
- service employment, through sport and leisure as well as cultural and media industries and financial services
- training and education.

Was this the agenda of a modern city?

IMPACTS – DECLINE OR MODERNISATION?

Strategies and regeneration

The various strategies and organisational arrangements set up in Sheffield during the 1980s and early 1990s combined to take the city in a number of directions. However, taking a perspective on these from afar, and casting an eye over the similar documents, slogans, and partnerships established in most other urban areas of the UK in this period, leaves an impression that Sheffield's approach was in no way unique. Strategy has always been victim of opportunism, uncertainty, and a degree of impotence. However, at the heart of each strategy were a number of common and recurring features: image, investment, innovation, and institutional capacity.

A consistent objective has been to replace the past image of Sheffield linked to historical and industrial associations with a new image of the city based on modern activities, infrastructure, and cultural activity. Visions have underpinned most strategies, rather than fixed plans, and these have often been associated with new catch phrases and logos. An increasing importance has been given to selling the city in recent years as the competition for both public and private capital has increased (Ashworth and Voogd, 1990). In a study of Sheffield's approach, the overall impression gained was that inward investors had no image of the city but, where they did, the image was likely to be a negative one (Crocker, 1994). The study concluded that any new image must accord with reality, and it was clear that the reality observed by both national and local investors was poor. Crocker (1994) argued that changes were required to address this problem which were more fundamental and long term than could be resolved by a new slogan or public relations campaign.

Local regeneration strategies have recognised the need to attract inward investment. Insufficient capital exists within an area to carry out the massive rebuilding and restructuring required. The successful attraction of an inward flow of capital also signifies new global relationships and an international competitiveness. Following the economic collapse in the early

1980s, new investment slowly returned to the city. The remaining businesses, still dominated by the metals sector, invested in new plant and machinery and there was also considerable acquisition behaviour, often leading to new European investment in local businesses. Several major urban regeneration projects were proposed during the 1980s, but most never came to fruition. Property investments actually implemented remained relatively small. The major single investments were the Meadowhall retail/leisure centre and public schemes of various sorts, including the WSG. No major international investment was attracted. The potential sites for major developments, such as a Toyota car factory, were limited, and the city faced an increasingly competitive situation from more favourably grant-aided adjoining areas (Lawless and Dalgleish, 1992). However, the availability of labour remained an important attraction, as illustrated by the decision of Norwich Union to come to the city.

Strategies usually express a desire to develop the indigenous capacity of an area through the release of innovative efforts and by designing innovative projects or schemes. Sometimes this is expressed through business development measures, on other occasions by supporting the soft infrastructure of education, R&D, knowledge, and culture. Sheffield was no exception, establishing Science and Technology Parks, a Cultural Industries Quarter, a Product Development Initiative, workshops for co-operative businesses, and the Way Ahead document proposed a Regional Technopole and a National Centre for Popular Music. Obviously, many of these schemes were small in scale compared to the extent of the problems, but also sought long-term goals. Perhaps the greatest innovation in policy was to develop new strategic service sector activities, such as leisure, sport, and financial services. To a great extent, these strategic goals coincided with prevailing market trends, but the scope and nature of activity attracted to the city represented a structural shift in resource allocation and job opportunities.

The importance of local capacity building in organisations concerned with urban economic development has been clearly established (Bennett and McCoshan, 1993). Sheffield, like other areas faced by economic restructuring, but also experiencing social and political change, underwent a major shift in the way efforts were made to bring about regeneration. In 1981, the city council stood almost alone and in conflict with central government. By 1994, there were over fifteen agencies promoting economic development in the city, including two significant new actors in the form of an urban development corporation and a training and enterprise council. This proliferation led to greater organisational complexity in the city and to an increase in agendas, but also to the development of partnerships. Initial partnerships were city council dominated, but over time central government has come to influence the shape and constituency of these arrangements, for example, in bids for resources via City Challenge, the Business Link scheme, and the Single Regeneration Budget.

Each new approach attempted to secure a greater private sector involvement. Perhaps the remaining institutional weakness in 1994 was the lack of a clear regional voice or organisational structure.

The impacts of change

The extent to which these strategies have brought about the regeneration of the city is a complex question, and one that can only be fully considered with the passage of time. A useful benchmark for such an assessment is a report on the economic position of South Yorkshire prepared in the light of the Single European Market to be established in 1992 (Université de Louvain, 1989). The report considered how competitive the region was in terms of future business and economic trends. The report made a number of critiques, each of which is examined in turn here.

Concentration of traditional industrial sectors and absence of growth sectors

By 1994, the city's employment relied less on the traditional sectors, but metals related activities were still dominant within manufacturing. However, this analysis belies the increases in productivity and competitiveness in these sectors and the nature of the markets which many Sheffield companies served. These were increasingly modern and likely to exhibit export-based growth, such as aerospace, oil exploration, automotive, and construction. Individual growth businesses were emerging, but perhaps too few to form the basis of a new sector.

Poor development of small and medium enterprises and inadequate support networks and services

This was still largely true with the rate of growth in small businesses being generally below the national average and other urban areas. While a number of medium-sized businesses existed in the city, the level and nature of such activity was not equivalent to the German experience, for example. The support networks for businesses had expanded, but the proposed establishment of a Business Link in the city highlighted the need for greater co-operation and targeting of assistance.

Technological marginalisation, poor track record of innovation and advanced technology, lack of technological R&D capability of international standard

Individual companies in the city have developed innovative processes and products. New, technology-based companies have set up in the city and grown. The two universities maintain strong reputations in certain areas of applied research and continue to attract research funds. The National Transputer Centre was attracted to the Science Park. However, these do not present a coherent R&D presence of international scope, and efforts to increase technology transfer were largely unsuccessful or achieved very limited objectives. This fault is largely not of the city's making, but rather the outcome of national policies which have reduced R&D expenditure and continued the spatial concentration of government research and grant funding in the South of England.

On the periphery of the European market and poor integration into high-speed transport networks

The strategies adopted at each stage of regeneration emphasised and gave priority to projects which would increase the accessibility of Sheffield to Europe. By 1994, none had come to fruition, including proposals for a city airport and modernisation of the rail route to London. The impact of opening the Channel Tunnel is difficult to foresee as the final configuration of links is uncertain. While companies such as Avesta Sheffield have used the freight services to ship stainless steel into Europe, the integration of Sheffield into the new geography of Europe depends largely on central government policies towards the deregulation and privatisation of services and to public infrastructure investment.

Industrial dereliction and urban decay and blight

Many individual sites and derelict buildings have been redeveloped as public investment occurs and levers in private investment. Certain areas of the city have been physically transformed, and investment continues. This was always a large and slow task, and often new developments stand as oases among vacant or derelict areas. Given the nature of the property market in Sheffield, there has been a particular problem in securing major redevelopments (Henneberry, 1993). In addition to this, there is emerging evidence that some new developments, in particular Meadowhall, are causing severe negative impacts on areas such as the city centre. The down turn in consumer spending combined with the construction of a major new light rail scheme has left many areas of the central area vacant or with an appearance of decay.

Critical lack of information technology and advanced communications infrastructure

The deregulation and privatisation of telecommunications provision in the UK was one factor that stimulated a growth in this sector of 6 per cent per annum during the 1980s. These trends were mirrored in Sheffield where leading edge technology was provided for major users such as Norwich Union and the Midland Bank. The city also benefited from investment by the Yorkshire Cable Company in 1994. By the early 1990s, the condition of the information technology and communications infrastructure was less of a barrier to development. Its maintenance and development remained a necessary condition of growth, however, albeit not the critical factor. More important is the development of services and users to create further investment in these technologies. A study of telematics in Sheffield concluded that, in the 1990s, the city was being reinforced as a national node of networks, rather than a node of international transactions. The main underlying feature of telematics in the city was to accelerate business processes in order to gain competitiveness and responsiveness in increasingly dynamic and uncertain operational environments (Dabinett and Graham, 1994).

Thus comparison with the Louvain Study findings shows a city that was obviously changing, but did this represent decline or modernisation?

The case for modernisation

Criticism has been made that the regeneration efforts in the city have been based on weak foundations. Concern has been expressed at the way in which investment has largely been encouraged through short-termism of the property market, social benefits have relied on the trickle-down effect, and many new activities are based on cyclical and fashion-based consumer behaviour (Totterdill, 1989; Dabinett and Ramsden, 1993). Here, though, an attempt is made to reflect on the longer-term impacts and direction of change, rather than the immediate beneficiaries of the modernising environment occurring in the city.

Modernisation has seen changing relationships between global and local relations through new markets, the control and flow of private capital, and the shrinkage of time and space through communications and computing technologies. These have impacts on specific localities, and most measurably on employment patterns. Sheffield has moved away from a male and manufacturing-based labour market. There has been an increase in female, part-time and service employment. Table 10.2 compares the employment profile of Sheffield TTWA in 1991 with other cities and major employment areas. First, the proportion of male and part-time employees reflects the national average, with little variation between areas. Sheffield has, if anything, converged towards the norm. This may be seen as modernisation if the movement from the traditional activities has also accommodated changes in practices and organisational behaviour rather than a simple shedding of jobs. Ratz (1990) has claimed that there was widespread interest in increasing labour flexibility and employee involvement in the

234

Table 10.2 Urban employment in Great Britain by TTWA in 1991

Urban Areas	Employment 1991				
TTWA	Total (000)	Male (%)	Part-Time (%)	Mnfr (%)	CFBS (%)
Sheffield	230.5	52	25	24	16
Manchester	648.3	52	25	20	21
Birmingham	647.5	53	24	27	18
Glasgow	517.7	51	23	18	18
Liverpool	358.4	49	27	18	18
Newcastle	316.9	50	27	19	15
Bristol	309.3	53	25	19	24
Leeds	308.4	52	26	20	20
Nottingham	288.0	52	26	28	14
Edinburgh	279.7	50	24	13	25
Leicester	230.0	51	24	32	13
London	2,894.1	53	20	11	32
Heathrow	635.1	55	21	15	29
Watford/Luton	299.3	52	26	24	20
Hertford/Harlow	205.2	52	28	24	16
Dudley/Sandwell	233.5	56	24	36	12
Coventry	206.7	54	24	32	13
Great Britain	21,568.0	52	26	20	18

Sources: Census of Employment/Department of Employment.

Note: Mnfr. = classes 2–4 (1980 classification); CFBS = communications, financial and business services, classes 7 and 8 (1980 classification).

city, and practices in Sheffield changed in similar ways to those observed nationally during the 1980s.

Secondly, the most significant feature of Table 10.2 is the sectoral distribution of employment. It is possible to comment on the nature of the service sector in Sheffield and the role of manufacturing. One strength of the manufacturing economy that previously existed in Sheffield was the ability for the business base to draw wealth into the city via its range of products and markets. Do the new and emerging modern activities provide the same engine of economic prosperity? The picture that emerges from the table, albeit a static snapshot, is that the new service base in the city is unlikely to achieve such impacts based on its configuration at the beginning of the 1990s. This comment is based on the presumption that the activities most likely to generate new and additional wealth creation are the communications, financial, and business services. These are well represented in both modern areas such as Heathrow and Bristol, and international and national centres such as London, Edinburgh, Manchester, and Leeds. Sheffield is poorly represented in these activities in terms of employment, and its overall profile most closely matches that of the Hertford and Harlow TTWA. Again this signifies a considerable shift to a broader-based economy, but one where the inherent engine of growth lies predominantly outside the region.

Sheffield is still a manufacturing centre compared to other major cities, but no longer has the concentration of employment in manufacturing found in the West Midlands conurbation and urban areas of the East Midlands (see Table 10.2). In absolute and relative terms, the extent of manufacturing employment matches areas such as the Watford/Luton and Hertford/ Harlow TTWAs, although these would have lost jobs in the early 1990s as a result of reductions in defence expenditure. The *extent* of deindustrial-isation in Britain and its urban areas is part of a wider economic debate (Green, 1989), but it is likely that manufacturing employment will continue to decline in Sheffield due to the adoption of new process technologies and work practices, irrespective of trends in markets and competitiveness.

The failure of the regeneration strategies to develop new growth sectors means the city is still dependent to a degree on businesses where an over-capacity exists within Europe (for example, steel) and others where competition will continue to increase from newly industrialised areas (for example, hand-tools). Existing companies will become increasingly linked, directly or indirectly, into global patterns, but the long-term manufacturing base may depend increasingly on inward investment and new entre-preneurial activity, both at a low level in the early 1990s. When compared to other global developments, such as successful technopoles and Japanese urban development led by technology-based programmes and investment (Castells and Hall, 1994), then the inherent disadvantages of location, history, and weak national policies appear to overwhelm the city's efforts to manage the restructuring successfully.

Any long-term regeneration will rest on the development of a highly skilled workforce and flexibility in the labour market. As growth picks up, new and local companies could be confronted with shortages of specific skills, some of which will reflect national rather than local labour market conditions. Generally, the changes discussed in this chapter have seen the Sheffield labour market converging with wider regional and national occupational structures. However, most projections indicate future in-creases in the number of managers, administrators, qualified scientists, engineers, and associated technical staff, while Sheffield still has an over-supply of unskilled construction workers, plant and machine operatives, clerical and secretarial workers. The latter occupations are all projected to decline (Sheffield Training and Enterprise Council, 1994). This leaves the city with some important human resource issues:

- unemployment remains a serious problem with young people dispro-
portionately affected, and levels of long-term unemployment continuing
to rise
- while school leavers are increasingly opting to stay on in education,
levels stay below the national figure and compare poorly with other
countries
- there has been a dramatic increase in the number of students at the two
universities in the city, but as few as 25 per cent of graduates find
employment in Sheffield.

Thus, as the city modernises, the opportunity to extend labour market
flexibility offers benefits and threats. Providing jobs can be created in the
city with a high level of skill and high wages, then increasing education and
training could lead to clear and wider benefits. The transition to such a
position needs clear labour market strategies and the management of such
growth. However, the city still has to catch up with other competing areas
in terms of its overall skills base and levels of labour demand. As a result,
it may fall into the trap of being a net exporter of skilled labour, and the
greater flexibility in the labour market will be used to advantage by
industries providing jobs associated with unregulated conditions, low skill
levels, and poor wages.

CONCLUSION – A MODERN CITY?

Sheffield is a changing city. Change is neither a new nor a modern
phenomenon, but developments now occurring such as South Yorkshire
Supertram, Sheffield Combined Heat and Power, Cable TV, Meadowhall,
new office developments and activities, new technology applications in
steel processing and engineering, university expansion, science and technology parks and a technopole, all create modernising images. However,
such examples exist in most British and European cities. The nature and
purpose of employment has also changed, with new work practices, new
management techniques, and personnel, and new ownership structures
occurring in much of the city's economic base. The competitiveness of what
remains has been transformed from fifteen years ago in 1979. Although the
impacts from events during this period were often large in scale and scope,
it must be realised that the process of change, restructuring, and falling
competitiveness had begun much earlier.

Levels of employment have declined. Skills and trades have been lost.
Unemployment, social problems, and inequality have increased in the city.
The evidence would suggest that the processes of change have shifted
Sheffield away from a traditional industrial area towards a broader-based
economy whose profile in many respects is more like the national average.
In this sense, further decline or modernisation is even more linked into
national performance and policies than ever before. To continue the

237

modernisation within the constraints or opportunities of national government policies, the managers of the city have to ensure that:

* manufacturing industry remains competitive, but is strengthened by additional inward investment and entrepreneurial activity
* higher level services develop in the city to broaden the scope for wealth creation and retention; in other words, the service-based employment being transferred to, or created in, Sheffield needs to involve high level tasks, such as decision-making and policy-making, rather than being simply low level, routine bureaucratic tasks
* the human resource base is developed to successfully transfer skills and knowledge to the local economy
* the evolution and development of new institutional arrangements continue within the city, and between the city and its region
* the quality of life, environment and service provision is maintained, if not improved.

REFERENCES

Amin, A. and Robins, K. (1991) 'The Re-emergence of Regional Economics? The Mythical Geography of Flexible Accumulation', *Environment and Planning D: Society and Space* 8, 1: 7–34.

Ashworth, G.J. and Voogd, H. (1990) *Selling the City*, London: Belhaven.

Audit Commission (1989) *Urban Regeneration and Economic Development: The Local Government Dimension*, London: HMSO.

Bennett, R.J. and McCoshan, A. (1993) *Enterprise and Human Resource Development*, London: Paul Chapman Publishing.

Bennington, J. (1986) 'Local Economic Strategies: Paradigms for a Planned Economy?', *Local Economy* 1, 1, 7–24.

Binfield, C. Childs, R. Harper, R. Hey, D. Martin, D., and Tweedale, G. (eds) (1993) *The History of the City of Sheffield 1843–1993*, Sheffield: Sheffield Academic Press.

Blunkett, D. and Green, G. (1983) *Building from the Bottom: The Sheffield Experience*, London: Fabian Society.

Brotchie, J. Batty, M. Hall, P., and Newton, P. (1991) *Cities of the 21st Century*, Harlow: Longman Cheshire.

Castells, M. and Hall, P. (1994) *Technopoles of the World*, London: Routledge.

CEST (1992) *Industrial Dynamics Working Paper 1*, London: Centre for Exploitation of Science and Technology.

Cochrane, A. (1988) 'In and Against the Market? The Development of Socialist Economic Strategies in Britain 1981–1986', *Policy and Politics* 16, 3, 159–68.

Crocker, S. (1994) 'Image Study', *Urban Transport Investment Studies 13*, Sheffield: Sheffield Hallam University.

Dabinett, G. (1990) 'Local Economic Development Strategies in Sheffield during the 1980s', *Centre for Regional Economic and Social Research Working Paper 10*, Sheffield: Sheffield City Polytechnic.

Dabinett, G. (1991) 'Local Policies Towards Industrial Change: The Case of Sheffield's Lower Don Valley', *Planning Practice and Research* 6, 1, 13–17.

Dabinett, G. and Graham, S. (1994) 'Telematics and Industrial Change in Sheffield, UK', *Regional Studies* 28, 4, 604–17.

Dabinett, G. and Ramsden, P. (1993) 'An Urban Policy for People: Lessons from

Sheffield', in R. Imrie and H. Thomas (eds) *British Urban Policy and the Urban Development Corporations*, London: Paul Chapman Publishing.

Duncan, S. and Goodwin, M. (1988) *The Local State and Uneven Development*, London: Polity.

Ernst, H. and Meier, V. (eds) (1992) *Regional Development and Contemporary Industrial Response*, London: Belhaven Press.

Gibbon, P. (1989) 'Recessions, Restructuring and Regeneration in Sheffield During the 1980s', *Centre for Regional Economic and Social Research Working Paper 1*, Sheffield: Sheffield City Polytechnic.

Green, F. (ed) (1989) *The Restructuring of the UK Economy*, London: Harvester/Wheatsheaf.

Hausner, V. (ed) (1986) *Critical Issues in Urban Economic Development*, Oxford: Clarendon Press.

Henneberry, J. (1993) *The 1980s Property Boom and Sheffield*. Unpublished Research Paper for Joint Initiative of Social and Economic Research, Sheffield: Sheffield Hallam University.

Kirkham, S. (1990) *Sheffield Development Corporation and the Lower Don Valley*, Unpublished Research Paper for Joint Initiative of Social Economic Research, Sheffield: Sheffield City Polytechnic.

Lawless, P. and Dalgleish, K. (1992) 'The Relocation of Economic Activity Within the UK', *Centre for Regional Economic and Social Research Working Paper 19*, Sheffield: Sheffield Hallam University.

Lawless, P. and Ramsden, P. (1990) 'Sheffield in the 1980s: From Radical Intervention to Partnership', *Cities*, August, 202–10.

Ratz, N. (1990) 'Employment Practices in Sheffield 1981–89', *Centre for Regional Economic and Social Research Working Paper 4*, Sheffield: Sheffield City Polytechnic.

Seyd, P. (1990) 'Radical Sheffield: From Socialism to Entrepreneurialism', *Political Studies* 38, 2, 335–44.

Seyd, P. (1993) 'The Political Management of Decline 1973–1993', in C. Binfield *et al.* (eds) *The History of the City of Sheffield 1843–1993, Volume 1: Politics*, Sheffield: Sheffield Academic Press.

Sheffield City Council (1982) *Tackling the Employment Crisis – a New Initiative*, Sheffield: Sheffield City Council.

Sheffield City Council (1984) *Steel in Crisis*, Sheffield: Sheffield City Council.

Sheffield City Council (1987) *The Uncertain Future of Special Steels*, Sheffield: Sheffield City Council.

Sheffield City Liaison Group (1994) *The Way Ahead: Plans for the Economic Regeneration of Sheffield*, Sheffield: Sheffield City Council.

Sheffield Development Corporation (1989) *A Vision of the Lower Don Valley: A Planning Framework for Discussion*, Sheffield: Sheffield Development Corporation.

Sheffield Economic Regeneration Committee (1989) *Sheffield Vision*, Sheffield: Sheffield City Council.

Sheffield Economic Regeneration Committee (1990) *Sheffield 2000*, Sheffield: Sheffield City Council.

Sheffield Training and Enterprise Council (1994) *The Annual Labour Market Assessment 1993/94*, Sheffield: Sheffield Training and Enterprise Council.

Totterdill, P. (1989) 'Local Economic Strategies as Industrial Policy: A Critical Review of British Developments in the 1980s', *Economy and Society* 18, 4, 479–526.

Université de Louvain (1989) *Socio-economic Consequences for the Traditional Industrial Regions of the European Community Arising from the Completion of the Single Market, Report to RETI*, Brussels: Commission of European Communities.

Watts, D.H. (1991) 'Plant Closures, Multi-locational firms and the Urban Economy: Sheffield UK', *Environment and Planning A* 23, 37–58.

11

CONCLUSIONS

Royce Turner

A number of common themes emerge in the chapters of this book. The first, and most obvious, is the dramatic and rapid change that has been taking place in the British economy in the 1980s and 1990s. Contraction in traditional industries has probably been the most salient, and has perhaps had the most direct impact on individuals, communities, and, indeed, on the physical environment.

The changing nature of British business and industry is examined throughout the book. Much large-scale traditional industry has seen considerable reductions in the numbers of workers employed and a contraction in the number of plants. The deep-mined coal industry, for example, has almost disappeared except from a handful of sites in Yorkshire and Nottinghamshire. Other sectors of the economy have been transferred into foreign ownership. The most obvious example is the motor car industry, where none of the major manufacturers in the 1990s are in British ownership. Morris argues that the Welsh economy has been transformed from a 'duo-industry domination' to one which has far more of a service-based orientation, and far more of an international orientation (chapter 3). Even in defence, which retains its status at the time of writing as a major British industry, Lovering notes in chapter 5 that:

> it is a very different entity from that of the Cold War era. Employment has been cut, industrial relations and payment patterns have been reconstructed.

In many ways, this restructuring represents a new 'model' of industrial organisation being implemented by large-scale business organisations. The contours of this are familiar and well recognised. First of all, there is less recognition, and far less power, for the trade unions. The agenda of both the Conservative government and the senior managers and owners of companies was clear, in this respect. From the late 1970s onwards the 'management's right to manage' was pursued as an emblematic totem of management power. The view of Malcolm Edwardes, for example, executive chairman of BL (the forerunner of Rover) between 1977 and 1982, was that BL had no chance of success until the unions were broken (Edwardes, 1983). One of the major symbolic battles was with the NUM, in the mid-1980s, as the mineworkers tried to resist deindustrialisation. Alongside the moves to reduce union power, 'flexibility' became a buzz word. This was a flexibility that related to time, numbers and status of workers, and working tasks. This might have helped some companies become more competitive, but for those workers failing to achieve 'core' status it meant a considerable lessening of job security and, very often, diminished working conditions.

The nature of the way places actually *look* has been changed by the economic and industrial transformation. The pit head winding gear has been swiftly removed from the mining villages. Urban Development Corporations – the flagship of inner urban policy in the 1980s and early 1990s – have been particularly important in the transformation of many industrial sites, and in their conversion for other uses. In many cases, the contribution of UDCs in this direction has been positive: near derelict industrial sites in Liverpool, Sheffield, Salford, and London, for instance, have been transformed into modern centres for offices, retail developments, and leisure pursuits. The extent, and economic impact, of these physical transformations, however, remains a point of debate. Vast industrial dereliction persists elsewhere, particularly in some of the coal mining areas, and the inner city localities.

Change is often feared, but is not always of negative connotations. If there is a benefit to the contraction of the coal industry, for example, it is that less miners will be subjected to what is often an unpleasant job, and subjected less to the debilitating diseases that were associated with it. It was once commonplace in mining areas – and the legacy of it remains – to see former mineworkers unable to walk a small incline, gasping for breath and pretending their reason for stopping was to admire the view, when really it was emphysema or pneumoconiosis that was inhibiting them. As time passes, fewer will be incapacitated in this way.

The problem with industrial change of the dramatic kind that was seen in the 1980s and early 1990s, is the economic dislocation it causes. Very often an adequate social mechanism for overcoming that dislocation is not in place. Redundancy payments *were* an attempt at alleviating the hardship caused by economic dislocation on a temporary basis. In other words, the payments were there to tide workers over a major change in their circumstances. The expectation, however, was that workers would, in time, find another job. It is worth remembering that the Redundancy Payments Act 1965 was introduced by a Labour government in times of near full employment. By the 1990s, instead of helping people *transfer* from one job to another, in a relatively buoyant labour market, it was often used as a mechanism whereby people's transition *out* of the labour market altogether was effected. This is clearly represented here in the data collected from a number of industries, and a number of different regions in the UK. There is considerable evidence of substantial 'exiting' from the labour market by workers displaced from traditional industry: in Wearside, in South Wales, in what were the former coal mining areas. Moreover, while the 'modernised' sectors of British industry that remain may be leaner and fitter, there are many who have suffered individually in this process of transformation. Lovering, for example, is unequivocal in his assessment in chapter 5 of the impact of defence restructuring: 'Within Britain, few workers and fewer communities have benefitted. On the international level, the reconstruction of the arms industry is not a cause for rejoicing.'

One of the – sometimes unnoticed – effects of economic transformation, then, has been the numbers of people more or less coerced by circumstances into leaving the labour market. For many, this meant that life chances they had come to expect in the advanced industrial economy that had been built in the UK in the post-war era were removed from them, often over a very short space of time.

One of the central forms the change has taken has been the transformation from an economy based very largely on manufacturing to one based on services and on lighter industries. There is an extent to which some change in this direction was perhaps inevitable, and was merely the outgrowth of an evolving economy. The central question, however, relates to how the implementation of dramatic such changes is *managed*. The management of change can be smooth or harsh, in terms of its impact on the individuals affected. In some of the industries that have faced contraction, significant sums of money were made available for some displaced workers. Thousands outside those industries also lost their jobs, however, and there were few ameliorating circumstances for them. The implementation of change can be effected by a number of different agencies, in the public or private sectors. For example, it would be theoretically possible for all changes to the economic structure to be left to the private sector. Under this approach, there would no intervention by government at all in either the implementation of the changes or the management of their impact on individuals and communities. In the UK, however, it was the government that was often the instigator of change, and sometimes the body seeking to alleviate its worst effects. It was the government, for example, which sanctioned or organised restructuring and rationalisation in the nationalised industries, prior to their privatisation. Such industries included steel, coal, shipbuilding, car manufacture. And it was only the government that had the resources and administrative power necessary to make an impact in areas economically devastated by such restructuring.

Some areas had closer links to the manufacturing economy than did others, of course. Birmingham was one such place, perhaps the premier manufacturing centre in the UK in the post-war era. Martin charts in chapter 9 the fascinating story of the attempt in Birmingham to engage in a metamorphosis from a manufacturing centre to a service-based economy. And, of course, it is evident that considerable success *was* achieved in this direction. Birmingham could boast, as of the 1990s, a number of prestigious international hotels and conference centres, and an expanding section of its population involved in the service sector. However, it is worth noting that Martin argues that the efforts in Birmingham have brought little benefit to the long-term unemployed in the poor parts of the city. He notes a 1994 survey which reported living conditions in parts of Birmingham as being the fifth worst in the country. This relates earlier to the point about the *management* of change: if the management of change is such that there are damaging consequences for large numbers of people, perhaps there is a case for changing the method of policy implementation.

Clearly, not only have the sectors of specialisation in the economy changed – away from manufacturing and towards service-based activity – but also the kind of people involved in those sectors has changed as well. Frequently, the chapters within this work refer to the displacement of the male worker and his replacement by the female worker. Morris comments, for example, on the feminisation of the workforce in Wales (chapter 3). Much of this is, as he states, due to the structural transformations in the economy: the change from heavier to lighter industries; the advancement of the service sector. Dabinett, also, puts forward the view that Sheffield 'has moved away from a male and manufacturing-based labour market' (chapter 10).

Crucial to an assessment of whether or not the 'new', developing, sectors of the economy have adequately replaced the 'old', and what the 'old' provided, is some appreciation of the employment consequences of the change. In straightforward terms, are the new areas providing sufficient jobs, of reasonable quality, to replace the jobs lost in the traditional sectors? There *have* been areas of growth – the numbers of jobs in the banking and finance sectors increased substantially in the 1980s and early 1990s. Stone, for instance, notes an increase of employment in this sector in Wearside from 2,300 to 7,300 between 1973 and 1991 (chapter 8). Morris also refers to rapid growth in the relative proportion of the workforce in services and, within that broad category, 'with much faster employment gains in banking and financial services' (chapter 3). Much of the work reported on in this book, however, sounds a note of pessimism. Dabinett argues, for example, in relation to Sheffield in the 1980s and early 1990s, that 'service sector employment grew in relative and absolute terms, but not at a sufficient rate or scale to off-set industrial job losses' (chapter 10). In the former coal mining regions, the evidence is similarly clear: at least as far as displaced mineworkers are concerned the picture as of the early 1990s is depressing. Stone sees *some* success in Wearside – 'improved growth capacity' – but also adds a note of caution: the modernisation has been 'not one sufficient to fill the employment and income gap left by the demise of the old industries' (chapter 8).

A connected point relates to the prospects for the accumulation of wealth – collective and individual – within the 'new' economic sectors. Dabinett's view on Sheffield, in this context, is that its former range of products and industries drew in wealth from elsewhere (chapter 10). He argues, however, that the 'new service base in the city is unlikely to achieve such impacts based on its configuration at the beginning of the 1990s'. The point hardly needs any elucidation: firms producing things for export to other parts of the UK or to other countries is somewhat different from a situation in which hordes of people – very often from the nearby locality – just walk about the out-of-town shopping centre (Meadowhall) built on the site of former steelworks. The latter may be providing some jobs in the retail sector, though many of these are very often low paid. The impression conveyed, however, is that this is an exercise limited to recycling local money.

A further area in which considerable change is evident is in the area of industrial relations. Morris points out, for example, that 'single union, "no strike" type deals are now the norm for new manufacturers locating in Wales' (chapter 3). And this is in an area in which, at least in the once heavily predominant industries of coal and steel, trade unionism was strong. Derecognition of unions, and constriction of their activities, are not confined to Wales. Stone notes here that smaller new production centres in Wearside are, in the 1990s, likely to be non-union, and the larger plants are very often single-union in which there are severe restrictions on what the union can actually do. This pattern of industrial relations was becoming common in the industrial economy of Britain in the 1990s.

The theme of this book is the transformation of the British economy, and whether or not the changes that have taken place constitute what could be called 'modernisation'. Clearly, there *are* aspects of modernisation that can be seen. Geddes and Green, for example, have noted the 'upskilling' of the workforce in the engineering industry: this has involved both the *professionalisation* and the *multi-skilling* of the workforce (chapter 6). On most criteria, this would be judged as a positive development. Lovering also notes the 'upgrading' of skills in the defence industry in that the 'occupational profile of the defence industry tilted sharply towards high level occupations' (chapter 5). Importantly, in the car manufacturing sector also, Rhys notes in chapter 7 that the production level record of 1.9 million vehicles produced in 1972, will have been exceeded by the mid-1990s. As far as motor manufacture is concerned, Rhys has considerable optimism: he sees the motor industry in Britain 'competing strongly with German-based manufacturers for the custom of European car buyers, and being set for major growth'.

Another form of change that has taken place has been an increasing internationalisation of the British economy. This has taken a variety of forms. One of them is the increasing globalisation of markets: it has become easier for companies to trade in some international markets. For example, following the Single European Act, it is easier, in theory at least, for companies based in any other the member states of the European Union to trade in the Single European Market that became operable at the end of 1992. On another level, the British economy has become a major recipient of inward investment from foreign multinationals bringing with them their own ways of organising and managing production. On yet another level, many British companies have become more international in scope, expanding production and overseas orientation.

In relation to inward investment, there are positive factors associated with it, and a number of areas which were formally associated with traditional industry have been recipients of substantial levels of inward investment. Stone, in chapter 8, finds that the role being played by inward investors in 'modernising' the Wearside economy is significant, particularly in relation to 'manufacturing techniques and the labour process'. It is important to recognise, as Stone acknowledges, that decisions on which changes in organisation of work practices to introduce are not made in a political vacuum. The context in which many of them were introduced was explicitly connected to reducing the power of organised trade unionism. On the strictly economic side, Stone's overall view remains somewhat pessimistic: there *has* been modernisation on Wearside, this has enhanced the region's chances of economic growth, it has not enhanced them sufficiently to provide the jobs and the income which had been provided by the now departed traditional industries.

Globalisation and internationalisation have altered the configuration within which business in Britain operates. Thus, for instance, Rhys makes the point in chapter 7 that the UK no longer has a 'national champion' in car manufacture. And it was, after all, 'national champions' that ordinary people identified with as being symbols of national economic and industrial strength. Moreover, this concept has been reflected in government industrial policy of the late 1950s and 1960s. It was seen earlier how the 'modernisation' strategies of both Labour and Conservative governments focused upon encouraging mergers in order to promote 'national champions' that could compete effectively worldwide. Hence, when Rover passed into the hands of the German company BMW in 1994, many saw this as being symptomatic of national industrial decline. And yet, perhaps in the new economic configuration, economic 'nationalism', if indeed nationalism it is, might not have the practical relevance that it once had. It is clear from Rhys' work, for instance, that the car major manufacturers in Britain are operating to world class standards of efficiency, despite the fact that they are in foreign ownership.

It is probably important to recognise that internationalisation has been crucial to survival of some companies. Lovering makes the point in chapter 5 that the defence suppliers in Britain that will survive are the ones that have globalised/internationalised. Rhys argues in chapter 7 that internationalisation has been central to the survival of motor manufacturing in Britain. A case can be made that internationalisation of this kind represents at least some form of 'modernisation'. There are, on the other hand, many companies in major industrial sectors which have yet to transform themselves. Rhys comments on the need for productivity gains in the motor components industry, if companies are to survive. Lovering notes, that there are many in the defence supplying industry that will not survive unless they are diversify. Diversification would, in itself, form a part of 'modernisation' but, as Lovering also notes, there is no major British company that has engaged in defence conversion in a big way.

It is also clear that some regions of the UK *started off* this whole process of transformation having more modernised economic sectors than did other areas. Geddes and Green note in chapter 6 the extent to which the South East of England has a higher proportion of its workforce involved in the non-manual sectors of the economy than have other parts of the UK. If non-manual occupations are to be taken as a symbol of 'modernisation' then, clearly, the South East could be classed as being more 'modernised' than other areas. It was noted earlier that areas which had been associated with the coal industry had a smaller proportion of the workforce working in high-technology industry and producer services. Similarly, many of the areas seemed to be underdeveloped in relation to the size of the small business sector.

Lovering also demonstrates, in chapter 5 that the important elements in the defence industry remain located in the South East of England. The headquarter sites of the major companies are located there, and the bulk of R&D is carried out there.The largest proportion of spending on defence is directed towards the South East and South West.

The economic prospects for different regions vary, but it is important where regions are positioned structurally. It is easier to maintain some semblance of economic prosperity if a region starts off in a position where it has economic sectors which have at least a chance of survival. This does not bode well for areas such as coal mining areas, where those sectors which have at least a chance of maintenance and development in the future might feel discouraged from locating, and which lack an adequate physical and social infrastructure to build a successful post-coal economy based on other sectors.

There is evidence elsewhere of a lack of modernisation in some sections of British industry. Baker reports in chapter 4, for example, that modernisation in that sector of the textiles industry examined as part of his study was limited. For a start, Baker notes workers facing a 'lack of high quality training'. Clearly, modernisation on any definition would see a highly trained workforce. Rhys notes in chapter 7 that, in the motor manufacture industry, 'total unit labour costs are comparatively low by European standards'. Low wages are also prevalent in these sectors of the textile industry examined here. In the Hinckley area, this has resulted in a 'tied', low paid workforce that lives on the doorstep. The industry itself is as dependent on this workforce as the workforce is dependent on it. The pattern is replicated elsewhere in another locality, this time the inner city, traditionally associated with textiles: Nottingham's Lace Market. It is a pattern, however, which sits uneasily aside the concept of a 'modern' economy. Most definitions of a modern economy would have wages being paid at a decent level, and a workforce which is not 'tied' to one particular industry and to one particular geographical locality.

Baker notes also the inadequate premises often used by textile manu-facturers, and a lack of introduction of new working practices and, in many cases, a failure to make the leap to the production of high quality garments (chapter 4). Many of these factors are also replicated in Nottingham's Lace Market, the east end of London, and elsewhere in the textiles industry. Instead, the pattern of production of low value-added garments remains, in contrast to the situation in Germany and Italy. The latter, in particular, has enjoyed considerable success in its textiles industry. Baker's findings contrast, however, with what is reported to be happening in other parts of the textile industry in the UK. Inward investment, for example, has featured in the textiles industry as in other places. Toray, for example, a Japanese multinational, entered production in the British textile industry in the late 1980s through the purchase of a subsidiary of Courtaulds. A little later, Toray announced plans to build a textile plant on a greenfield site in an area associated historically with the textile industry – Mansfield (Strange, 1993). There is, then, a clear division in the British textile industry between the 'old' and the 'new'. The 'old' is represented by small, very often, family-run businesses, frequently operating in areas traditionally associated with textiles, such as the East Midlands or Lancashire. The new is repre-sented by the computerised mills owned by British multinationals like Courtaulds or, indeed, by foreign multinationals such as Toray or the Taiwanese multinational, Hualon. Hualon announced in 1994 that it was to build a giant plant to manufacture fabric in Northern Ireland, with govern-ment assistance of £61 million (*The Guardian*, 4 May 1994). The new plant would obviously work to the highest technological standards, aiming to produce fabrics which would compete directly with imports and displace them. There was an important, political, aspect to this instance of re-industrialisation. The development of the plant amounted to a partial reversal of the trend for multinationals with bases in the UK to source their production overseas in low wage economies. In the areas with a long standing association with textiles, the industry still had a huge bearing on the local economy and on employment levels. For example, the textiles and clothing industry combined employed 25 per cent of the manufacturing workforces in East Midlands and Northern Ireland in 1993. Moreover, despite the large variations in 'modernity', the industry could still boast a major input into the balance of payments, contributing exports worth £4.8 billion in 1993 (*The Guardian*, 25 November 1993). This emphasises the extent of contribution which traditional industry – which much of the textiles industry remained, despite its 'modernised' sectors – still makes to the economy.

The debate on the precise causes of relative economic decline in Britain, as noted in the introduction, are legion. It is unlikely that widespread agreement will be reached on reasons for relatively poor industrial performance in the 1960s and 1970s. The issues are too value-laden and too political. One of the most prominent reasons put forward, however, has been that the owners and managers of British industry have failed to invest sufficiently in R&D, and the performance of British companies therefore fell behind the performance of companies in economies with which the UK is often compared, such as Germany's and Japan's. The argument that is presented normally is to argue that 'modernised' and 'modernising' economies would see a relatively large proportion of GDP invested in R&D. A number of the authors in this book have comments to make about the strength of R&D in parts of the UK in the early 1990s. In relation to Sheffield, Dabinett notes in chapter 10 that while 'new, technology-based companies have set up in the city and grown', the attempts to enhance high tech 'do not present a coherent presence of international scope, and efforts to increase technology transfer were largely unsuccessful or achieved very limited objectives'. It is worth making a point of contrast with the Sheffield of the early twentieth century and earlier: companies and individuals in Sheffield were pioneers of industry and R&D, as noted in the introduction in chapter 10. Similarly, commenting on the Birmingham economy in the mid-1960s to the late 1970s, Martin noted that 'indigenous businesses were also slow to invest in new technologies and few moved into high technology sectors or new markets' (chapter 9).

There is an argument, however, that the emphasis on the level of R&D being carried out within an economy, and the impact of that on company performance, is far too simplistic an analysis (Edgerton, 1993a). This argument has a number of strands. First, it is wrong to argue that the levels of spending on R&D are parsimonious, as is sometimes put forward. According to Edgerton (1993b), for example, companies in Britain were spending about the same on R&D as industry was in France in the 1990s. It was spending more than industrial companies in Italy and Spain were. The argument runs that because the USA, Germany, and Japan are the three largest economies, it is axiomatic that more will be spent on R&D within their economies. Edgerton's (1993b) view is that:

The US and Japan account for more than half of the top 100 R&D funding businesses in the world. But Britain is in third place with ten companies, compared with nine German and eight French (although these nine German businesses are much bigger spenders than the ten British firms).

Edgerton (1993b) goes on to point out that the amount of money devoted to R&D by British companies increased considerably in the 1980s, even though it declined as a proportion of GDP. The important aspect to Edgerton's standpoint is that he argues, cogently, that different economies do, and should have, different development paths. None could share exactly the same development path, otherwise the 'law of comparative advantage', arguing that we all benefit by economies specialising – so beloved of classical economists – would cease to operate. As Edgerton sees it, more domestic spending on R&D by British firms might not always be the best way forward:

> No such universal rule applies to all countries, or all firms, at all times. No one would suggest Spain could only grow by raising its R&D:GDP ratio to Japanese levels.

Spain, of course, might seek to increase economic growth through increasing tourism, which might not be an option available to all economies, and which might not require much in the way of R&D. But also, companies or governments in Spain could simply *buy* in new technology rather than developing it through indigenous R&D. Edgerton's point is that 'Britain was overtaken in industrial efficiency by countries whose firms spent less, not more, on R&D'. And these economies, such as 'Germany, Japan, France, and even Italy,' managed this feat 'not by massive investments in R&D, but by importing new ideas, products, and processes'. It is obvious, however, that particular companies, and particular industries, *will* need a certain level of R&D simply in order to survive in an increasingly globalised market, with companies providing the market with increasingly sophisticated products. Lovering makes the point in chapter 5, for instance, in relation to defence, that: 'R&D is all the more necessary for British firms since it is only through technical ingenuity that they will be able to compete against competitors who can draw on much cheaper labour.'

The fact remains that, according to a report published in 1994, £104.4 billion was spent on R&D by the top 200 international companies, and they paid out £36.9 billion in dividends to shareholders. This compared with £7 billion spent on R&D by the leading 362 British companies, who paid out £14 billion to shareholders (Company Reporting, 1994). Clearly, the British firms were more keen than their foreign counterparts to pay out dividends to shareholders, rather than invest in R&D. It is important to note, as well, the argument that at least part of relative economic decline in

Britain has been a result of the allegedly disproportionate amount of R&D spending here devoted to the defence sector. This argument is, of course, heavily connected to the critique of British foreign economic policy which holds that a commitment to a long gone role as a world economic and military power has been held by the UK far beyond the time when she could afford to carry out such a role (see, for example, Gamble, 1981).

Aligned with attempts to make the 'high-tech' connection, often, are efforts by governmental, or quasi-governmental, agencies, or indeed, companies themselves, to upgrade the skills level of the workforce. Martin, in chapter 9, notes that in Birmingham, the city council set itself the objective in the mid-1980s of 'clos[ing] the gap between training needs and training provision' and 'developing "high technology" initiatives for the city'. Again, presumably in a 'modernised' economy, the workforce would be a highly productive, highly skilled workforce. Training policy at national level has changed in the 1980s and 1990s – and has had to change – because the institutional structures that had ensured its provision in the 1960s and 1970s were considerably weakened. In other words, the companies that had provided training in the past either simply no longer existed, or were so much reduced in size by the 1980s, that they were no longer providing training on a large scale. Stone, for example, notes in chapter 8 that shipbuilding in the 1960s in the North East had provided 'skilled jobs' and that the shipbuilding companies 'were heavily committed to training through apprenticeship schemes'. By the 1980s, of course, much of that was gone. Moreover, many of the nationalised industries – such as steel and coal – that had provided excellent training schemes, had also disappeared or, in much reduced form, been transferred to private ownership. The government therefore lost the considerable ability to influence the training that this had provided. The major policy change in the late 1980s was the introduction of Training and Enterprise Councils (TECs). Here, public sector money was directed at training activities by organisations led very often by private sector managers. This afforded an opportunity for employers to influence training policy using state funds. One of the perennial problems of the British economy in the 1980s and early 1990s was the existence of skill shortages alongside unemployment. If the right policies had been pursued it should have been theoretically possible to go some way to overcoming both. It is too early to tell what the impact of the changes in training policy will be on the economy. The objective within a 'modernised' economy would be to have a highly skilled, highly trained workforce. There is obviously still some way to go. Rhys, for example, argues here that in the British motor components manufacturing sector, in order to improve competitiveness, a further investment of training of both managers and workforce is necessary.

It is clear from the chapters in this book and from evidence elsewhere that there has been what can be termed a 'productivity revolution' within

British industry. This was widely trumpeted by the Conservative government as being a reflection of their success in micro-economic policy. And Lovering demonstrates in chapter 5, for instance, that in 1992, at Rolls-Royce aerospace, sales per employee were up by 13 per cent. Notable increases in productivity also have taken place in car manufacture and steel manufacture. Geddes and Green here note the 'above average rate of increase in labour *productivity* in engineering'. In coal, productivity doubled. In 1985/86, the first full year after the strike against pit closures, output per manshift for underground workers (the standard productivity measure in the industry) stood at 3.4 tonnes. By 1992/93 it stood at 7.43 tonnes (British Coal, 1993). By 1994, following further colliery closures, the figure had increased still further to over 9 tonnes per shift. These compare with horror stories of lagging productivity in the 1970s and 1980s. For example, British Steel used to argue that, in the late 1970s, its workforce was managing output of steel at 141 tonnes per man year compared to 237 in Germany (Iron and Steel Trades Confederation, undated, circa 1980). Rhys notes here that productivity in the UK motor industry increased by 9.1 per cent a year over the period 1984 to 1994, almost twice as much as productivity increases in Japan of 4.8 per cent over the same period. There has been a dramatic turnround in this area, therefore, with companies in Britain overtaking productivity increases in some of the most advanced economies. It is crucial to appreciate, however, that increases in productivity have been bought at the cost of redundancies and dramatically increased unemployment. So, while productivity can be described as being one aspect of 'modernisation', many thousands have been excluded from that modernisation. Moreover, in relation to the motor manufacturing and component manufacturing industry, Rhys argues that 'productivity . . . is still too low in some enterprises' (chapter 7).

Importantly, the dramatic increases in productivity have a bearing on the wider debate relating to the prospects for a return to full employment – or something approximating to it – in the UK. The Labour Party made the commitment to full employment a central element of its economic policy in 1994, reinforcing the message at its 1994 conference. The productivity revolution, however, made demonstrably clear that even if there were a major boom in industrial production, industry would not need the same numbers of people as it did in the past. Those days have gone. If anything like full employment is to be returned to the jobs will not be found in industry. If jobs are to be created, they would have to be created in other sectors.

The policy framework of the Conservative government since its election in 1979 has emphasised the efficacy of the free market approach to business. The best the government could do was to provide a political and economic environment which was conducive to the growth and development of businesses. It is evident, however, that the government has been prepared to override its belief in the free market in order to achieve other objectives. This was clearly the case in relation to privatisation, for instance, where gas, telecommunication, electricity, and water, were changed from being public sector monopolies into private sector monopolies. Although there were some moves later to develop competition within these industries, much of this was restricted to business customers. Competition, the touchstone of free market economics, is hardly enhanced by measures such as these. In chapter 5, Lovering gives the further example of the government conspiring to consolidate the British defence industry around a few, small, giant groups. Rather than providing an environment conducive to business growth, at least in relation to defence, Lovering argues that the political environment in the mid-1980s was 'turbulent', which made it 'difficult for defence companies to plan for their own modernisation'.

Something of a consensus emerges within these chapters on the belief that there is a need for a 'national industrial strategy' in Britain. A national industrial strategy would almost certainly envisage a role for government far more pro-active than that allowed for within a free market position. On the post-war development of the defence industry in Britain, for example, Lovering notes that:

> no one ministry and no single government post was ever respon- sible for overseeing [defence industry development] policies and ensuring that they hung together coherently. This strategic "gap" was symptomatic of the wider lack of institutional apparatus within the British state which was geared to economic development.

Geddes and Green also report in chapter 6 on the calls by both the NEDC and the EEF for a more pro-active industrial strategy for the engineering sector, involving an enhanced role for government. The perceived need for this is emphasised by the key role of engineering in the economy – in both the UK as a whole, and in the South East in particular – and also by the need to respond to the opportunities presented by a car industry in the UK rejuvenated by inward investment. It is obvious that if maximum economic benefit is to be derived from inward investment in this direction, domestic car component manufacturers have to respond successfully to the new challenges.

The overall picture, in terms of the elusive concept of 'modernisation' is, not surprisingly, mixed. Quite clearly, there are business and industrial sectors that *have* modernised, and could meet almost any definition of that. In defence, for example, Lovering notes in chapter 5 'remarkable success' in 'technological leadership, exports and corporate adaption'. Rhys argues in chapter 7 that, in relation to motor manufacture, 'the industry is among the world leaders', although he adds the rider that 'the variations are too great and improvement still has to be made'. Yet considerably less numbers are working in the car industry. There are many thousands who have been totally excluded from whatever levels of modernisation there have been. Some of these have sought a way back into the labour market and the economy via self-employment. It is not clear just how many of these would have *voluntarily* chosen this 'enterprise culture' route to an economic livelihood, however, had there been other, traditional, types of employment available. Many thousands of others have been forced into low pay, part-time jobs, as part of a 'flexible' workforce. It is easy to put forward a case, in these circumstances, that a great deal of the cost of modernisation has fallen on workers either on the margins of the labour market, or excluded from it altogether. If there has been partial success in modernisation, to the exclusion of many, this in itself may raise difficult issues for government. The social and political problems of a dual economy with a minority of the workers in secure, high technology companies, earning decent money, with a substantial proportion of people either excluded from the labour market altogether, or on very low pay, are potentially catastrophic.

REFERENCES

British Coal (1993) *Report and Accounts 1992/93*.

Company Reporting (1994) *UK R&D Scoreboard 1994*, Edinburgh: Company Reporting Limited.

Edgerton, D. (1993a) 'More R&D is not answer to Britain's blues', *The Guardian*, 30 August.

Edgerton, D. (1993b) 'Research, Development and Competitiveness,' in K. Hughes (ed) *The Future of UK Competitiveness and the Role of Industrial Policy*, London: Policy Studies Institute.

Edwardes, M. (1983) *Back From the Brink: An Apocalyptic Experience*, London: Collins.

Gamble, A. (1981) *Britain in Decline: Economic Policy, Political Strategy and the British State*, London: Macmillan.

The Guardian (1993) 25 November.

The Guardian (1994) 'Commission Approves £61 m Aid for Belfast Textile Plant', 4 May.

Hall, P. (1991) 'Structural Transformation in the Regions of the UK', in L. Rodwin and H. Sazanami (eds) *Industrial Change and regional Economic Transformation: The Experience of Western Europe*, London: Harper Collins Academic.

Iron and Steel Trades Confederation (undated, circa 1980) *New Deal For Steel*, ISTC.

Strange, R. (1993) *Japanese Manufacturing Investment in Europe: Its Impact on the UK Economy*, London: Routledge.

INDEX